friends: a love story

friends: a love story

ANGELA BASSETT
COURTNEY B. VANCE

WITH HILARY BEARD

Recycling programs
for this product may
not exist in your area.

FRIENDS: A LOVE STORY

ISBN-13: 978-0-373-83121-0
ISBN-10:   0-373-83121-8

www.kimanipress.com

Printed in U.S.A.

For Our Mothers—thank you!
For Lloyd Richards & Golden Wall—
thank you for showing us a more excellent way!
For Bronwyn Golden & Slater Josiah—
thank you for coming!

Therefore shall a man leave his father and his mother, and shall cleave to his wife and the two shall become one flesh. And they were both naked, the man and his wife, and were not ashamed.
—*Genesis* 2:24-25

He is the half part of a blessed man,
Left to be finished by such as she,
And she a fair divided excellence,
Whose fullness of perfection lies in him.
—William Shakespeare,
King John

ACKNOWLEDGMENTS

Like many of you, it took a very large village to raise us and for them we are eternally grateful. This book and our marriage is a testament to our village continuing to teach us how to love and how to allow ourselves to be loved, God's way. To that end we are still in process and every day we are in awe of our blessings. It is the journey not the destination that is our focus and we thank you all for encouraging us along our way!

Special thanks to Bishop Charles E. and Mae Blake, Pastor A. R. Bernard, Dr. Frank Little, George Browne, Earle Gister, Hilary Beard, Darrell Miller, Chris and Tracy Jackson, Mavis Allen and our agent, Manie Barron, for planting the seed.

HILARY'S ACKNOWLEDGMENTS

I thank God for showering me with grace yet again, and for blessing me with the faith and courage to leave "safe" jobs behind so that I could pursue my calling to be a writer.

Angela and Courtney, you touched and inspired me through your work long before I ever imagined I'd know you. Count me among your many fans whose spirits have been bolstered by your unwavering commitment to portray our community with love and integrity. I am grateful, too, for the kindness, grace and trust you showed in opening your inner sanctum to me, and for your courage in laying your lives bare so that others might see themselves and feel inspired to achieve their greatness. Lord knows you could have kept all of this private.

Manie Barron, you're a genius! What vision it took to conceive of this project. We've been on an amazing ride. I can't wait to see where we're heading next.

Mavis Allen, you laid your eyes, heart and red pen upon these pages in such a thoughtful and loving manner. Many thanks to you and the Harlequin/Kimani team for believing in us.

Kailey, Alex, Jadon, Jonathan, Alison and Jennifer Beard, I am so proud to be your family. And no words can express my appreciation for my deceased parents, Charles Beard and Peggy Lanton Beard. I am grateful to all of my forebearers, whose prayers paved the path I stumbled along until I found my present life. Your strength and dignity inspire me to push past my small places.

TABLE OF CONTENTS

Chapter 1

I Ain't Average

It was a hot and sticky August day when I came into the world in 1958—at least, that's how I imagine it. Angela Evelyn Bassett is the name I was given—my middle name in honor of Aunt Evelyn.

But I've gotten ahead of myself. I need to start my story with my parents.

Mama didn't have the best luck when it came to men, but she always protected me from them. After she graduated from high school she migrated from St. Petersburg, Florida, to New York City, where she lived with her father's brother, Uncle Charles and his wife, Aunt Evelyn. That's where she met my daddy, Daniel Benjamin Bassett, who'd moved to New York from Winston-Salem, North Carolina. They met, dated, got pregnant with me, married and lived in a small apartment in Harlem. I think it was on Seventh Avenue across from Small's Paradise.

My father was very bright, a self-educated kind of man—he could talk to anyone about anything. Yet I always thought of him as a jack-of-all-trades but a master of none. He made his money working in the neighborhood, fixing jukeboxes and other electrical things. My mother, Betty Jane, was a nurse's aide or something like that. I have a really pretty picture of her in her white uniform. With both of them working, they didn't have much—even before I was born. Times were hard for black folks in the late 1950s and early 1960s.

Ten months after I was born my mother got pregnant again. Of course, that only made things harder. I don't think my parents had considered how they would handle two babies, living in New York and both of them having to work. My mother never speaks poorly of my father, but sometimes she says he was frugal or stingy. According to her he was the kind of person where if she would say, "The baby needs shoes" and those shoes cost $4.72, he would count out $4.72—not $4.73—not a nickel more. Maybe he was broke, I don't know. I'm certain times were tight.

On top of struggling financially, my parents' relationship was troubled. My mother once told me a story of how she tried, or pretended to try, to leave my father in her trademark melodramatic style.

"We're leaving your daddy. We're leaving that man," she sang as she packed me into the car. His friends apparently reported to him, "They're in the car, and she's telling the baby she's leaving." He rushed home.

"What?" he said. "Get back in the house! You ain't leaving."

I also have a vague childhood memory of playing with a little white windup dog that flipped over and barked. I remember thinking the dog was fun. My mother was cooking greens. There was an argument about money—my daddy didn't want to give her money for food but he was eating the food—then a fight. A window got bumped then somehow my father's head was out the window. That's the only memory I have of being in that apartment. Maybe that was the kind of behavior my mother was trying to get us away from.

After Mom got pregnant with my sister D'nette, my parents shipped me down to Winston-Salem to stay with Daddy's sister Golden. Aunt Golden and her husband, Grover, didn't have any children of their own, but she was someone who loved children, and she was good with them—they were her background, her education, her love. And Uncle Grover didn't mind me coming to live with them. He was a barber and had his own barbershop, Sanitary Barbershop. Cutting heads was his thing.

I stayed with Aunt Golden and Uncle Grover in the little redbrick, two-bedroom house he had built on Graham Avenue near Winston-Salem Teachers' College, now Winston-Salem State University. The house had a porch with an aluminum glider on it and a magnolia tree in the front yard, a weeping willow in the back. I liked to play in the basement and was a good kid, from what they say. Aunt Golden and Uncle Grover had a committed and consistent relationship. They were good, God-fearing people who loved, supported and took care of each other. I never heard a harsh word said in their home.

My aunt Golden was a teacher, so she was gone during the day. While Auntie was at school I would stay with my grandmother, whose name was Brownie. Grandma Brownie lived in a little house across the street from the school. On Sundays I would go with either her or Auntie to Goler Metropolitan AME Zion Church. Auntie always dressed real fine and wore hats to church and all that stuff. She would dress me like a little doll baby in little frocks with gloves and little hats. As a small girl I was always repeating, "Praise the Lord!" and "Hallelujah!" which I heard at that church on Sundays.

Across the street from Aunt Golden and Uncle Grover, I had a girlfriend, Debra. I would play with her and her cousins, and we all went to church together. I probably heard Debra or my other little friends calling their mothers "Mommy"; I remember on several occasions attempting to call my auntie "Mommy" or "Mama." Now, I don't believe I ever tried to call Uncle Grover "Daddy," but I did try to call Aunt Golden "Mommy."

"Angela, I am not your mother," she would tell me in a

gentle voice. "You have a mama. I am Auntie." I would get upset and twist up my face. I wanted to have a mama.

One day when I was four I was in the basement playing when Auntie called me upstairs. "Angela, your mama's on the phone."

"Hello…"

"Hi, Angela. This is Mama," said the voice on the other end of the line.

"I ain't got no mama," I shouted and threw down the phone. I remember feeling upset that the woman I lived with and loved was not my mother, yet here was this voice on the phone saying that she was my mother. It is the only telephone conversation I remember with my mother while I was living with Golden and Grover. I guess back in those days, people wrote letters, but I was too young to read.

The next thing I knew (I'm sure some days or weeks had passed), there was a knock on the door and a pretty, brown-skinned woman—my mother—was standing in the door frame. My mother looked nice, and I imagine my auntie told me at least a little something to expect—I don't remember it being traumatic. But the next thing you know, I was gone, headed to St. Petersburg, Florida, with her and my little sister, D'nette. To hear my mother tell it, while she was living with my dad she had a couple of nervous breakdowns and ended up in court. The judge told her to take her children and go home or he'd take us or put us in foster care.

"I'm going home," she told him. "I'll go home." That's when she left my father; although they didn't divorce until years later.

In St. Pete's we stayed with my mother's parents, Grand-mother Emma and Granddaddy Leroy, whom we called Mama and Daddy. My mother got a job as an aide in a hospital. My grandmother took care of me while mother was at work. We'd sit and watch soap operas together. She'd have her coffee and I'd have my mug filled with coffee, which was really milk with a teaspoon of coffee in it. When her stories were over I'd fill up her green-stamp book, putting all the little stamps in their places. That was fun! When I finished that we would walk up to the little store and get my grape snow cone. Then I'd get into her big bed and take my nap. That was my day.

At night my mother went to secretarial school. She hadn't done well in high school—she said she was always slacking off with her girlfriend, skipping class and smoking, and barely graduated with Ds and Fs. Now she was paying for it and having to play catch-up while she had two little girls. We'd sit on the bed together and play a game where D'nette and I would show her flash cards with shorthand characters on them while she learned and figured them out. Eventually she got very good at all those squiggly lines and dots and stuff. Between that and the steno pad, she would do her thing.

D'nette and I got along well. She was fun and cute and happy to have a big sister. Being older I was always one step ahead of her. One time when we were home at Mama Emma's, I remember finding some scissors and playing barbershop just like Uncle Grover.

"Let's play barbershop," I said to D'nette, and cut off all her little plaits. When I finished, she smiled and said, "Now let's do yours." I said, "No, let's do something else." When my mother came home from work that day, she beat the daylights out of me. I was always outsmarting D'nette like that.

"I have five moneys and you have one money," I'd say. "I'll give you my money for your money."

"Okay." And of course my money was a nickel and a couple of pennies and hers was a quarter. Then she'd want to have her turn.

"No," I'd say and change the subject. "Want some cookies?"

So we lived with my grandparents for maybe a year. My mother got along with her dad—she was a daddy's girl—but didn't get along with her mom at the time. There was a lot of "get-down"—arguing—between them. Maybe it was because my grandmother had become a Jehovah's Witness, with all its tightenings and restrictions.

When my mother couldn't stand living with her parents anymore, we moved out of Grandmom and Granddaddy's house and into a little dinky shotgun apartment on the other side of the railroad tracks that ran behind the "beer garden." A beer garden is a saloon, one of those little joints where the barflies hang out. They've got peanut hulls and sawdust on the floor. For fifty cents or maybe a dollar you could get a crab, a red potato and half an ear of corn wrapped in newsprint. My grandmother's sister Viola and her husband, Hiram, owned and ran it. You know how it goes: Mama Emma was the pious church girl, Viola ran the beer garden and the baby girl, my mother's youngest sister, Inez, was a teacher. Anyhow, our little house must have been cheap, cheap, cheap, cheap, cheap—Oh God, it was po' and nasty! We had indoor plumbing but there were roaches and all that stuff. It was funky, tired, to' down, wretched and just awful!

Daddy Leroy would come see us all the time while we lived in that shotgun shack. He and my grandmother lived together and seemed to get along just fine, but Grandmom was way off into her Jehovah's Witness thing. My maternal great-grandfather Slater Samuel Stokes, whom we called Papa, was a preacher. But apparently Grandmom never received answers to her spiritual questions in her father's church. *Whoever comes along and meets you where you are, that's where you go.* In Grandmom's case, to everyone's dismay, the people who she "met" were Jehovah's Witnesses.

Meanwhile, my grandfather just wanted some "peanuts," as my mother called sex. He had a "girlfriend" who lived across the street from the projects in a two-story shack building. He would see her and then come visit us. We knew Granddaddy was married to Grandmom, but we also knew that he had a woman on the side.

Before long, my mother moved us out of the shanty and into the Jordan Park Projects a few blocks away. We had a one-bedroom apartment on the second floor. We didn't have much. We were on welfare. We got blocks of government cheese and peanut butter. I remember taking money out of my mama's purse and going to the store every day and buying honey buns, candy and soda. It wasn't much at the time—maybe a nickel—but it was still stealing. I would buy my honey bun and a soda and maybe some candy cigarettes or a candy necklace. Or I might get a peppermint or grape or green-apple Jolly Ranchers hard candy and stick it down into a dill pickle and suck the dill pickle for a sweet-and-sour taste. Later we moved into a two-bedroom, ground-floor apartment with a porch. D'nette and I shared a bedroom that looked out onto the clothesline. No matter what direction you looked you were facing a brick building. At least the kitchen looked out at Jordan Park, the all-black elementary school we attended. We would cross the street, flip ourselves over the fence, walk across the playground, climb over the monkey bars and go on up to class.

My mother may have struggled in school and early in her life, but she had an excellence about her and passed it on to us. Mama didn't want us to suffer her fate and she would tell us as much. She made sure we looked nice. She made sure we did well in school. She raised us up to love God. On Sundays we would walk together to Stewart Memorial CME Church where we attended Sunday school and service. I was part of the youth choir and had a great time singing. Ma was a deaconess. She sang in the adult choir. Her favorite song is "His Eye Is on the Sparrow," which she sang as a high soprano with her typical melodrama. I would be so embarrassed. One of my favorite memories is watching Papa sing "Take Your Troubles to the Lord and Leave Them There" while he was standing in front of the altar of his church. He took this white handkerchief out of his pocket and threw it across his shoulder like it represented his burdens weighing down on him real heavily. When he finished the song—*Take your burdens to the Lord and leave them there*—he took the handkerchief off his shoulder, threw it over the altar with a flourish and turned on his heel and walked away lighter. I remember sitting there rapt. "Wow, *Papa!*" It was great acting and great theater. I come from a very dramatic family.

At home I played with my baby dolls and cut out patterns for them. I had lots of dolls. When I was a little girl I had white dolls—that's all there were. I remember little black girls with white baby dolls. But after James Brown came out with "Say It Loud, I'm Black and I'm Proud," I remember black dolls coming out on the market. Aunt Golden sent me and D'nette these two black baby dolls—they were two or three feet tall. You could hold their hands and walk with them. I always thought the black baby dolls were pretty; it was nice to see a baby doll that looked just like me. We'd comb their hair then my cousin cut their hair— then we needed new dolls. There were some black girls who still wanted white dolls—that's what they were used to. Personally, I never had Barbie dolls because they didn't look like me.

We watched *Julia, Bonanza, The Monkees* and *Tarzan* on TV. Mom would have us sing and perform together Motown hits that were popular on the radio. The latest single would come out, "Papa Was a Rolling Stone" or "Say It Loud, I'm Black and I'm Proud," or "You Got Me Going in Circles," and she'd have us act it out. Then one of the ladies in the neighborhood who liked kids helped us form a little dance group. We'd make up dances and sing to songs like "Kung Fu Fighting" and perform them at the local Delta Sigma Theta mixer. I laugh when I think back on how much all this would aid me as a lip-syncher later in life. Mom would also take us to the movies. We saw *Lady Sings the Blues,* which my sister loved—after she saw it we had to learn all the Diana Ross songs. We also saw *The Ten Commandments* and *Superfly*. I was in love with the Jackson 5 and daydreamed I would marry one of them—probably whoever had the cutest, roundest Afro at the time. In my imagination we would have children and live in a real house.

Every summer my mother would send us to North Carolina to visit Aunt Golden and Uncle Grover. I loved going to visit them. We would stay for about a month and come back with boxes of clothes. They helped us out because my dad sure wasn't providing anything. We got *no* support from him. I guess Daddy just didn't know how to be a father. Now that I think back on it, I realize that when my dad didn't fill his role, the men on my mother's side of the family, like Daddy Leroy and Papa, stepped in. Our relationship with these men was reflected in what we called them. Daddy Leroy and Papa were my grandfather and great-grandfather, but we called them what Mama would call them.

When I was about seven or eight, we traveled up to North Carolina to go to Grandmom Brownie's funeral. That's where I saw my father for the first time since I was a very little girl. I remember thinking that he was cute. He had a pencil mustache, big daddy hands and a little wave in his hair. I also met my half sister, Jean, the daughter from my father's first marriage. She was about twelve at the time, and really pretty with dark skin and long black hair. Jean lived in Winston-Salem. She must have thought my father and mother were still together, because I've heard she told my mother, "He's not going to stay with you, either. He didn't stay with us."

Several years later, while visiting Aunt Golden and Uncle Grover, I would meet Jean's half sister, Lynn, who is not related to me biologically because she's not my father's child. She and Jean have the same mother and were raised together. I grew to love Lynn as a sister, nonetheless. Lynn is about five years older than me. To this day I'm not exactly sure who her biological father is. Yet in the tradition of my family, she called both her mother and Aunt Golden mom, and Uncle Grover dad.

Over the years my mother worked herself up into better jobs. She got a job at Family Services—"the welfare," we called it—doing data entry. We were on assistance until my mother started working at "the welfare." I guess you couldn't be on welfare if you worked for welfare. When she began hearing from other people about the process of getting child-support money, she learned the ropes and realized she didn't have to provide everything for us. She ended up getting sixty dollars a month from Daddy. We said, "Yeah! Go, Mom. You really did something—you made the system work for you." My mother was always there for us, raising us, providing for us.

But I'm also thinking she probably wanted some quality companionship, along with needing help with raising us. My mother had welfare, she had her secretarial job and other gigs, but my daddy wasn't sending the sixty dollars consistently. During my childhood she had a couple of boyfriends. There was the young boyfriend, Billy. I remember one time somebody broke into a gas station and he called my mother up and told her to come by and help him take some cigarettes and things. He looked at it like a windfall, a blessing—like somebody else had done a deed that he or my mother would never do, but since the deed was done they could take advantage of it.

"Oh, no, no, no, no, no!" my mother said. "There's right and wrong, and that is wrong."

When I was about eleven, my mother and Billy were planning to get married. One night about a week or two before the wedding—the justice of the peace was already hired—I woke up to discover Billy touching me. He stopped as soon as I awakened and, I guess, went back into the room with my mom. I just remember that it was the longest night in creation. I thought, "I can't wake my mama up now. I have to wait until daylight until he's gone." When Billy left I raced into her room.

"Mom, B-Billy, Billy was feelin' on me last night," I cried.

My mother listened carefully and was calm and concerned.

I don't remember ever sensing that she didn't believe me. I knew she was on my side. That evening Mama set me in a chair. She and Billy sat across from me on the sofa.

"Angela, now Billy and I are going to get married," she said. "What do you think?"

"Mom, I know you were going to get married and that you love him, but I don't think you should," I told her.

"Okay," she said, then turned to Billy and said, "Get out!"

Perhaps Billy's fondling of me happened out of the blue. Until he felt me up, he had done nothing to make me feel uncomfortable; I had no indication that he was looking at me funny. Today I wonder if maybe he didn't want to get married and that was the way he got out of it. Maybe he didn't have the courage to say, "I don't want to do this," so acted out so he could get out of it. He chose one hell of a way. Mama must have been absolutely devastated, but she protected me anyway.

Then Mom started dating this old guy. He was a yard man. He had a lawn service and a truck with a lawn mower in the back of it. He worked hard. He had integrity. He was always helping and very nice. And you could always get him to give you thirty-five or fifty cents. He worked his full, hard day and at the end of the day he would relax with a drink. It seems like he drank about a pint of some clear liquid every day. Anyhow, I woke up in the middle of the night one night, and *he* was feeling on my butt! Well, this time I couldn't wait until morning. I just went right into Mama's room, crying.

"Ma-Ma-Mama, he—he was feeling on me." Nothing happened as dramatic as that other time, but that was the end of that one, too. The old guy stayed around as a friend but their relationship was over. My mother stood up for me once again. Because she empowered me at that moment, neither situation seemed to scar me.

Mama didn't have the best luck when it came to men, but she always protected me from them. Now that I'm older I sometimes think back on the situation. Mama had two children, but she was still a young woman. She was working overtime for the state to earn anything extra she could. She had to be lonely. She had to want a relationship. But on two different occasions she chose to believe her baby—her kid—over her man. You hear stories all the time about women who side with the boyfriend. Women who choose to believe him, choose not to see what's going on under their nose. If my mother had chosen to look the other way and didn't take my word for it, ain't no tellin' how jacked up I would be right now, how that would have played out. My life could have gone in an entirely different direction. By believing me she gave me such a gift!

Fortunately, I was around other good and decent men like Daddy and Papa and some father figures at school. Yet both times I was violated, the men walked past my sister's bed to my bed. I was fourteen months older than D'nette and have always appeared a little older, plus I was more developed. But she never had those issues. I started wondering, "What is it about me?" I have never quite answered that question.

Sometime around then my mother started talking to me about sex. She tried to give me the information I needed without giving me a license to experiment. Some folks are very free sexually—that was never her vibe. In her book, sex was fine when you got married. Until then, there were certain things that weren't proper, that you did not do. Laying up in your mama's house with your boyfriend was one of them. That demonstrated a lack of respect. Having a boyfriend was one thing. Shacking up was another. But she did give me conflicting messages. On the one hand, she was very "don't you bring no babies in here!" But at the same time, whenever we were at Eckerd's Drugstore, she would show me, "Now this is a condom—and if he don't want to use it, fuck him. I mean, don't fuck him!" People would be walking down the aisles. I was sure they were listening. I would be so embarrassed.

One time she told me, "Okay, do you know how to excite a man? You grab his penis."

"Oh, Mom. No, you don't!"

"Yes, you do."

"Oh, God, really?"

"Yeah, and you rub it."

I was in the seventh grade or so at the time—very young. Way younger than when I was potentially going to do it. So I guess she felt it was safe for her to talk about it. Because the closer I got to the age when I could potentially be doing this, she got stricter. "Don't do it! You better not bring no babies in here because I am not taking care of them."

Now, while this all was going on, my mother allowed Mama Emma—the Jehovah's Witness—and her friend to come over and instruct D'nette and me spiritually every Wednesday night. We never went to Kingdom Hall and Mom never took part in this particular activity, but she allowed us to sit there and read whatever their little book was. The book had these pictures of people running from destruction and hell and brimstone. It would scare us to death because the world was supposed to be coming to an end in 1976 and it was 1973 or '74. "Oh, Lord, I got but two more years to live!" According to what my grandmom told us, only 144,000 were going to be saved. That seemed like a big number—but not that big. I didn't think I was special enough to make the cut. Then again, I thought, "She doesn't seem too frightened by it. Is it really going to happen?" We were not a very receptive audience.

After I graduated from Jordan Park Elementary School, I was bussed out of our neighborhood to attend Disston Middle School to attend seventh grade. It was 1970—the first year bussing was implemented to integrate public schools in St. Pete's. I distinctly remember the little faces of my white classmates whose parents couldn't flee during "white flight." I hadn't been around many white people before, other than people like the clerks at the grocery store or the shoe salesman over on Central Avenue. (I remember D'nette lying on the carpet while we were buying shoes one time and just wanting her to stand up straight and act "right" around all these white people.) Once I got bussed to Disston I remember hearing rumors about "race riots" at the high school and white students bringing dogs and something called brass knuckles to school. I remember thinking, "Oh, my gosh!" Thank goodness, in the seventh grade we were sweet little kids and were all just interested in each other and getting along. "Hi, excuse me, thank you."

The next year I was bussed to Azalea Middle School, where I attended eighth and ninth grade. The principal was a red-headed white man named Mr. Kreiver, who used to be an army sergeant. Although the world around us was racially charged, at Azalea everything was cool. Academically, my mother's sense of excellence was starting to kick into full gear. She stayed on top of our grades. After struggling through her life, she started telling us we were going to go to college. "You ain't gonna go through this thing, here," she'd say about her own life. Mom would come to school with her steno pad to talk to the teachers. She would be very regular at home, but she'd show up at school and pull up and act "queenly"—an interesting duality. "What is she doing in your class? Um-hum, um-hum," steadily taking shorthand notes—bip, bop, bip.

When I was in ninth grade, I got my first boyfriend, Ricky. My mom let him come over on weekends. She would go get us Burger King and we'd sit on the couch and listen to Al Green on the eight-track tape over and over. We'd kiss, and then he'd try to unbutton my little shirt and get into my bra. I'd jump, button it back up and say, "You can do whatever with those other girls over there, but we're just going to kiss and that's where it's going to end." I remember him playing "You Got It Bad Girl" by Stevie Wonder.

When you believe in a feeling,
And it's holding you back from my love,
Then you've got it you got it bad...

"Well, I'm just gonna have to have it bad. Because I'm gonna be somebody one day!" I'd tell him. And I remember laughing to myself and thinking, That's not gonna work on me!

Sometime during this time my mother got a new boyfriend. His name was Theodore Slaughter and went by the name of Teddy. Teddy seemed to be nice, one of those quiet dudes. He built swimming pools for white people. They dated for several years. I always liked Teddy, he was always nice to me. And I was a good kid. I never disrespected him. If Ma told me to be home when the streetlights came on, that's when I hit the step.

Over the summer between ninth and tenth grade, Mommy and Teddy got married. A day or so before the wedding we moved into Teddy's home. After spending most of our lives living in the projects, it was our first time living in a house! D'nette was especially happy about the move up and that we were getting a daddy. D'nette was always talking about wanting a father. When she would get mad at our mother, she would say, "I want to go live with my daddy." I'd remind her, "Well, your daddy ain't here. He ain't sent no birthday card, no money or nothing. Mama has to take care of everything. And now you're mad at Mama and want to go with your daddy? Do you think things will be better with him?" Then she'd quiet down and reconsider her fantasy life with Daddy.

Mommy and Teddy got married on a Saturday. The next day she sent us up to Winston-Salem for our annual summer vacation. Seven days later she called to tell us she was getting her marriage annulled.

This is the story she told me about the annulment. It had been raining "cats and dogs" in St. Pete's one night that week. My mother went to her girlfriend Mattie's house. They were picking out patterns and sewing. When Mommy came home, Teddy asked, "Where have you been?"

"That's for me to know and you to find out," she answered. It was very much like my mother to say things with a lot of attitude. ("It ain't what you say, it's how you say it," she would tell us.) Well, a little altercation ensued. All of a sudden he's beating and slapping her and whatnot. Now, my mama done talked "smack" before they were married, she done talked and said whatever she had to say, and he never raised a hand to her. But here it was a week after getting married and he was beating her up. I guess maybe it was his idea about what being husband and wife meant. My mother told us she had rollers in her hair and that every roller got knocked out, save one. In the process of beating her, he fractured her nose. Afterward, he took her to the hospital.

Now, to get to this one particular hospital you had to go down a cobblestone road that ran by a little crick. I don't know the actual name of it but we called it Bugga Crick. It was dark there, with overhanging trees—mossy, swampy, spooky. Well, Mama says that while they were driving by Bugga Crick, Teddy told her, "And somebody's gonna kick Angela's ass, too, 'cause she's just like you!"

Now why he would want to speak that destiny on a sixteen-year-old girl, I will never know—I never did anything to him. When I found out about it, it hurt my feelings. Mama told me, "I wanted to defend you, baby, but we were going down Bugga Crick and it was dark. I thought if I said something he would run off the road and kill us both. I told myself, 'Just let me shut up until I can get to the hospital and away from him.'"

When Mama got to the hospital, she got taken care of and then called us up to tell us the deal. She also filed charges against Teddy. Of course, D'nette was upset because she had always wanted a daddy.

When we came back from North Carolina a few weeks later,

we thought, "Where we gonna live now? Oh, God, I guess it's back to the projects." But the preacher at Stewart Memorial, where we had gone to church for all these years, had a parsonage he didn't live in on the other side of town. He let us live there for a while. But even after we moved in, my mother just lay on the couch, crying. She just couldn't do anything. You had to bring her water and everything. Now that I think back on it, I'm sure she was crushed, but, of course, being dramatic, Mama milked every moment out of it.

Apparently Teddy tried to reconcile—or at least reason with my mother to drop the charges against him. I remember Aunt Viola, who owned the beer garden, coming over to talk to Mama while she was lying on the couch.

"Betty, now, Hiram has hit me, too, you know," Aunt Viola told Mom. "But we're still together. It's no big deal. Forgive and forget it."

"Heck, no, no, no, no, no," my mother said to Viola. "If Hiram beat you, that's on you. With all due respect to you, I'm not going through that. No, no, no, no!"

Then Teddy wrote my mother a letter—"Please, Betty, forgive me. I'm sorry," he wrote—blah, blah, blah, blah. He made the mistake of writing it in red ink. I saw it and thought, "Oh, no, here she goes."

"He wrote the letter in red ink," my mother shouted. "That's my *blood!* His name is Teddy Slaughter and he tried to slaughter me. His last name isn't Slaughter for nothing!"

Being a teenager, after a while I thought, "Get up! Get up! I'm tired of being your slave. Just stop crying and being all sad. You don't want to go back to him but you won't get up."

Now, for some reason, around that same time my father came to St. Pete's for the first time. He came for the weekend and spent time with us. My mother gave him her bedroom and she slept on the couch. He said, "Why don't you sleep in here?"

She said, "Hell, no! Them days are over. You are here to see your children."

Well, one evening while Daddy was visiting, Teddy came by the house. My mother told him, "I don't know you. Just keep driving by."

I peeked out at him from the front picture window as he walked back to his car. I saw him reach in and start to pull out something long and dark.

"Oh, my God!" I said. "He's got a shotgun." I figured he was about to shoot the picture window.

"Get away from there!" my mother shouted.

D'nette ran and hid in the closet. I thought, "My daddy's here and he's going to kick his behind!" and kept on peeking out the window. But Daddy went and stood over by the closet next to D'nette. Teddy's outside and Daddy's inside, but there was no protection nowhere! Fortunately, it was just the long part of a car-jack that Teddy pulled out of the car. Did he throw it? It's now been so long, I can't remember.

That fall I was bussed to Boca Ciega High School. Race relations at Boca Ciega were a whole different story from Disston and Azalea. The black kids and white kids there had been having altercations so Mr. Kreiver, the former sergeant, was transferred to Boca Ciega. The school paired him with a black vice principal, Mr. Anders. They squashed the race problems from day one and won the respect of all students because they were fair. No one felt unjustly treated. My mother got tight with Mr. Anders. He was like a father figure to everyone. Between Mama and Mr. Anders they had their eye on me. "You make sure she's doing what she's supposed to," my mother told Mr. Anders and he stayed on the case. He would tell Mama, "Miss Betty, Angela can be this. Angela can be that. Angela can go to college."

In the meantime, my mother was laying down the law: "A is

excellent, B is above average and C is average. I don't have no average children. Don't bring home no Cs," she'd say in her usual melodramatic way. Mess up academically, and you'll be off of cheerleading, off of this, off of that.

"I ain't average," I started thinking. I hadn't considered this before. "I'm above average—excellent!" My mother implanted such high academic expectations in me that I began to believe her. It was a real turning point. She had prepared me to be independent. "You're going to college," she would say. She thought fly, fly, fly, little bird. Drop the eaglet out of the nest and she'll flap her wings before—splat!—she hits the ground. And then she'll pick herself up and try to fly again. I think that was her intention from the beginning.

So I did well in school—I was the first black person in my high school to be admitted to the National Honor Society. But I didn't work too hard—I did my academics enough to impress the teachers and Mr. Anders. I was popular and hung out with everybody. When I got off the bus in the morning at school I'd go to Bible study with the good, straight Bible kids. Then I'd hang out in the dining room with the nerdy kids. When I started reading poetry and performing monologues and doing little plays, I'd hang out with that crowd. I also hung out with the cool kids—I was a cheerleader until I pulled a hamstring and couldn't do the splits anymore. I hung out with all different groups of people. I wanted to be good, but I also wanted to hang.

But all this monitoring by Mom, Mr. Anders and even Mr. Kreiver made me feel like, "Ugh, I can't do *anything!*" Unlike D'nette, who back then was a goody-goody, a drag—she's the life of the party now—I was the kind of kid who wanted to get my foot up to the edge, hang it over and then come back before it got too dangerous. My mother smoked, so I would steal her cigarettes and hide them in the tears in the sofa cushions. When D'nette wasn't home, I'd smoke my mother's Winstons. My head would be swimming. Mom didn't have any liquor around so I didn't drink. I wouldn't try reefer even though I was around it a lot because of something my mother told me.

"Do you know what grass is?" my mother would ask.

"Noooo," I'd answer, knowing full well I did.

"Grass is not the stuff outside. It's called marijuana and kids smoke it," she'd say. "Once my cousin Connie gave me some and I didn't know my ass from a hole in the ground."

I thought that was amazing—that she didn't know her ass from a hole in the ground. What did it do to you? I wondered. But then she'd go on this long talking jag with you—it could be for hours—about smoking marijuana. She'd be in the kitchen cooking and you just had to sit there at the table and listen. I didn't want to try grass after that.

At parties I'd be around people smoking reefer, which most of the kids were doing at the time. D'nette, who my mother made me take everywhere, would sit there with both hands over her nose and mouth—at the party!—trying not to breathe.

"They're smoking reefers in here!"

"Yes, they are, but we're not," I'd whisper. "Why do you have to act like that? Can't you be cool? You're gonna embarrass me."

I also started to straddle Mama's rules concerning boys. In tenth grade I got a new boyfriend, David, and we liked each other a lot. During this time my mother, who had always told me not to get pregnant, tried to be close to me. She started talking to me about men. I remember that she'd warn me, "The ones you don't love will love you, and the ones you love won't love you." She also started talking about the first time I'd have sex.

"Angela, I want to know. I want to be there," she'd say to me.

"Really, Ma—physically?"

"No, not physically. But I want to be there for you."

The morning after I lost my virginity I told my mother about it.

"Ma, I did it," I said while we were at the breakfast table.

"You had sexual intercourse! With who, David?"

"Yeah."

"Why? *Why?*" she demanded. "Did he threaten to break up with you?"

"*No*, Mama!"

"Come on, let's go for a ride."

"Ma, can I come?" D'nette asked.

"No, D'nette, you stay home," my mother told my little sister.

Then we drove around and she talked to me for what must have been seven or eight hours—until I was blue in the face. All that openness up front, then after it happened, "Oh, no!"

After that I decided having sex was not worth braving my mother's tirades. I thought, "Forget this. I'll wait and have sex when I go to college!"

In eleventh grade there was a little college boy who liked me. I'd tell my mother that I had to go to rehearsal for a play I was in. I'd go to rehearsal and do my four lines then my boyfriend would pick me up. We'd go back to his dorm room and start kissing, kissing and hugging and rubbing and kissing. Oh, I could kiss like crazy, but there was no way I was having sex! Each night it would be kiss, kiss, hug, hug, rub, rub and then, "Stop! Take me home." This went on for night after night. The young man was nice. He wouldn't push and he always took me home when I asked him to.

When I was in high school, I also participated in Upward Bound, an academic and cultural enrichment program for underprivileged kids. We didn't see ourselves as underprivileged. In fact, in St. Pete's we were the cool kids. David Davidson was captain of the football team and very smart. He wanted to be a lawyer. Kenny Leon had a mom and a stepdaddy and he was in the program. Today he's a Broadway director. He directed the version of *A Raisin in the Sun* with P. Diddy in it. In Upward Bound, I got to meet kids from around the city and different high schools. We did African studies, little plays, read poetry, got tutored—that kind of thing. When I was fifteen, George Langhorne, the program's director, informed me that he had handpicked and submitted me for a special program. I was being invited to attend the Presidential Classroom for Young Americans. It was supposed to be a great honor, and it was a total surprise! Mama and Miss Mattie got my wardrobe together, bought me a coat and sent me up to Washington, D.C. I lived in a fancy hotel room for a week with three white kids from around the country and around the world. I had never been away on my own, I had never stayed in a hotel and, other than going to North Carolina, I had never really gone anywhere. It was a rite of passage of sorts.

The Presidential Classroom program was about government, government, government. "When there's a war, inflation goes up, down or whatever…." "I have a question, Mr. Senator…." Political, political. Well, I didn't have any questions. I was just sitting there thinking, What the heck are we talking about? This is boring. Are we gonna see some monuments? Then we'd go look at monuments. I took a lot of pictures. Later, I showed them to Mama, who has a way of describing things that could hurt your feelings if you took it that way. "It looks like a stick in the ground," she said about the Washington Monument.

One night they took us to the Kennedy Center to see a play, *Of Mice and Men,* starring James Earl Jones. I was touched and moved by the play, and James Earl Jones, who played his character so beautifully. It was just great! And when he, as the character Lenny, got shot on that stage, I cried. The theater had emptied, the people were gone and I was just sitting there, boo-hooing. "How can these people just leave?" It was like a spark had gone off inside me. If I could make people feel as passionately as I feel right now, I thought, that would be a wonderful thing!

After that I started participating in the drama society at

school, if you want to call it that—we didn't really do a play or anything. When I was a senior, the society held an evening of monologues. I remember doing one from *A Raisin in the Sun* of Mama talking to Benita.

> *...when do you think is the time to love somebody the most? When they gone and made things easy for everybody? Well then, you ain't through learning—because that ain't the time at all. It's when he's at his lowest and can't believe in hisself 'cause the world done whipped him so!*

I put on my great-grandmother's blue-and-white dress, stuffed the bosom full of paper and made up my hair and face to look old. I remember people applauded and received my performance well. It touched them. I thought, Oh, maybe I'm good at this! I'd perform at church in the talent contest, I'd get with Kenny and we'd do a scene from a play together, and we had arts nights at Upward Bound—that kind of thing. I'd read Langston Hughes poems: "Madam and the Rent Man," "Madam and the Phone Bill," "Madam and the Minister."

At the library I found a recording of Ruby Dee reciting the poetry of Langston Hughes. You know, Ruby Dee is good—she can do poems! So I just copied her and was good at copying her. I really connected with the sentiment of one poem in particular that she did entitled "Final Call." It was powerful and had a great rhythm.

I performed "Final Call" at a CME Church conference one time. I was so nervous after my recitation that my knees buckled. But then people started applauding. I received a standing ovation from the crowd of more than one thousand people. Experiencing the rush of applause from so many people almost blew me backward—it made me feel good. Later I entered and won a oratorical contest put on by Optimist International. Experiences like these made me feel validated and assured and confident in my abilities. I had a sense that God had given me a gift. The works of these great black artists that I read and performed heightened the sense of excellence my mother had implanted in my spirit. They also connected me to the rich cultural legacy of African-Americans, and made me aware of black people's strength, struggles and accomplishments.

At the beginning of my senior year, my mother received a letter on a yellow legal sheet of paper from Mr. Langhorne, my old Upward Bound director. He had gone on in the world—he was in the army and had been stationed elsewhere—and hadn't been in contact. But he sent my mother a letter telling her where to have me apply to college.

Dear Betty, I know it's time for Angela to start applying for college. Have her apply to the University of Virginia, University of Miami, Harvard, Yale, University of California at Berkeley...

Until then, I had been thinking about going to Howard, since it was a very prestigious black institution and I had visited D.C. before. Then somebody suggested that I apply to Mount Holyoke, an all-girls' school in Massachusetts.

I didn't know what other schools to apply to. I'd been to Florida A & M University; that was okay. I liked the food—they had greens and fried chicken—but the dorms were kind of old and they had roaches in them. I didn't think I wanted to go there. Where should I go? Close by? Far away? California seemed kind of far…. The counselors at school were no help. If you didn't ask them to get in your business, they didn't get in it and you went wherever you went.

Since Mr. Langhorne had sent this letter, I applied to the schools he suggested, along with Mount Holyoke and Howard. I got into Miami first, and was awarded the Martin Luther King Scholarship and only had to pay four hundred dollars to attend.

Then I got into Howard but had to pay five thousand dollars, which seemed like a million dollars. I got into the University of Virginia but not U.C., Berkeley. I also got into Mount Holyoke.

"That's a girls' school and there are two kinds of lesbians—born and made," my mother warned.

I didn't know what she was talking about; we'd never had a conversation about lesbianism. But I figured she didn't want me to go there.

When I got the acceptance letter to Yale my mama started screaming, "My baby's going to Yale! My baby's going to Yale!" She fell onto the bed, started kicking her feet into the air and having a fit. I was just sitting there reading, "You have been accepted out of nine thousand applicants…." All I had to do was get a thousand-dollar loan—from them. So I guess I'll be going to Yale and not Howard, I thought. But I was very intimidated. I remember trying to push to the back of my mind the thought "they're supposed to be smarter in the North. I may not be able to cut it." I did, and decided, Well, I'll go for a year. But if I can't cut the mustard and get kicked out, then I'll go to Howard, which is where I wanted to attend anyway.

Of course, after I told my counselors I got into Yale they were proud and thought it was wonderful. I remember one of them saying, "You're going to Yale! That is the best drama school in the world!"

Ah hah!

Chapter 2

Where the Heart Is

I come from a family that took what life dished them and made the best out of it. My father, Conroy Vance, was from Chicago, where he was raised in a foster home. His biological parents had given him up when he was three or four—old enough to remember them and to have been traumatized. I don't know why his folks didn't raise him and don't know if he did, either. He never recovered from the abandonment, yet he lived a full and meaningful life.

My mother was the oldest daughter of Lloyd and Virginia Naomi Daniels. She had one sister, Lois Ann, right behind her in age, then eleven years passed before her brothers Lloyd and then Lee were born. My maternal grandfather—everybody called him Pappy but I called him Granddad—was president of the longshoreman's union in Chicago. Between his income and my grandmother's clerical work for the Chicago Department of Treasury, they and their children lived decently, as the lives of black folks in the 1930s and 1940s went. Working on the waterfront was difficult and dangerous, and in the winter when Lake Michigan would freeze over there wasn't much work. As head of the union, Pappy would tap into the treasury to help members out during those frigid months. To hear family members tell it, when my mother was in her late teens, Aunt Lois's new husband insisted on working on the docks. Pappy didn't want that for his son-in-law. But he gave my grandfather an ultimatum: "If you don't let me work, I'll sit at home." Pappy relented, and apparently, one winter, gave him some money to tide him and Lois over. Someone reported Pappy to the authorities. The police came after him. Pappy evaded the cops for six months. But while he was on the run they harassed his family, banging on the door of my mother's childhood home at all hours of the day and night. After a while, my grandmother couldn't take it anymore. She packed up the kids and moved to Boston, where she had grown up (she was born in Washington, D.C.). When my grandfather turned himself in, he was locked up for two years. Once he was released, he went back to work on the docks, but my grandmother and the children stayed put in Boston. Yet it wasn't a split in the traditional sense. Grandmother and Grandfather spoke several times a day and Grandfather was always in Boston for the holidays. However, the separation had a deep impact on the family, especially the boys, who had been very young when my grandparents split.

My mom attended DuSable High School before she moved to Boston. That's where she met my father. Daddy planned to go to college. His biological parents had left him a sum of money that he was to use to further his education. He had dreams of becoming a lawyer. But when the time came to go to school, the money was gone. His foster father had spent it, thinking it was "money for me to raise the kid." Dad saw that as a tremendous betrayal. Believing he had college money, he had messed around in high school. He had to go into the air force instead. He was bitterly disappointed. For a while he was stationed in Alaska, then Maine. When he got out, he went to Boston University on the G.I. Bill. At that point he and my mom hooked up.

* * *

My parents got married in 1955. My father wanted to have five children—he wanted a big ol' family. My mother didn't want to have children immediately. Because of the age difference between my mother and Aunt Lois and their two younger brothers she felt that she and her sister had had to raise their two younger brothers. Despite these reservations, Cecilie was born in 1958. A year or so later they moved to Detroit, when Daddy was offered a job managing a low-income housing development, which meant we could live there at reduced rent.

Right after they arrived in Detroit and while my mother was pregnant with me, someone tried to kidnap my sister, Cecilie, whom people say was an "exceptionally pretty baby." Mommy was shopping and turned away for a moment to look at some groceries. Cecilie, then a toddler, started to wander—until a woman said, "Ma'am, is that your baby?" My mother turned around just in time to see a man holding Cecilie's hand and walking toward the door. Mom started screaming. The man dropped my sister's hand and kept walking out the door. Thank God, my mother got Cecilie back. I was born in 1960. Shortly thereafter someone else almost took Cecilie. My folks weren't about to let anything else happen to their children. They were determined to get Cecilie and me into environments where we could grow up unscathed.

Cecilie (I often call her Cec, pronounced "Cess") and I were very close. She was the big sister, charged with looking out for me. I was her "little brother." My mother would tell her, "Make sure you take care of your brother." Most times that was cool, but, of course, sometimes she didn't want to.

"Just make sure to do it," my mother would say.

During the first few years of my life we moved around the Detroit area about every two years. We lived in a small house in Inkster, Michigan, across the street from a small park. Cecilie and I would play on the playground. One time Cecilie climbed feetfirst through the handrail at the top of a sliding board. Her lower body got through but her head got stuck.

"Help me, Court!" she cried. I looked up. Her feet were dangling in the air and she was hanging by her hands. But I was too small to help her.

"DADDY!" I screamed as I lit out for the house. When Daddy and I returned, Cecilie was barely hanging on and her hands were trembling. She couldn't hold on anymore. He pushed her back through the bars and basically saved her life. He was so proud of me that day!

I was a very curious child—I just liked to see how things worked. But Daddy wasn't very happy with me when I put my blocks in the toilet to see what would happen. It stopped up the toilet on Fourth of July weekend so they had to pay a plumber triple double time to repair it. My mother and father took turns "beating" me. They were so hot they probably even let Cec get in a couple of licks! Then there was the time my father took Cec and me up into the attic. "Stay on the beams," he told me. Curious about what would happen if I stepped off the planks, I ventured onto the pretty, pink insulation. It gave way. I grabbed onto Cec. Next thing you know, we were both falling through the ceiling. Cec landed first and "cushioned" my fall. Needless to say, she was very unhappy with me. My mother was mad at my father for taking us up there. Another time I sprayed Lysol on the concrete basement floor and lit a match. *Whoosh!* I just wanted to see what would happen.

When I was about six, my parents moved into Detroit proper onto West Grand Boulevard, one of the main drags. We lived in a formerly all-white moneyed area that black folks had come to inhabit, where huge houses had been subdivided into two-family and four-family homes. If you had a two-family you had an entire floor. I think we lived in a four-family house. Still, to us it was really big. The lawns were fifty to eighty feet deep. "Hitsville," the headquarters of Motown, was about eight doors down the street. We used to sit on the stairs of the house next door to Motown and watch the people come and go. We were too young to know who they were but old enough to know we should watch them.

As long as I wasn't causing minicatastrophes, my mother encouraged my curiosity. When I was six years old, she read me a book called *Henry the Explorer.* It was about a little boy who read a story about polar bears, then set off to explore his town with his dog, Laird Angus McAngus. I loved *Henry the Explorer!* It taught me to be curious about the world—that whatever I could read in a book or dream, I could go visit. When I was little, the only world I knew was my block, so I explored my block. My mother would make me a peanut-butter sandwich and tie it up in a bandanna. I'd tie the bandanna to the end of a long stick and carry it over my shoulder, just like Henry did. Then I'd go to the parking lot two doors down the street, where snowplows had created huge mountains of snow. She always kept a close eye on me. "Don't look! Don't watch me," I would tell her. (Of course, she watched me through the window like a hawk.) When I got to the corner I would climb one of the mountains of snow, sit down and eat my sandwich, then go back home.

Although Cec didn't always feel like being bothered with me, she'd beat you up if you tried to mess with her "little brother!" I remember a time when we went trick-or-treating and some bad boys swooped down on us to take our candy. As I cried, "They stole my candy!" Cecilie took her flashlight and started hitting them to protect me. She gave them so many bumps from her big flashlight that they let her keep her candy and ran off. Daddy was so proud of her that night.

But during the summer of 1967 life on West Grand Boulevard changed. I stood on the front porch of my family's home as a long line of army tanks rolled down the street. I didn't know what was going on—I was just excited because G.I. Joe was on my street. "G.I. Joe—there he is!" I'd shout as National Guard tanks rumbled by. G.I. Joe was my favorite toy—I loved G.I. Joe. I had all the G.I. Joe figures and stuff. The troops were headed toward the Twelfth Street area of Detroit, where black people were rising up against the lack of jobs, horrible housing and widespread police brutality. Their neighborhoods were being bulldozed to make way for I-75. The Detroit Riots changed the city—and our lives—forever.

During the five-day uprising, I could feel the tension and apprehension in the air. Sometimes G.I. Joe would stand guard along our street. One day I walked up to one of the soldiers to say hi. He turned and pointed his bayonet at me! I was shocked and traumatized. That night, my parents powwowed and decided to get out. They didn't want us in the middle of all the mess. Making matters worse, the riots deprived Daddy of his livelihood. The Bi-Lo grocery store he managed farther down West Grand was one of the businesses burned to the ground.

As was his habit, my father rolled with it. He found a job as a foreman at the Chrysler plant. For the next eighteen months he and Mommy socked away money so they could buy a house. For a while we stayed in a very small apartment on Dundee Street, until June 1969, when we moved into our family's new house, a five-bedroom dwelling on Appoline Street.

Until that point we had lived in a segregated, all-black world. Racially, Appoline Street was mixed—predominately white and Catholic with a few black families. My parents were ecstatic and felt they had made an incredible move. They wanted to be a part of integration and to raise Cecilie and I in a multicultural environment where we could learn how to deal with living in a "white world." Now we lived between two white families. To Cecilie and my delight, one of them had ten kids!

The neighbors on Appoline Street were tight and looked after each other and all of us kids. Our house was in the perfect location. We were one block up and across the street from the public school we went to and the playground where we played "pom-pom touch." Pom-pom was a game where you raced from one side of the fence in the schoolyard to the other side while you tried not to get tagged by whoever was "it." If you got tagged you had to go to the center of the field with everyone else who got caught. The kids in the center would call "pom-pom" and everyone who hadn't been tagged yet would race to the other side. The goal was to be the last one touched. On top of playing pom-pom, my friends Clarence, Greg and Darren and I played touch football in the street. The driveways were the first downs and two light poles were the touchdowns. You couldn't keep me out of the street!

We all played together without incident—black children and white. I don't ever remember being called "nigger" or any other racial slur. But the adults around us were going through it. Black folks were all about "black power." White folks were scared and moving out of the city in droves. That June, when we moved into the neighborhood, "white flight" wasn't happening on our street. By the time we went to school in September, the neighborhood had "flipped." The white folks who could get out, got out. By the first day of school the neighborhood had turned predominately black. Only a handful of whites remained. We couldn't leave at that point. My parents thought, "What have we done?" They knew they'd never get their money out of the house. In just three months their dreams of raising us in a mixed neighborhood had gone up in smoke.

But from my nine-year-old perspective, I didn't see "white flight," I just got new friends to play with. The neighborhood was still a great place for Cecilie and me to grow up in. The street stayed very neighborhoody, and black and white families looked after each other. Cecilie and I were the neighborhood's little "stars"—everybody loved us. We were quick and could run fast, but we were also cool and got good grades. When we played pom-pom we never got caught—and if we did end up in the middle, we were quick enough to catch everyone else.

* * *

In spite of all the hard knocks he'd endured, my dad worked hard at his job at Chrysler. Daddy was wise. He liked to read though he didn't have much time. He was also very gregarious—he was the center of attention in any room, a life-of-the-party type of guy. My father loved to talk and explain and debate and look at things five and six different ways. He really should have been a lawyer. I didn't like all that debating and arguing. When I would try to keep up, he would talk me down. I would just get confused and get mad. Cecilie could hang with him; her mind was nimble like that. But while they were debating and arguing, I'd say, "This is boring. I'm gonna go play some ball."

On weekends my father hung out with his family and fixed things. Dad was very handy. He could fix anything. He'd read fix-it books and might take a couple of weeks to figure the thing out, but he would figure it out and then head to the hardware store. He was the kind of man who wanted to have the tools in the house *just in case* he needed to fix something. I was Daddy's boy—he used to drag me all around. "Courtney, roll with me." We'd go food shopping and run all kinds of errands, but we'd always end up hanging out in the hardware section at Sears. When he was ready to tune up the car or fix whatever, I was his helper. He didn't show me how to fix anything myself, but I knew all the tools to hand him. He'd tell me, "Courtney, hand me the Allen wrench," and I'd give it to him.

My dad was also independent. He was one of those black men who, perhaps because of his life circumstances, was determined to do everything for himself. Most of the time he did—and did it right. But he could be independent to a fault. If he made a wrong turn or we got lost in the car, he hated to ask for directions. I remember driving around in circles, with my mother going, "Conroy, will you stop at the gas station, please?" Cec and I would be in the back seat. "Oh, gosh, Daddy, please stop."

My father and I hung out a lot together. But our interests were different. We didn't have a lot of things in common, and emotionally we weren't on the same page. I was rough-and-tumble on the outside, but I was also very sensitive. Daddy would laugh at my tenderness. I remember back in the days of the natural and Afro, he gave me an ultimatum: comb my hair or it all comes off. It hurt to comb my hair, so I didn't like to do it. He told me I'd have to suffer the consequences: the dreaded "bald head." I remember feeling embarrassed after getting all my hair cut off. I didn't want anyone to see me just yet. As we rode our bikes home from the barbershop, I asked Dad if we could go down the side streets so my friends didn't see me. My plan worked beautifully right until we reached the beginning of my block. One of the young twin boys a few doors down saw me. "Ooh, look at Courtney," he hollered. "Look at the bald head." I broke into tears. My father laughed so hard he just about peed himself. When I was older—I was in high school—my first girlfriend broke up with me. I was just destroyed. I ran into the house saying, "It's over, it's over!" Daddy burst out laughing again. I ran upstairs and into my room. He wasn't very good at dealing with feelings. Between his insensitivity and the kids on the playground, I learned not to show my emotions often.

Dad also didn't know how to have one-on-one conversations about some of the more personal aspects of life. That included the birds and the bees. Beginning when I was about nine or ten, he would come into my bedroom on occasion and ask me if I liked girls. I would just say no—what kid wants to talk about the birds and the bees with his parents, especially at that age? It was territory that I certainly didn't want to go into. But in reality my little buddies and I had been noticing girls since we were six or so. The first love of my life was a pretty little girl named Gina. She and I developed a crush on each other and everyone thought it was cute.

Now I'm sure Mom sat Cecilie down on several occasions and went through the birds and the bees speech, but Dad never said, "Son, let's sit down and talk." Instead, he put the burden of whether or not we'd have "the talk" on my shoulders. Because I had no intention of bringing it up, I missed out. I effectively avoided that speech for my entire childhood.

I had, however, stumbled onto my father's stash of *Playboy* magazines back when I was six. Dad hid the magazines in the basement in his office. Back then, *Playboy* was soft-core porn—breasts, side views, hands strategically placed. But no genitalia. Still, the centerfold was enough to make me say, *"Whoaaa... This is cool!"* They were secret. Taboo. And they were in *our house!* Of course, the fact that I was secretly peeking at my father's hidden pornography only made me feel more uncomfortable about talking about my sexuality. But today I realize that his difficulty getting below the surface was chiefly because of his background. There was an unspoken understanding when I was a child that certain questions about his childhood were off-limits. As I got older I became curious about finding his parents, but although I suspect Dad knew some things about them, he never expressed any interest in finding them.

My mother was very nurturing and always took care of us. She was the family's implementer, following up behind the scenes after my dad gave his directives or did his life-of-the-party thing. She made sure we did our homework and finished our chores. Mom was an educator and a librarian. She was always reading books. To this day she reads or listens to more books than anyone I know. We were always around books. In our home there was an unspoken rule that you'd better read and do well in school. After school, Cec and I would usually hang out at the library where she worked. The library was our touchstone, our sanctuary—and the place we went to bug her, especially after she transferred from the main library to a local branch five minutes from home.

"Mommy, Cec is doing this…"

"Mommy, Courtney's doing that…"

Physically and educationally, the library was huge in our lives. I used to explore the stacks and try to figure out where books on different topics were located. There were fun things to do there after school and on Saturdays. When I got older I'd write my school papers there. As a librarian, Mom was involved with all kinds of groups all over the city—literacy groups, homeless groups, Habitat for Humanity, book clubs. Long before publishers sold books on tape, Mom would read aloud and tape stories so people could hear them. A whole community of people in that library system supported each other and helped lift us up.

Cecilie and I didn't always go to the library after school. When we were younger, we might stay home with a babysitter. When we were older, we'd stay by ourselves. Sometimes when we didn't go to the library, we would sneak and watch *General Hospital* and *Dark Shadows*. Cec was a TV junkie. But the only time we were actually allowed to watch TV was cartoons on Saturday morning and *Jacques Cousteau, Wild Kingdom* and *Disney* on Sunday nights. From the example my mother set, I learned the power of lifelong learning.

Because my mom was so nurturing, I felt that I could always go to her and just talk about whatever was going on—I didn't have to have a debate. If Cecilie didn't do what she was told, I would go to Mom and tell on her. Cec was a little fireball. You couldn't tell her or make her do nothin'. When I was eleven we got two dogs, Rana and Pepper. We were supposed to walk and feed them, but when it came time to get up in the morning, Cecilie would say, "I ain't getting up, Court. You get them." And I would.

Although Cecilie could keep up with my father in debating, she and my mother were close, as well. They talked about everything. However, once Cec became a teenager they became like oil and vinegar. They would often bump heads, but always came back together.

We were your typical lower-middle-class, black-American, slightly dysfunctional family. Our parents believed in kids having chores. On Saturdays, Cec and I cleaned the house. I would take the upstairs, she would take the downstairs and we would do the basement together. I might rake the leaves, mow the grass or help shovel a neighbor's sidewalk for allowance money. Our parents also believed in discipline. We grew up with spankings and punishments. We didn't think of raising our voices. Sucking your teeth or rolling your eyes were grounds for Lava soap on the tongue, which has to be one of the worst punishments ever devised by parents! After a while, Cecilie and I were self-checking—our parents only had to look at us and we would fall in line.

After our chores were done, my parents always had ways of keeping us busy. I would go to the boys' club and play bumper pool or basketball or peewee football, and they would take us to museums and the theater and other safe environments where we could dream and learn. Sometimes we would go ice-skating at the Jack Adams Memorial Arena near our house. On Sundays we went to church, although when I was twelve we just stopped going. I never knew why, yet I missed it. We didn't go on family vacations, probably because my dad worked all the time. Plus, traveling was expensive. But when I was a teenager, Pappy came and got us and took us out to Boston. There I met my extended family. We talked to my maternal grandparents on the phone three times a week and definitely on Sundays. I grew up in a family where my grandparents had the longest long-distance relationship I'll ever know in my life. That's what we knew—really keeping in touch. We were on the phone all the time.

On the downside, my parents argued about money. They

had this thing about "this is your money, this is my money." As best I can tell, they never worked that out. Mom just chose to let Dad manage the family finances. And my dad always seemed to have a lot of secrets. He closed himself up in his office a lot. My mom would retreat upstairs.

Other than that, we were a tight little unit—our family did everything together. Mom and Dad protected us and kept us close. They instilled in us the spirit that we could do what we wanted to do and be what we wanted to be. If we could think and dream it, we could do it. But that was tempered with a you've-gotta-work-it ethic. "Things are not going to come easy, but you can work for them." They couldn't protect me from the harsh realities of being a black boy, but my parents knew that if they armed me with education, knowing right from wrong and the knowledge that I was loved, I would do all right.

Over that first year or so that we lived on Appoline Street the climate began to change. The peer pressure shifted from being about school, good grades and running fast, to what you were wearing and how well you could fight. You had to fight to defend yourself and your reputation. Now, it wasn't like today, where if someone is bullied, they might turn around and say, "I'm gonna kill you," and mean it. It was more like, "I'm gonna get my cousin and he'll beat you up," or "I'm gonna get you after school," and the whole school knew, gathered around and almost forced you to fight.

When we played, we played hard! Pom-pom one-hand touch gave way to pom-pom two-hand touch and finally to pom-pom tackle. In pom-pom two-hand touch you had to touch the person solidly with both hands at the same time. If you touched them with one and then the other, that was considered pitty-pat, and pitty-pat didn't count. Of course that led to a lot of arguments!

"That was pitty-pat!"

"No, I touched you two-hands solid!"

"No, you didn't!"

"Yes, I did!!!"

To make sure you didn't pitty-pat, you had to hit somebody solid and might even push them over. And if someone called, "pom-pom tackle," hey, you just had to do it. You had to tackle somebody on the gravel, which, of course, my mother hated because it would tear up my clothes. Needless to say, all the pushing and tackling led to a lot of altercations.

Fighting over pom-pom was one thing, but during the first semester of fourth grade, I was peer-pressured into fighting in school. Fred, a friend who was also my nemesis, called me out one day in homeroom. I can't remember what he said, but they were definitely fighting words.

The entire class said, "Oooooh!"

I told him, "You can't call me that!"

He said, "I did!"

The whole class was asking, "Whatcha gonna do, Court?"

I remember the teacher saying, "Courtney, don't you get up!"

But I had been called out. I had to get up for my reputation's sake. Next thing I knew, we were fighting and getting sent to the principal's office. Now, this was back in the days when there was still discipline in the schools. Teachers could spank kids, and all the paddles were different thicknesses and had different names. But there was no abuse. You'd get paddled on your hands or your bottom at school, then get a spanking when you got home for doing wrong in school. Back then, parents accepted that if the teacher paddled you, you must have done wrong. And they were right; we were always trying to get away with something. I know that if those paddles were not there we would have overrun those teachers. For that incident I got paddled and suspended for three days.

Now, when I got in trouble for fighting in class, my parents knew that something was really wrong. I was "Courtney-Boy," as my mother called me. I was a nice kid and well behaved. I was not a person who fought—that was not like me at all. And worse than the fact that I fought at all was that I fought *in class*. My parents went down to school and had a conference with the teacher about what had gone down. Then they came home and had their powwow with each other. They came to the conclusion that they had to get us out of that school. If they didn't, they knew that something was going to go down that would be out of their control.

Cec and I got wind of the fact that they were thinking about putting us in a different school and we were going to run away. We packed our bags and hid them under our beds. As usual, our parents scooped us; somehow they knew what was going on. While we slept, they pulled our bags out of their hiding places and put our clothes away. The next morning we were on our way to a brand-new school—a Catholic school called Mother of Our Savior. Because it was a Catholic school, my parents would have to pay tuition. It wasn't cheap and they couldn't afford it but they figured out a way, although it increased their financial stress. The world Cecilie and I lived in changed overnight. This was our first experience at a mostly white school, an environment I would remain in for high school, college and grad school.

I finished out grade school at Mother of Our Savior, followed by St. Mary of Redford for middle school. I did well academically at both places and although they were basically all white, my experiences were, for the most part, uneventful. I had my white friends at school and my black friends at home—except for one black girl at school named Marie Hollis. Boy, did I have a schoolboy crush on Marie! I remember pining over her. One day I slipped a note in her math book and waited anxiously to see if she liked me, too. Unfortunately, she didn't. But we ended up being good friends. I learned that you can't make somebody like you; some relationships are just meant to be what they are.

On weekends and over the summers I continued to hang out at the Boys' Club. I went to Boys' Club camp and even became a youth counselor. The adult counselor, Mr. George Browne, was a teacher and the track coach at a prestigious and expensive private school called Detroit Country Day School. One day he told my father, "Your son is pretty smart. He should apply for a scholarship." I did, was accepted and got a partial scholarship. My father delivered the surprise.

"It's going to be a sacrifice but you're going to Country Day," he told me in the basement just before school began.

I was very excited! Ever since I had seen the campus I had wanted to go there. Country Day was located in the suburbs. The campus was huge to me. There were a lot of fields, it was open and the people were nice. They had glass backboards on their basketball court, which was a big deal back then to a little jock like me. And the fact that I now would have to travel twenty miles to school each day had activated the "Henry the Explorer" in me. As I got older my world got a little larger, and I would explore my neighborhood on my iridescent yellow, single-speed bike with the banana seat.

Now that my world would include a school located twenty miles away, I was intrigued about the route out there. Riding in the car with my parents, I observed that the service road along the highway went all the way out to the suburbs. It made me want to explore on my bike. I couldn't ride on the freeway but I could take the service road, I thought. That summer between middle school and high school I went exploring. School was out, so there was no big hurry. When I'd come to a place that was unfamiliar, I'd say, "Hmm, how am I going to do this? Well, I can go over there..." I didn't read maps; I plotted it until I figured it out. Once football practice began in August, I knew how to ride my bike to school. My parents said, "Call us when you get there, boy." Thinking back on it, they were pretty brave. They could have said, "Stay in the neighborhood." Once school started, my parents paid a student who drove to take me to school. When I turned sixteen they handed down our little clunker station wagon to me and I had my first car and my freedom!

On top of exploring the route to Country Day, while I was a teenager I explored all of Detroit. I became a bike-riding fool! I'm still a bike-riding fool today. I'd tell my parents where I was going and what route I was going to take. Then I'd pack a lunch, get on my bike and call them when I got there. They let me ride around the whole city, which is pretty amazing. I guess they knew that I liked to explore and wasn't gonna do nothing—I just wanted to ride around. It was pretty dangerous, though. I always stayed on the sidewalk but I could have gotten hit by a car or truck—and it wasn't like there were cell phones back then.

Looking back on it, I realize that "Henry the Explorer" changed my life. "Henry" was huge to me because it was all about dreaming. And letting me explore the world around me was a wonderful gift my parents gave me. The things I discovered as I explored reinforced the things they were telling me about how whatever I could see in my mind, I could be. It also meant that when I could, I would be leaving Detroit.

If ever there was a kid who was excited about going to a high school, it was me. I was really excited and thankful that my parents were allowing me to go to there. I loved going to school at Country Day because there were all these great classes and a lot of activities and there was no peer pressure about clothes or fighting. I became a Country Day boy—I took advantage of everything! Academically, I was a B/B+ student. I struggled with math and science because my Catholic-school curriculum hadn't been as rigorous. But the teachers tutored me and didn't abandon me and made learning fun and exciting. And by my junior year I *got* it and ended up with an A in chemistry, my most difficult subject.

On top of my academics, I played football, basketball and ran track. Eventually, I captained all three teams and became three-sport All State. Mr. Browne, the track coach who had been my boys' club counselor, became a good friend and mentor and grew very close to my mom and dad. When I was a freshman I was given the chance to make an announcement about a tennis tournament. I had never heard or seen foreign names like Pancho Gonzalez before, and the fact I couldn't pronounce the names became a funny thing to everyone. After that tournament, I started reading the homeroom announcements. I did lunchtime skits and parodies of teachers with the other kids. I did student council, I sang in the choir—I did everything you could volunteer for. I did so many things when I was at Country Day that my parents, who came to practically every event—my dad often left work early—practically lived at the school.

Compared to the white kids with their precise way of speaking, when I arrived at Country Day I guess I talked kind of "country." But the more I spoke in public at school, my diction, English and vocabulary improved. I stopped sounding as country, but after being around so many white kids for so long, I started getting a little confused. After a while my sister asked, "Courtney, why do you talk 'white'?"

"What?"

I didn't understand what she was talking about. "I don't talk 'white'!" I'd tell her.

It was a confusing time, and I could have used a little assistance from my dad to help me with these very different worlds I was navigating. Cecilie went to Catholic school with white kids for a few years, then went to Cass Tech, the best public high school in Detroit and an integrated, although mostly black, environment. She had a big Afro, was all about black power and wore POW bracelets. I wore a shirt and tie to school. I had been a black boy in white schools since the fourth grade. Yet I lived around black folks. Nobody had talked to me about how to hold on to my sense of myself as a black child immersed in a world of white folks. Nobody had ever asked me, "Courtney, how do you feel going to an all-white school?" I was a child. It was just, "This is where you're going to school." Back then integration was a big thing and our parents wanted us to go to integrated schools. And black parents weren't talking to kids about that kind of stuff—how to be a black kid in a "white" world—least of all my father, given his background.

So there I was in the classroom every day, dealing with being the only black kid. I had no one to talk to about how I felt about it, nor did I know that it was even something we could have been talking about. My parents had raised me with such love and confidence that wherever I was, I liked everyone and everyone liked me. It wasn't until I got older that I began to have a real hard time dealing with the feeling that I wasn't wanted.

My black friends with wealthy black parents who were Country Day "lifers" didn't share my enthusiasm for the school. They thought, "I don't know why Courtney is doing all those things. I'm just trying to finish, I'm tired of Country Day." I didn't understand why they weren't into it. But they had been there forever and knew the negative kinds of things that were going down and could go down behind the scenes.

It wasn't until my senior year that I got a taste of what they may have been talking about. I had been playing three sports for three years and I was exhausted. I wanted to play football, prepare for and take the SATs, then run track. When I announced that I was not going to play basketball for my senior year, word got all the way to the headmaster of the school. He called me into his office.

"Courtney, I hear you're not going to play basketball this year," he said to me.

"No, I'm going to rest and focus on my studies and get ready for track."

"Well, Courtney, we want you to play," he responded.

"But I don't want to play," I told him.

"We *want* you to play."

"But I *don't want* to play."

"*Courtney*, we *want* you to *play*."

"Well what if I *don't* play?" I asked.

"We will revoke your scholarship," he said as he stared at me over the top of his bifocals.

"What do you mean?!"

"We *will* revoke your scholarship if you *don't play*."

"I didn't know I had an athletic scholarship."

"Well, you do."

I walked out of the office in shock. I had made Country Day my whole life—I was a Country Day boy! Now the headmaster was trying to intimidate me. When I told my parents what had happened they couldn't believe it. They thought I had a needs-based scholarship, too. The headmaster may have been lying—I don't know. My family had a powwow. We probably could have pushed it but it was 1977 and my parents were hard-pressed to pay what they were paying. We didn't want to risk what could happen if the school took any money away from us. We agreed that we'd put the incident behind us and I'd suck it up and play. Needless to say, it was a long season. On top of that, our team wasn't very good. But I didn't get an attitude—I played and played hard.

That year I had a girlfriend, Kristin. Because there were very few black students, we had known each other the whole time. But all of a sudden during senior year it was different. "Wow, it's you!" Kristin and I both lived in Detroit but didn't see each other outside of school. We practically lived at Country Day; we were both there for fifteen hours a day. I would see her during the school day, when we were studying, when she would come by practice and at Country Day parties. We were tight. This was when I first learned that sometimes when the timing is right a friendship can turn into a love relationship.

I kept doing my thing and keeping my eye on the sparrow— I had decided I was going to Harvard. My mother's brother Lee had graduated from Harvard back when I was eleven. That's when I decided I wanted to go there. Now, I didn't know anything about Harvard—Uncle Lee had gone there so I wanted to go there. But as far as Country Day was concerned, I decided, "Y'all can try to do to me what you think you're going to do. I'm going to Harvard and I'm not letting anything get in my way."

Neither my college counselor, nor the teacher who was the Harvard rep at Country Day, thought I would get into Harvard. He focused on helping the white kids. My counselor tried to steer me toward applying to smaller, less prestigious schools. The lack of confidence they had in me really did not make me question myself. I applied to Harvard, Brown, Northwestern, University of Pennsylvania and Michigan, even though my counselor told me I had a very low chance of getting into any of them due to my test scores. But as the acceptance deadline loomed, I did play with the idea of applying to one or two "safety schools." That April, my mother called me at school to tell me that an envelope from Harvard was waiting at the house. That same day there was a big invitational track meet after school. And all of a sudden the Harvard rep was acting nice to me. He was handing out the first-place tabs for the preliminary, semis and final races (of course I was coming in first in my heats of the hurdles). That's how I knew I had gotten in. I was admitted to every school I applied to. We talked about it as a family. I got more financial aid from Brown than Harvard. But my mother's people were in Boston. My parents felt more comfortable with me going there. Once again, even though it would cause strain, they decided they would make the sacrifice. Kristin was going to Swarthmore, outside of Philadelphia. We decided we would wait for each other. My dad told me, "Courtney, that's going to be tough; you're going to college now. But do your thing."

After all my hard work, solid academic achievement and school spirit, at graduation I got an incredible surprise: I was awarded the Headmaster's Cup, the highest honor a Country Day student could receive! Everyone stood up and clapped for me. My mother told me later that my father had been in tears. That summer I got a little parchment with my name written in calligraphy in different colors, saying I'd been admitted to Radcliffe, Harvard's former sister school for women—someone obviously thought that with the name Courtney I was a girl! Later they sent the parchment for Harvard. I got them framed and still have both.

Chapter 3

In My Element

That summer of 1976, I visited Aunt Golden and Uncle Grover in North Carolina then she took me to Yale and deposited me there. That was the first time I had seen the campus. Before classes started I attended the two-week preregistration orientation program for minority students, so I had friends and knew my way around the campus before everyone else invaded. I definitely felt intimidated when the other students arrived, though not as much as I might have. When I heard where these other kids had gone to school—prep schools like Andover and Exeter—I started thinking again that they were smarter. Everybody seemed to have taken years of ballet and flute and piano. They were all so talented and said they were majoring in subjects like premed and political science. I was the only person thinking about being a drama major, and I was fighting that at the time. I remember thinking, Well, they say schools in the North are better than the schools in the South. But then I'd see how the kids acted and say, "But they don't seem to have much going on in the common-sense department."

I had three white roommates. They were nice enough. The young woman who shared my bunk bed was from Chapel Hill,

North Carolina. I remember thinking they washed their hair a lot. And I had to get used to the whole climate thing—I didn't know anything about layering. I remember freezing, and lying on top of the radiator and waiting for that *tick, tick, tick* as it warmed up. When I bought boots, I got the wrong kind. Everybody kidded me as I trudged through the snow in my yellow rain galoshes. For my work-study job I washed dishes in the cafeteria and tutored kids from the community in math and English. I didn't have much money and Mom didn't have any money to send me, yet I came home every Christmas. One time I brought my roommate Deedee with me. Her mother had passed away while we were in school, so I said, "Come on, Deedee, and come home with me!" After we bought our tickets we only had seven dollars between us.

Academically Yale was difficult. I never needed a tutor or anything but I remember having a lot of self-talks in the mirror.

"Are you gonna quit? Are you gonna drop out?"

"If you drop out you can say that you came and you stayed for a year."

"What are you gonna do?"

"Are you gonna stay up all night? Then stay up!"

"Well, go on and cry if you want to cry. But then what's that gonna help?"

"Okay, now get up and wipe your face."

But then I got my first A or did an all-nighter and got a B. Then I felt okay.

Socially I was popular, but dating was pretty hard. There were certain girls the guys liked. We'd call them the "stars." They'd usually be fair-skinned with long pretty hair. I didn't look like that. After the "stars" were taken, the boys might look over our way a bit. But when you were a lowly freshman, you couldn't get nobody. When I was a sophomore, I dated a freshman. Then he broke up with me. It just seemed that for some reason the black girls and guys couldn't get together. The boys were up and down the road going to different schools. We girls had to scheme to get kisses from them.

"You like him? All right, let's see how we can help you get into a romantic situation." I guess none of us seemed as provocative as the girls somewhere else.

I remember one time I was talking to Mama about some guy whose attention I was trying to win or keep. She was just not impressed.

"Shit, *you* the prize!" she told me. "He ain't shit, he ain't all that. *You* the prize."

I hadn't thought about that before, but it stuck—it resounded. It resounded. *I'm the prize!* I recall thinking, "Oh, that's a good way to think of myself"—not that I was better than anyone else, but that I was worthy of being respected and treated nicely and loved and thought highly of and taken care of. Since my father hadn't been around to tell me I was his beautiful little girl, his princess, or to model how a good and proper man should look and behave, I hadn't had an example—well, at least nothing that felt warm and familiar. So when I went out into the world I hadn't already seen a good man or known what he looked and felt like. Still, I wasn't out there looking for it, trying to make up for it. I didn't have a brother, uncle—nothing. Just my great-grandfather, Slater Stokes—and Granddad Leroy, whose girlfriend lived right across the street, but that was a bit of a mixed message. Then there was my mother's uncle who ran the beer garden, but I was young and couldn't go up in there to see him running his business. The other men in my family who were good and up to something lived someplace else. On a daily basis, I saw my teachers, the principal, the pastor of my church, my best girlfriend's daddy—one of them had a daddy.

The idea that I was a prize was very new to me. I practiced it to varying degrees. I remember one boy asked me not to be mad at him for something he had done. I recall thinking, You poor nothing, you unintelligent person. You're not worthy of my time. Don't even think of me—don't think of me at all. Don't even look my way! I was definitely overreacting but that's how I interpreted valuing myself, being the "prize." Plus, I was proud that I had come so far with fewer resources than the average person; at one time I hadn't had anything and now here I was at Yale—not that I was consciously trying to be more than I was. My male friends called me on my stuff, though, which wasn't too hard to do. It was like I was wearing a miniskirt but my judgment "slip" was showing all the way down to my ankles.

But in spite of my academic challenges and lack of a love life, I have to admit I partied in college. We partied—literally—from Wednesday to Sunday, whether playing bid whist (I was a lousy fourth hand for someone desperate), going to a house party where one student's brother was the DJ or hopping the train to New York City. My roommates and I would go to the latest and hottest clubs. We could dance all night long in our four-inch heels. Then we'd nearly fall asleep in Grand Central Station waiting for the train home and get back with our feet hurting and back all out of alignment. Our counselors wondered how we were going to graduate. We burned the midnight oil—both ends of the candle and the middle, too.

Once I got to college I started to perform in a lot of plays. There are twelve different colleges at Yale. Each had its own drama society and would put on different productions. Then there was the University Theater, which was beautiful and reserved for the biggest plays. I was doing plays every semester—myself and one other black girl, Cheryl Rogers. Our friends would come see us in *Hedda Gabler, Uncommon Women* and other plays they ordinarily wouldn't have come to see, and enjoy them. I also performed at antiapartheid demonstrations to pressure Yale into divesting from South Africa, which were going on all the time. I didn't know a lot about the politics. I couldn't run down the statistics. But I could find poems that would relate and get up and perform them in the Commons area of campus. It would go over very well and when I was performing, I was in my element!

At one point Auntie Golden advised me not to waste a Yale education on a theater degree. By then I was aware that it was the graduate drama school, not the undergraduate theater program, that was the best in the world. Still, I thought, I'm here and the drama school is right up the street! Thank you, Lord! And I'd walk down the street and—Hey, that looks like James Earl Jones! and it was. He was performing at the Yale Rep in *A Lesson from Aloes.* So for the first three years I tried not to major in theater. Instead, I studied administrative science— business. That seemed to be more practical. But I was just not into statistics and trigonometry and math that looked like artwork—squiggle, squiggle, triangle, equals sign. At one point I told myself I needed to put my priorities in order and focus on my studies. I didn't do any plays that semester, but I found myself still doing all-nighters. I thought, Well, I might as well do my plays if I'm going to do all-nighters anyway.

Eventually I went down the list in the Yale course directory: classical studies, women's studies, history, molecular biophysics… None of those seemed to be much more practical than theater, and it seemed like a B.A. or B.S. didn't get you too far and that everyone would need an advanced degree. Otherwise, what were you going to do with political science or economics? I wondered. I had heard that you could get into business school with a degree in any major, so I decided to throw myself into theater. If it didn't work out at least I'd tried, then perhaps I'd apply to Wharton, a prestigious business school.

By the time I figured all this out, it was too late to change my major to theater. So I majored in African-American studies/ theater, which caused my appreciation of black people, our culture, achievements and struggles—some of the most dramatic of which had unfolded during my childhood—to deepen. My knowledge of our history and culture would shape my attitudes and beliefs about the opportunities I would later seek and accept. I also squeezed in a lot of drama courses and did a performance thesis in addition to my regular thesis on the history of the Negro Ensemble Company, down in New York, the first major theater company to focus on black life, and offer black writers, directors, producers, actors, playwrights and craftspeople the opportunity to produce works that reflected their cultural values and determine their own destiny. Lloyd Richards, one of its founding members, had just come to Yale to become the dean of the drama school. I got to meet him and asked him to get me an introduction to Douglas Turner Ward, head of the Negro Ensemble Company. The folks at NEC opened their files to me.

I didn't get the chance to come to New York often; however, as I traveled in and out of the city during my college years, I did get to spend a little time with my father. He lived in the Washington Heights neighborhood of Manhattan. Several times I spent the weekend with him and his longtime, live-in girlfriend. We'd usually travel over to Teaneck, New Jersey, where Uncle Jerry lived, and we'd all hang out. They'd put on music, drink Crown Royal and we'd laugh and shoot the breeze. The first time we got together, Dad tried to suss out where I was and act cool.

"What do young folk do today?" he asked me. "Want some reefer?"

"I don't smoke reefer! I don't do drugs."

I noticed he didn't offer D'nette reefer when she came to visit—he'd had a velvet picture painted of her; he didn't have one drawn of me. I remember feeling closer to Uncle Jerry than my dad.

As one such weekend was drawing to a close and I was about to return to campus, I remember having a conversation with my father about our relationship.

"Yes, you are my father," I told him, "but I haven't spent time with you. Getting to know each other is a process. After nineteen years I can't just run and jump on Daddy's lap."

Well, that did not sit right with him. He said, "No, I am your *father!* I'm your dad." To me, his response felt like "Bullshit! No, it doesn't take time. I'm the father, you're my daughter. Daddy, daughter—we are close!"

"Yeah, you're my father and I love you and you're half of why I'm here. But to have a relationship, it takes time to get to know each other."

He said, "No, it doesn't."

He was drinking and it wasn't going so well, so I figured I'd let it go.

"All right, Dad, I'm leaving," I told him. "Give me a kiss."

When I went to kiss him, he put his tongue in my mouth. I pulled back—I *shot* back! I was *shocked!* I was *mortified!* I was *FUCKING MORTIFIED!* My father had kissed me like a woman—that crossed the line! Your boyfriends put their tongue in your mouth, I assume my father put his tongue in his woman's mouth, but—drunk or otherwise—a father shouldn't put his tongue in his daughter's mouth—*EVER.* If I had known what was going to happen I would have had the presence of mind to slap the *shit* out of him. I would have slapped him sober! But I was shocked. I didn't say anything. I just got out of there as fast as I could.

On my trip back to New Haven, I began to process what had happened. I was furious! That was *fucked up!* I couldn't believe it. Then again, he *was* drunk—he had drunk a lot. I didn't know if he thought that was okay to do or whether maybe in his drunken state he was confused about who I was. It really didn't matter though. My rule about drinking is: you control it; it doesn't control you. And drunk or not, in my mind that was just more evidence to me of the lack of the relationship between my father and me. His relationships had never been father/daughter; they'd always been man/woman. Perhaps in his very inebriated state he reverted to what he knew. Whatever was going on with him, it was some kind of interesting human nature something or other. I wasn't going to let it fuck with my head for too long. Life with my dad was just what it was. I came to the conclusion that this was just part of what happens when a family isn't at its best—the way God designed it to be: a mother, a father, the children. Some men just don't know how to be fathers. My dad was one of them. He didn't have a clue. I never brought the incident up—we never talked about it. But I paid a price for my silence. Between not having a father figure and having so many men try to take advantage of me, it definitely colored the landscape of my relationships. I don't think I was as strong as I could have been in saying no to men whose behavior didn't measure up to the standards I had in mind. Thank goodness I had acting to channel all these emotions into.

As for my dad, I didn't ask for another kiss until he was on his deathbed.

For my performance thesis during my senior year I directed and acted in Ntozake Shange's *For Colored Girls Who Have Considered Suicide/When the Rainbow is Enuf*. I was The Lady in Red. I applied to perform the show at the University Theater on what would have been parents' weekend. They didn't pick us for the main show that ran on weekends—probably because we weren't doing *South Pacific*. But they did give us the Monday through Thursday before the big parents' day show. We figured that they felt we weren't good enough to be the stand-alone show for parents' weekend. But now I understand that it was incredible validation of our talent that Yale University—where the white sons and daughters of privilege prepared for the world—permitted us to perform on their main stage. Still, we put on the play and featured all these wonderful women who were strong, passionate, talented and had an artistic flair. The show was so moving and engaging that the university asked us to extend it for another four days. On top of that a black church and a community organization wanted us to do it for them. After a while it seemed like the play kept going on and on, but it was very well received. Auntie Golden came up to see it. "Wow, you're really good!" she told me. That was very affirming, since she once thought pursuing theater would be a waste.

So during my senior year I was acting and directing on campus, in and out of New York researching my thesis, and talking to theater greats like Lloyd Richards and Douglas Turner Ward. I also made friends with some of the graduate drama students, like David Allan Grier, Reg E. Cathey and Izzy Monk, who were actors (David's also a comedian); Jim Simpson, a director, who went on to marry Sigourney Weaver; and OyamO, who wrote *The Resurrection of Lady Lester*. I performed in *The Resurrection* with some of the grad students at the Yale Cabaret that students put on. That year I decided to apply to both Yale and NYU drama schools, but when I went to NYU to visit, I realized I wouldn't apply in time to get financial aid. So I had to put all my eggs in one basket. Jim Simpson agreed to critique my monologues. I did two—Lady Anne from *Richard III*, and Frankie from *Ladies in Waiting*. Then I auditioned for and applied to the prestigious Yale Drama School—and got in!

Unfortunately, my mother was never able to afford to come to Yale to see me act. But she did make it up for graduation. She was so proud of me and I was grateful she had encouraged me to attend. My dad also came. I was a little reserved. "Oh, hello…" Still, it was cool to have them both there together, along with Auntie Golden, who definitely wouldn't miss it. It was cool, it was definitely cool.

I started drama school at Yale that fall of 1980. There were about seventeen students in my class—about ten men and seven women. Of those, there were two black guys and two black girls: Charles Dutton, Roger Guenveur Smith, Sabrina Le Beauf and me. Two brown skins, two light skins. Our class was like the little orphan class. We didn't have any big stars or any pretty, pretty, pretty girls or any handsome, handsome, handsome guys. By industry standards we were just a hodgepodge of regular-looking interesting/character people—you know: tall, skinny, bald, comely, black; no one voluptuous or blond. At twenty-one or twenty-two I was about the youngest in our class; the median age was around twenty-seven or twenty-eight. Most of the students had been out in the world. When someone would tell them, "You go from this class to that class, then take a test, then break down the set, then go to rehearsal and you will go from morning 'til night," they thought, "Oh, please! I'm fully grown. I don't feel like doing that. I'm sleeping in." Or they had opinions and would challenge the teachers. "I don't particularly like voice class and don't see why it's all that important. I'm tired, I'm going to miss class today. I'll go next week." They upset the traditional dominant-subordinate roles of professor and teacher. I think that after our class the program was composed of mostly younger students.

By and large, acting school is a really exciting time. You're breaking a script down, you're chatting about the characters and good and bad performances, you're doing a play, you're sitting around at the "gypsy" bar where all the grad students hung out. You're into something you love and want to dedicate your life to. You aren't out trying to find yourself; you didn't say, "Let me try to do something practical instead of what I love to do." You've found it—and it didn't take thirty years! Everyone is training so they can hopefully survive in this impractical profession where people are always telling you that only five percent or ten percent of Screen Actors Guild (SAG) actors actually make a living, and the other ninety percent are doing other jobs.

Even though it's very exciting, drama school is very hard

work. Everyone loses weight the first year because you don't have time to sit down and eat. I existed on coffee, Snickers and bagels. Academically, we had classes, scene study, the history of theater, voice class, singing class, movement, fencing. When I was not in class I was at my work-study job. After first semester, on top of academics, you have to do things like put on a Shakespeare production in ten days—build the set, sew the costumes, learn your lines, rehearse with your classmates, everything. When I think back on it, what we accomplished was amazing. It was so awesome—I was in love with it. And there were so many talented students, like Sabrina, Roger, Charles, John Turturro, Jane Kaczmarek and Kate Burton, daughter of the famous actor, Richard Burton.

Unlike out in the real world, race in drama school was, for the most part, a non-issue. You were supposed to grow up and be a teacher, a doctor, a lawyer, those kinds of jobs. We were already different—young, artsy, ain't none of us gonna make no money right off the bat. Race didn't make that much difference. We might deal with it in the context of a scene, like if we were performing something of Athol Fugard's, the great South African playwright. But for the most part we would deal with race later, in the real world, the marketplace. While we were in school any conflict we experienced was mostly interpersonal. We rarely allowed race to restrain our feelings, our intuition, our delving into the psyche and human emotions. I'm the mama, the white girl's the daughter and you're the audience. We believe it and we say it is, so you believe it, too. And no one was talking about, "Okay, when you graduate, some of you are not going to work. It's not because you're not talented, it's because you're black or Latino." Or whatever the 109 other reasons are why people don't work, like you're too tall or too short. For the time we convinced ourselves, "It's going to come down to talent, right?"

* * *

In October of my first year, my father's girlfriend called me with the news he was in the hospital. He hadn't been taking his blood pressure meds and came home from work with a really bad headache, which wasn't like him. She took him to the hospital, where they learned he had a brain aneurysm. I didn't know what a brain aneurysm was—I now understand that he was having a stroke—but it was brain stuff and sounded serious enough that I tried to get there. Kate Burton was one of the few students with a car. When she heard my dad was in the hospital, she offered me a ride to his hospital in the Bronx. She dropped me off and I found my way to his room. I remember he was very lethargic—I don't know if it was from the meds or the aneurysm. One eye was half-shut. We talked a little bit, and I spent the night somewhere down the hall in the hospital. Then I had to return to campus the next day. Before I left I said, "Dad, I'm getting ready to go. Give me a kiss."

"No, not today," he answered. "Some other time."

"You're really not going to give me a kiss?"

"Nah," he said—not mean, but real cool-like.

"You seriously aren't going to give me a kiss?"

"Maybe tomorrow...."

I was a little hurt. It wasn't like we were super-duper close, and especially given our history, I didn't *have* to ask him. He died two days later.

Daddy's funeral was held in a funeral home in New York. I remember going into a very small chapel, walking forward through the pews and seeing my father laying there looking all stiff and puffed up with formaldehyde or whatever they use, his hands propped up on each other on his chest—not in a position I'd ever seen him in before. I guess there's no way to make the dead look natural. As I looked at his body, a part of me was detached—"Wow! Look at you." That part of me wasn't sad and found it all very interesting. I remember wandering into the rooms with other dead people in them and getting spooked. I was thinking, "*Whoo!* Let me get out of here and back to the room where my dad is."

Another part of me sensed mortality. Finality. That part of me felt sad. I remember thinking, I didn't have years with you or the relationship I wanted or dreamed of with you, I had the relationship that I had. I knew you, spent some time around you, had some interaction with you, and my mother never spoke ill of you, but I longed for more. Yet all my disappointments aside, I was grateful for him. Despite all I did not get from him, I got life from him. All that's particular and singular and unique about me—half of it came from him, from his genes. And the family I did get from him—D'nette, Grandmom Brownie, Aunt Golden, my uncle Jerry, my sister Jean and her sister Lynn—all of that was because of him. Now he was gone.

While I was sitting there, my aunt Helen, Uncle Jerry's wife, tapped me on the shoulder from her seat in the pew behind me.

"Angela, this is your sister Lisa."

I turned around and looked into the eyes of this sweet-faced sixteen-year-old girl. I remember reaching my hand out, shaking her hand. "Hello, Lisa. You're so pretty!"

When I turned back around, I looked at my father in the casket, eyes closed. "Well, aren't you something else? This is some extra drama. *Whoa!* I have another sister I didn't know about, and she's sixteen and I'm twenty-one!"

My sister Jean was sitting next to me. She was just learning about Lisa at age thirty-three. She was visibly upset and shaken. "Oh, my God, this is so terrible! How does this happen that people die and you're meeting siblings at funerals. This is just over the top! This is not supposed to happen! This is so inappropriate!"

Lisa may have been a secret to us, but somebody knew about her; she didn't get from North Carolina to New York on her own.

During the funeral they played my father's favorite song,

"Danny Boy," an Irish song I imagine he loved because his name was Daniel Benjamin Bassett. That has to be one of the saddest dirges that has ever been written. It is so sad. So beautiful. I cried. It really took me there. Life and death were hitting me in the face at once. My father and I had both been trying to create a father-daughter relationship. But if you don't have the tools and you don't have the time, you just don't make it. We didn't make it. Now there was no chance of reclaiming our relationship. I was stuck with: my dad put his tongue in my mouth, my dad didn't kiss me to say goodbye and then he died. And now I'm meeting my younger sister at the funeral. You can't do that to someone! Thank God I was an actor and could use all these emotions and experiences in my characters. I had grown to expect a lot of drama and foolishness. It didn't bother me.

While I was a student, as far as I'm aware, not many of the male students were romantically interested in me. Some guy from the other side of town kind of liked me. He was much older—he had to be in his forties—and I was trying to be cool and deal with him. But he wanted to get me involved in stuff I didn't want to be involved in. You had to run for your life! One particular situation whose details I will keep to myself involved a massage, a piece of material (he was making swimsuits), some scissors—then out came the Polaroid camera. I shouted, "Put that down! I'm going to be somebody one day, I cannot be in these kinds of situations."

During my last year of school, Charles Dutton and I started dating. I needed one roommate to fill out my three-bedroom, three-bathroom apartment on Dwight Street in New Haven. The apartment was really nice—big, long, spread out, quiet and you didn't feel up on top of each other. It was also near campus. I wanted to keep it. I think Charles was a little reluctant at first; he already liked me. But he acquiesced, moved in and everything was copasetic.

I thought Charles was a fascinating person. He was about twenty-nine or thirty and street-smart. Before coming to Yale he served an eight-year stint in prison for fatally stabbing someone during a fight. While he was locked up, he read *A Day of Absence* by Douglas Turner Ward, one of Negro Ensemble's founders, whom I had met. It changed his life; he started doing theater while in prison. When he got out, he applied and was accepted to Yale. I admired Charles as an actor. He was—is—phenomenal, very powerful, compelling. He is a mesmerizing performer; you can't take your eyes off him when he is onstage. His performance begs you to watch. You want to see his character develop and unwrap itself, layer upon layer upon layer. I admired his instinctual ability—his approach seemed to be more intuitive than technical. He was certainly learning the technique from his studies but didn't always know how to break a script down into iambic pentameter—unstressed, stressed, unstressed, stressed. That didn't matter. He could get up onstage and speak as if he knew exactly how to break it down. He knew how to perform Shakespeare in iambic pentameter from somewhere deep in his core. That married with his passion, and usually his audience would eat it up. Some of our other classmates were brilliant students, but when they got up to perform they didn't have that richness. Their performances were dry compared to what he was able to do. He was definitely the best actor in our class.

Doing scenes with Charles was amazing. I have always enjoyed working with somebody who is very, very good at what they do: I am drawn to them, attracted to them, appreciate them. He and I could relate as actors. On top of that he could be very sweet. He would just talk and laugh—he has tremendous charisma. He can get you on board and excited about anything. I remember wishing I could engage people to the degree he could. He could be talking about a jelly jar and people would look at him like he was talking about a vase from the Ming dynasty. He would weave spells and have people enraptured. Maybe it was witchcraft on a level. I remember watching him, knowing what he was talking about and wanting to say, "It ain't all that—it's a jelly jar. He's got you caught up! Talkin' 'bout a Mason jar…." Observing him was when I really understood the meaning of the term "confidence man"—he had a tremendous amount of assuredness when he talked about his ideas. He could make you go along with him. I remember thinking it was a gift and wishing I had it. (Then again, since what he was talking about wasn't always quite true, it might have been a little like lying.)

Men seemed to respect Charles, whether students or male teachers. He didn't take no mess off of no one. Somewhere along the way, he had earned the nickname Roc. Charles would cuss people out one day and be, "talk to the hand" without saying it. The other students would ask me, "What's wrong with Charles? Is he okay? Is he all right?" I'd say, "Yeah, he's fine. Ain't nothin' wrong with him." But everyone would be concerned about how he felt, was he upset? The next day Charles would smile easy, light up the world and draw people back in. "Hey man!" It was amazing to watch him. I could never dissect how he did it.

I don't exactly remember when my admiration for Charles turned into romantic attraction. He was talented, charismatic and sweet; he was intimidating; he was a protector; he trained as a boxer and was physically fit. I don't like bad boys, but I do like a man with a little spice. I'm not one for bland food; overall, I like interesting people—interesting and attractive, naturally attractive.

One night he came home to our apartment while I was on the couch taking a nap.

"Hey, girl, why don't you get on up and go to bed?"

"Whaaat?"

I starting working my feminine wiles. It wasn't too hard. You know, you act cold, he warms you up, you fall into his arms. Next thing you know, you're kissing and it's on. Now you're a couple. Now you're together. Now you need another roommate.

My relationship with Charles had its ups and downs. In private, he was very, very sweet—baby talk, that kind of thing. He would call his mother every week. When I would complain about the phone bill, he'd say, "When I was in prison, I couldn't call." What could I say to that? He also loved animals—puppies, birds, fish, parakeets. One of our classmates bought a little white pit bull, Radar. Roc loved that dog; she had a built-in dog walker. He would get the dog and go jogging, groom him, walk around with him. Animals seemed to relax him. Maybe with animals you ain't gotta talk and explain yourself like you do when human beings are upset with you. It was truly a case of man's best friend. Today I hear he has a farm—goats and a lion—somewhere back home in Maryland. So he had this interesting duality about him—bad boy, don't take no mess, real dangerous; yet very gentle by and large.

Of course, in addition to his plus side, there were certain things about Charles I didn't much care for—"What? You're betting on pit-bull fights!" I didn't know about all that. And he had a Don Juan complex. There was another little girl in the class below us who found him attractive, as well. I remember fussin' with him about the time and smiles and positive energy he gave her—and whatever else might have been going on. They were awfully friendly over in corners whispering and talking. I don't know if he was trying to make me jealous but I was. And, on top of that, she was white. I couldn't stand it, I couldn't stand *her!* I turned into a green-eyed-monster girl—I was jealous as hell. Of course, he assured me they were just friends—friendly friends. But in my mind it was more than friendly talk. Everyone knew we were definitely roommates, living together, going together or whatever. Yet my intuition— my woman's intuition, my actor's intuition—said something wasn't right. "If she was just friendly, then I would sense that. But I sense more," I would tell him. One time we were giving a party at our apartment. The phone rang and Charles and I picked up at the same time.

"What you doing?" the woman asked.

"Oh, Angela's having a party," Charles answered.

"Well, how long is it gonna last?"

"Oh, I don't know."

"Will you come over?"

"What are you doing?"

"Oh, I'm about to take a bath."

When they hung up I called him on it. In private. I ain't crazy like that: I ain't gonna fight in public.

"Oh, *I'm* the one who's having the party. Now it's *my* party!"

"Angela, you always imagining things. I knew you were on the phone. That's why I said what I said."

My head was tight and about to explode. I had my great-granddad in mind as my frame of reference for what a good man was like. I loved Charles but didn't think he was as cool as Granddad. I knew our relationship would end one day.

I know there were things Charles wished were different about me, too. On top of complaining about my jealousy and insecurity, he would tell me that I tried to be "perfect": I prayed; I went to church; I sang in the choir; I put my money in the Bible. The Bible was by the bed and the money was in the Bible. I figured that was the safest place for it—safer than putting it in your sock drawer, your underwear drawer or under your mattress. My thought was, "Lord, it's in your hands. Lord, multiply it!"

Eventually my nemesis classmate and I were cast in a play together—the one where I'm the black mom and she's the white daughter. When we had to work with each other, see each other, be up on each other, sense each other and see each other for who we were, we were cool. We liked each other. We talked once in the library.

"I was mad at you," I told her.

"I was upset that you were mad at me."

"Well, I was mad because I thought you and he were up to something. Maybe I was afraid of you."

Something might have been going on between her and Charles, or he may have been trying to make it seem like something was going on when nothing was happening. Whatever. The way I thought about it, none of it was forever—it wasn't like either of us was going to be with Charles permanently. Yet we had become two women at odds and had gotten all pulled out of shape over this thing. When we finally talked, we realized, "Oh, you're feeling like that?" That's when I asked myself, Is it worth it? I realized she was cool and that we were more alike than not alike. I reflected on how I had gotten to this place where I was in graduate school trying to learn and grow, yet during part of my day I was just agitated whenever I saw her. I had enough to worry about just trying to get through school, yet I had allowed this one person to *a-gi-tate, ir-ri-tate* the *hell* out of me. Because of this guy. Over this man. After we talked I got past all of the bullshit that was making me insecure and maybe her insecure, too. From that point on we had a mutual-admiration society. We made peace, embraced each other, healed, grew to like each other and worked together well. I appreciated her as an actress. After that experience I realized that women are just wonderful, and it's not worth having a man in the middle.

While all this was happening, my classmates and I were preparing for the "League" auditions at Julliard in New York. All the drama schools—back then, it was Yale, Carnegie Mellon, Julliard, NYU, ACT, there are more now—would present their graduating class and invite casting directors and agents to see them. During our last year, we worked with a couple of partners on our scenes. I recall I had three—one with Charles, one with Sabrina and another with Elly Koslo. I think we performed versatile Shakespeare contemporary avant-garde. The setup for the Leagues was real simple: you'd go from scene to scene to scene. In total, there might be an hour of Yale's Class of '83 presenting itself. After you performed you could walk down the hall and look at a preliminary list of agencies who were interested in setting up an appointment to meet you; maybe they have a project they're working on and want you to audition. But the real goal was to get an agent. Back then, actors were moving to New York to do theater—very few people were moving to L.A. That's what actors did after drama school. There wasn't a lot of television filmed in New York, except for *The Cosby Show,* soap operas and industrial films. So the goal was to find an apartment, an agent and go on auditions. The Leagues helped you make the transition.

After the Leagues were over, we went back to school and waited for a more detailed list of students the agents were interested in interviewing. Some might want to meet you right away; others might want to see you a little later. I think I had about three or four people interested in seeing me. That wasn't a lot, but some classmates didn't receive any requests. One girl in our class—Sabrina Le Beauf—just blossomed. She became the star of our class, the star of the Leagues with around seventeen requests. (Later, she played Sondra Huxtable on *The Cosby Show.*) So I took the train back down to New York to meet these agents, from the big muckety-muck agencies to the smaller boutiques. I went to Associated Artists, a small agency, last. I remember one of the agents, Louis Ambrosio, remarking, "Oh, we didn't think you were coming. We almost forgot about you."

"Well, good thing you didn't do that," I replied. I was young, I was cocky, I was graduating from Yale. We talked and I guess they liked me. I ended up signing with the agency, which later became Ambrosio Mortimer.

Everyone—my mother, my auntie and uncle—came up to my drama school graduation. It was an exciting day, full of possibilities. I have a picture of myself somewhere, looking very young, idealistic and fresh-faced. I was also happy because I had received a scholarship to cover my grad school expenses. So I only had undergraduate school loans to contend with, which was a grand total of about four thousand dollars. Of course, that seemed like a lot at the time. (When I had signed for the thousand-dollar loans each fall, I thought, "Gosh, how am I ever going to pay this back?") Now I told myself, It needs to be whatever it needs to be and I'm easily going to be able to pay it back. I even took out a little extra loan because I knew I was moving to New York and wanted to have enough to cover rent. And I had some graduation money my family gave me.

Charles and I had decided to move to New York together. We had found a little rent-controlled apartment an older alumna was subletting. I remember Charles told his mom, "Look where Angela keeps the money." I felt like I had to think about that for both of us.

Late that spring of my third year, Charles, John Turturro and I took a prospective student to a pub to talk to him about "the Yale experience". The brother's name was Courtney B. Vance.

Chapter 4

A Million to One

My first semester at Harvard was tough. Seeing my parents walk down the stairs was really hard. I can't imagine what that is like as a parent—are you bereft or ecstatic, or a combination of both? All I know is that I really, really, really missed Mom and Dad that fall of 1978. I had a hard time adjusting to college and all the academic pressure. "What grade did you get? What's your major? What are you going to do?" Plus, I wasn't raised to be a party boy, drinking beer and hanging out, which it seemed everyone was doing. At least in October I got to go to Swarthmore to visit Kristin. But when I was there she started talking about how maybe we should break up. When I got back to school, a "Dear Courtney" letter was already waiting for me. But needless to say I was blue. I threw myself into my classes and my work-study job.

Because I had done so much stuff in high school, I was exhausted and had had enough of extracurricular activities. I decided I would just run track and focus on figuring out what I wanted to do for my career. Figuring out what to do was important to me. My dad didn't seem to enjoy what he did for a living. After watching him struggle, I knew I wanted to find something that I was happy doing.

My plan was to meet as many new kids as I could so I could find out what their parents did. I knew that not knowing what we wanted to do, we would talk to each other and figure it out. But when I got there, I learned that everyone but me already knew what they wanted to do.

"I'm gonna make the money, brotha."

"How do you know? You're only eighteen," I'd ask.

"What do you mean—how do I know?"

"Where did you find that out?"

I was shocked. I felt like I was behind the eight ball, so I went to the Office of Career Services and Off-Campus Learning. You could supposedly go there and tap into alumni for career advice in certain fields. I'd try to contact the alumni but all their phone numbers were no good.

"I feel like such a loser," I told the career counselor.

"What are you talking about? You're a freshman!" she said. "What are you doing in here?"

"I feel like I'm behind everyone else."

"There's nothing wrong with you," the counselor laughed. "Now, get out of my office!"

That fall I started training with the track team. Because of that, I was with the same group of guys all the time. I liked them, but I felt like I did that in high school—hang out with the same kids all the time. "This is not working. This isn't part of my plan." I felt like I needed to be with a new group of people if I was going to meet kids and find out what their parents did. That's when it hit me—that was the end of competitive athletics for me. I felt like maybe I could meet more kids if I auditioned for plays.

I hadn't done much acting before. Right before I graduated from Country Day, I had played the tiny role of Mr. Witherspoon in *Arsenic and Old Lace*. It was a lot of fun and I promised my teacher I'd try acting again. But at Harvard acting was a big deal. Every department, every house had a different dramatic society. If you wanted to act, you could go from show to show to show. There were hundreds of plays and musicals going on at one time—large, medium and small. Multiply that by all the different colleges in Boston and there were thousands of plays going on in Boston at any given time. I figured I'd try out for some of them. It wasn't about the acting; I wanted to meet new people so I could figure out what I wanted to do.

The first audition I went to was for a play called *Mars*. We had to pretend to be things like steam, mist, fire and darkness. While I was waiting to be called, a beautiful girl caught my eye. Whoa! I thought. Inspired by her beauty, I threw myself into my roles: steam, mist, fire, darkness! I got a part. And that girl, whom, to allow her some privacy I'll call Ahren Moore, ended up being my girlfriend for the next eleven years. Ahren was an actress and dancer and very graceful—tall, statuesque, gorgeous. She was a sweet girl. I really liked that she was honest, simple and positive. In her world, the glass was always half-full. Ahren was the picture of beauty, inside and out. Her character and beauty were exactly what I had been raised to look for. And she was just the right girlfriend for a young man who had walked out of his family's house an innocent, who didn't know about the birds and the bees.

After my freshman year I returned home to Detroit. Jobs were hard to find that summer. I was blue. I knew my parents needed me to earn money to help out. Something finally broke in July. My dad knew someone at GM who got me a job filing papers. I started thinking that I might want to work there one day, so I became "Henry the Explorer" all over again.

I'm going to read about the different offices at the world headquarters, I thought. Then I'm going to go to every office and tell them, "I'm going to be a sophomore at Harvard. I just want to know what you do."

All of GM opened their doors to me. I'd call the VP of Legal or Purchasing and say, "I don't want to take up your time, sir, but I'm a sophomore at Harvard and may potentially work here. Do you mind talking to me about what you do?"

I met so many people that summer. The guys I was working with would ask me, "What are you doing on your lunch break?"

"I'm going to a meeting," I'd say. Then I'd leave my paper-filing job to meet with the VP of Worldwide Purchasing. When I left to return to school, everybody loved me and wanted me to come back to GM.

During the first semester of my sophomore year, I got bitten by the acting bug. I had a hard time telling Ahren that I wanted to be an actor. She was a serious actress. I was reluctant to tell her. I thought she wouldn't respect me or wouldn't think I was serious enough. I didn't want her to think that I thought that I could just come in and do what I'd call "this acting thing." I thought she'd say, "You can't become an actor, Court. This is my thing. This is what *I* do." When I finally told her, she was glad and told me she thought I was good. It was a big relief.

When I went home that Christmas I still didn't know what I wanted to do for a living, but at least I felt like I had a plan. I told my parents, "I want to take a year off and act." I wanted to go to Banff, a famous drama and arts center nestled in the Canadian Rockies. I had the brochure all ready and everything.

My parents just looked at each other. Cecilie was caught up in the Vietnam protest movement and struggling to stay at Michigan State and now here I was, wanting to drop out and act. They had taught me that I could be anything I wanted, but I'm sure in their minds they were thinking, "Oh, God, no! Not that!" My folks didn't know anything about acting except that most actors were unemployed, especially black ones. But they couldn't go back on what they had taught me now.

"Son, we don't mean to diminish what you want to do," my dad said. "But you can't take a year off. If you do, it will extend our payments. Stay in school, finish up and then you can do that."

"But I really want to act," I pleaded to my mother. "I don't know what I want to do for my career."

"What happened to all your confidence?" she asked.

"It's just so hard. Everyone seems to know what they want to do."

"You're going to figure it out, son," she told me. "It's going to be all right."

I was really disappointed, but what they forced me to do was come up with plan B. I realized I was at Harvard to expand my mind and learn, so I would do that. But people had been telling me about this thing called drama school and it sounded like something I wanted to do. "I'll expand my mind and do shows while I'm here, then I'll go to drama school when I finish." To be able to do shows, I felt like I needed to major in something that didn't require writing a thesis. I just wanted to take a blue-book exam. For some reason, history didn't require a thesis so that's what I chose. Then I took courses in everything histori-cal I thought would expand my mind.

I finally knew what I wanted to do! For the next two and a half years I threw myself into acting. I started with shows at Harvard, but college drama departments are real cliquey. If you acted in the major plays, you were with the same people in every show; the same people got all the major roles. I decided to get off campus. I started doing all kinds of stuff—hand modeling, working with commercial agents and going to major theatrical organizations like the Boston Shakespeare Company and Theater-Works. From doing that, I started to meet a whole dif-ferent circle of folks. I did an acting workshop in Boston, and our final showing was in front of the artistic director of the Boston Shakespeare Company. He invited me to become an ap-prentice with the company, and by my junior year I was a company member doing major roles in major plays like *Hamlet* and *Rosencrantz and Guildenstern Are Dead*. I was a company member getting a small salary. I was a little acting machine. I finally knew what I wanted to do! So much for GM—I had a plan and I was working it!

Of course, the folks at Harvard didn't know about any of these things. People never saw me at Harvard. I had disappeared. I would spend the night with Ahren or with my aunt in town, get up at 5:00 a.m. and ride my bike across the Charles River—rain, sleet, snow or shine—in time to do my work-study job, which was delivering *New York Times, Boston Globe* and *Harvard Crimson* newspapers to the students in Harvard Yard. I didn't know the bus or the subway schedule; I was always on my bike. It was only by the grace of God that I didn't fall under some bus wheels during a blizzard. I would deliver the papers to the kids living in Harvard Yard because it didn't conflict with anything else. But I had to get there by 5:30 a.m.; if I got there late, the students would take my papers. And guess whose paycheck that had to come out of? From there I'd go to classes in the morning and rehearsals in the afternoon. I'd do shows and see Ahren at night. I got very little sleep but I was extremely excited and happy.

The summer of my sophomore year I returned to Detroit and worked at GM. On Sundays I was drawn to church. I went on my own. One time I was so moved by the service I walked down the aisle, ready to give my life to the Lord. But something held me back. "No, I'm not ready." I turned around and walked out of the sanctuary. I would answer the Lord's call at a later time.

During the summers of my junior and senior year Ahren and I auditioned and were accepted as members of Shakespeare & Company, a theater and festival in Lenox, Massachusetts. About fifteen students lived communally in stables that had been converted to apartments on The Mount, the estate of Edith Wharton, a twentieth-century American writer. In exchange for doing things like dusting the house, mowing the lawn, pulling stumps and laying down gravel, we got free acting classes. It was a wonderful exchange.

Shakespeare & Company's approach presented a complete mind shift for me. Up to that point I thought acting was all about using different voices. I was good at that. Actually, I was becoming kind of arrogant about it. I thought we'd be learning about the intricacies of the text and iambic pentameter, the rhythm Shakespeare used for much of his work, which I thought was the next level. We didn't do any of that. Instead, we were called on to use our emotions. I didn't know anything about emotions—how to tap into them or use them. In fact, I had spent much of my youth hiding my feelings so I wouldn't get teased. Once I learned that we had to explore them, I copped an attitude. "Why you gotta explore your emotions? What's up with that?" I didn't realize that sharing your emotions is what acting is all about. All I knew was that I was being asked to stand in front of a group of people I didn't know and share personal things about myself. In one particular exercise, they wanted us to share two things about ourselves we wanted them to know and two things about ourselves that we didn't want them to know. Where I came from, revealing any vulnerability—not to mention deep secrets—could subject you to relentless humiliation. But here, they didn't want you to hold back; you had to reveal things. As my classmates shared, all kinds of things came up. Tears would suddenly start flowing because people were talking about things they'd never told anyone before. I thought, "You mean I've got to cry?" I said to myself, "Oh, Lord, that's too much. I don't know if I want to know that." This kind of intimacy was extremely foreign to me.

My first summer at Shakespeare & Company I was out of my depth. "What does this have to do with acting? How does it apply to playing Shakespeare? Why can't we just say the play?" In the meantime, it seemed like Ahren was having a great time. Unlike me, she had an ability to roll with things. She was free; she went with it. She took to the work like a duck to water. I was jealous of that and that I had to share her attention with my other fellow apprentices. "Wait a minute! That's my girlfriend. What are you doing?"

"Courtney, we're here with fifteen other people," she'd tell me. "Stop trying to monopolize my time!"

I found living with all these people twenty-four hours a day way too intense. And the emotional work made my head feel like it was going to explode, like it was going to shatter! Once I snuck out of the stables in the middle of the night. I was so stressed out that I overcame my fear of the pitch black—we were deep in the woods; I was thinking "lions and tigers and bears!"—and felt my way tree-by-tree to the road. When I got there I shook a street sign to the ground and just howled and howled. When I was done crying and screaming, I walked the mile or so to back to The Mount, felt my way back through the woods to the stables and went to sleep. In class the next morning, while we were lying on our backs doing vocal exercises, one of my classmates said to me, "Did you hear that moose out there last night?"

My eyes got wide. Fortunately, we were lying down, so he couldn't see them. "Yeah, man, I did hear that. That was wild, right?"

"Yeah, man."

That scared me; I didn't go out anymore after that. But I had done what I needed to do—scream.

I struggled in front of everyone all summer. It was frightening. It was agonizing. Eventually I had a breakthrough. As I was performing in the balcony scene in *Romeo and Juliet,* the emotion that was supposed to accompany my text suddenly flowed through me and I blew up the scene. Everyone said, "Oh, my goodness!" My performance was so compelling, and I'd overcome such a block, that they rushed toward me and lifted me up in the air. As I began to understand how to access and use my emotions, I became a different person. Suddenly, I developed a newfound confidence. I realized that I didn't have to hide my emotions all the time. When I was confused or in pain, I could use them—I could put them into a scene. Knowing that was so very freeing; I was on top of the world with glee! At the end of the summer my family drove through Massachusetts on their way back from picking Cecilie up from her flight back from Germany, where she had been stationed for three years in the army. After her grades had dropped, she'd had to leave Michigan State. "Just pick which branch of the military you're going into," my father had told her, "because you're not going to just sit around here." Being in the army instead of college had taught Cee her lesson. She later graduated Phi Beta Kappa from Northeastern University in Boston.

During their visit with me they saw me carry a spear in the play *Twelfth Night*. My dad was thinking, "This is what you've been doing? Okay…." But I could tell he was proud of me.

By the next summer I received another grant to apprentice at Shakespeare & Company. I had become comfortable with my ability to let my emotions flow through the words, which is what the audience connects with and what makes a performance levitate. This gave me a way to channel emotions I was feeling but not expressing, personally. I just took off. I had discovered my gift and I was on fire! During that time I began to think more seriously about studying acting in grad school. My Shakespeare & Company voice teachers warned me to make sure it was what I really wanted to do. "Acting school is hard and very expensive," they told me. "And three years is a long time to remain focused if the real reason you're going there is to find an agent."

Now that I was receiving praise for my work and felt a lot more like a real actor, my ego, which had already begun to blossom, really began to grow. That second summer I publicly criticized the performances of some of the professional actors in the program. "I don't understand what they're doing. Emotionally, they're not doing anything." Whether my comments were right or not was beside the point. Who was I but some college kid who had a gift he'd recently discovered? And where did I find the gall to publicly expose that the pros were struggling? Among the equity actors I became a pariah. Being so insensitive as to publicly embarrass people who were more accomplished than me was just one example of how I struggled in my personal life. I didn't know how to deal with my feelings in life or in relationships. I didn't have the tools, so I depended on Ahren. She was much more prepared for life than I. She could never be defeated; she always had a plan A, B and C. If something didn't go my way, I didn't have the tools to say, "Oh, well," and shift gears. When it came time to come up with options, I would shut down. I didn't know how to solve problems. Instead, I would just sulk; I would get blue; I would get moody. Ahren would think, "Oh, God. He's down again," and would navigate around me. But when I was feeling crazed, Ahren would calm me. "Courtney, you're fine. It's going to be okay." She was my emotional center.

Come graduation that spring of 1982, I told my parents, "There are no awards. No big show. This isn't going to be like Country Day. The things I've been doing, nobody knows about it—least of all, the Harvard community. So just come and let's celebrate." And celebrate we did!

My mother arrived a few days before my dad, who couldn't get off from work. She got there in time to see me star in *A Lesson from Aloes* by the South African playwright Athol Fugard, over at Boston Shakespeare. I was too young to do the lead role, but the director and leading company actor, Henry Woronicz, was a big fan of mine, had said, "Just grow a beard and let's go." I was amazed when I was able to go onstage, finish the play and not blank out on all those lines. My knees were actually knocking. Mom saw the play with the rest of her family. She was blown away when I came out onstage in my sixties outfit—a hat, a suit and a narrow tie. She said afterward that I looked like her father. My mother came back and saw the play again with my dad. Until then, they had been thinking, "We spent all this money to go to Harvard and the boy wants to be an actor?" which I'm sure was a nightmare for them, although they never expressed it. Now they thought, "He's got a gift. He's got to do this."

Especially after doing such a big role I wanted some training so I'd learn how not to be so nervous as to allow my nerves to defeat me—that's why I wanted to go to graduate drama school. All the members of the acting clique at Harvard were applying to Yale down in New Haven, Connecticut. I knew that's where I had to go. Other than that, I didn't know anything about Yale, except that the actress Meryl Streep had gone there. My goal was merely to learn how to stand onstage without my knees shaking. Everyone was saying, "Courtney, you're going to get in. You're so good!" But I didn't know—I didn't know anything. Plus, I was burnt out from all that I done while at Harvard. I didn't want to apply right away. I wanted to take some time to rest, choose the pieces I wanted to perform for my audition and practice my lines. I also wanted to make enough money to visit Ahren, who was going out to the American Conservatory Theater (ACT) in San Francisco. For a year I lived with my uncle and friends and worked the midnight shift as a security guard at the Boston Museum of Fine Arts and the Copley Plaza Hotel.

Working the midnight shift left me free to deal with just the art and my thoughts. I practiced the lines of the scenes I'd use to audition while I walked the floors. As I rehearsed the monologues, I'd look for their emotional heat, since expressing my emotions was now my strength and I was so emotionally available. I said those pieces to myself for nine months. They dropped so far down into me that I knew every nuance in them. I reached a point where I couldn't say them anymore to myself; I needed to share.

It's funny, but as important as that audition was, I don't

remember the audition itself; I only remember that in the moments immediately before it, I was off in my own thoughts and some tiny little ol' dog with a big bark ran up on me from out of the blue and scared me so bad I almost peed on myself. Fortunately, nobody saw how high I jumped. However, Earle Gister, head of the acting department at Yale, and Larry Hecht, who headed acting at ACT, told me they will always remember my audition. A few weeks later I received my acceptance letter. I was standing on my friend's front porch, which overlooked a cemetery, and opened the letter and I said to myself that this can either be a very good day or a very bad day. But either way, because of this cemetery, I will always remember it. When I saw that I had gotten in, I screamed. It was a life-changing moment. But my joy was immediately tempered with, "What about Ahren?" I called her right away. We both paused, unsure of what to say. When we realized we had both gotten in, we screamed together. The odds of that happening seemed like a million to one!

Ahren's parents were paying for her schooling. Mine could barely pay for Harvard; I'd have to pay for Yale. I didn't get any financial aid since I was under twenty-five years old and the school wouldn't replace what they believed should be my parents' financial contribution. I would have to pay for drama school myself, but I didn't have any money. I couldn't believe I had gotten in but wouldn't be able to go because I couldn't pay for it. It felt like my wings had been clipped. I was distraught and started having what I now know were anxiety attacks. I was so stressed I was freaking out. At one point I shifted to working days, but dealing with all the visitors and their questions made me anxious. When I'd reply, sometimes I'd hear myself talking gibberish.

Frantic to figure something out, I talked to the dean at Harvard who used to run Yale's drama school, who was a supporter of mine.

"They're telling me I'm not going to be able to go there because I can't pay for it. Do you think there's some corporate sponsorship I could get?" (Oh, how naive of me!)

"Why do you want to go to Yale?"

I was shocked that he tried to dampen my joy.

"What do you mean, 'why do I want to go to Yale'? Because I want to get trained at the best school in the country!" I felt devastated. Betrayed. Just like the counselors at Country Day who didn't think I'd get into Harvard. I never sought his advice again.

I did, however, call the financial-aid folks down at Yale. They were a lot easier to deal with. They encouraged me, "Come down here and talk to us and we'll see if we can figure something out." We did. While I was on campus I met a few of the students. Charles Dutton, John Turturro and Angela Bassett took me out to the Gypsy, the drama school hangout.

It wasn't until after we arrived on campus that fall that the Yale drama school administrators learned that Ahren and I were in a relationship. They were in complete shock; apparently, that had never happened before. Earle Gister told us that they never accept student couples because it's hard on the rest of the class. But Ahren and I had gone to different colleges and applied from different coasts, so it never occurred to them that we knew each other. Hundreds of people from all over the country had applied to go to Yale. Only fifteen had been accepted into our class. Three of us were black. Ahren and I were two of them. And we were a couple. I thought it was amazing! We just knew it was a miracle. Between being immature and the big ego I was developing to hide my insecurities, it went right to my head.

The first week of school was amazing. We met the acting school's dean, Lloyd Richards. I hadn't known he was black but now that I knew, I took pride in it. Later I would learn he was also one of the most renowned master acting teachers in the entire United States. My voice teachers from Shakespeare & Company also taught at Yale, so I already knew them. And Ahren and I did well when we students performed our audition pieces in front of each other. In fact, I was so excited that I went out and cut my hair into a Mohawk.

"Why did you do that?" Ahren asked me when she first saw me post-haircut.

"I don't know—I just felt like doing something to celebrate!"

"But why?"

"Because I was happy. I was excited!"

"You know something, Court? You're wild."

"Yeah, it's crazy, right?"

I was really so excited that my dreams were coming true. In many ways life couldn't be more perfect. But though I appeared confident from the outside, on the inside I felt intimidated. I didn't feel that I belonged. I had participated in Shakespeare & Company but I had no technical knowledge about acting. Acting is emotional but it's also technical. You have to know the technique of it. Some of the other students knew more technique than me. The women in our class were very, very, very strong—dramatically, comedically and personalitywise. They blew most of the men away.

Ahren and I rented an apartment in New Haven about a mile off campus. I'm sure our parents were thinking, "Oh, they're shackin' up?" But it didn't faze me. My folks hadn't raised me in the church or put those types of values in me; they couldn't say anything now. Soon after that I came home with a puppy—a gorgeous, yellow shepherd Labrador we named Bottom after the character Nick Bottom in Shakespeare's play *A Midsummer Night's Dream.* On a typical day I'd go running with Bottom at six in the morning (Ahren wasn't a morning person); school would start at eight, we'd have classes until two and, after first semester, we'd typically rehearse until one in the morning. On top of that, I had a work-study job washing dishes at the Yale Cabaret and cleaning the Yale Repertory Theater, and we had to do our classroom work and learn our lines. I'd ride my bike to school and she'd take the car so one of us could return home to walk Bottom during the day. (How crazy was that? It was like we had a little baby.) Unfortunately for him and for us we didn't know the first thing to do with him. We'd be gone for over twelve hours a day. Bottom would tear up the house. But we loved him like a child. Ahren was always dragging him into bed with us. I counted on his playfulness to break my melancholy moods. Bottom was my lifeline. You couldn't break his joyous spirit to save your life. But with all this going on, by the end of the day I'd be a little numb. Fortunately, by now I had learned to share Ahren with my classmates. She developed her set of friends and I had mine, but we were all one class.

My favorite class was fencing, which is all about quickness—whoever attacks and gets back on defense the quickest will score the most points and will win. Initially, we were all loving and gentle with each other in fencing class. Eventually we realized it was a great place to take out our aggression. At that point, it was on! Between my athletic ability and competitive nature, I was one of the best in my class. Academically, I studied hard and soon took to the work. In acting class when we'd explore scenes, my partner and I would rework the same scene over and over and over, each time making it more dense and rich. Our classmates thought the point was to work a scene and move on to the next one. At the end of the class, Earle Gister, our first-year acting instructor, complimented my partner and me because we had explored that one scene so deeply. "Now, that's the way to explore a scene!" he told us. I could feel the whole class shrink. I achieved by the end of the first semester what I had set out to achieve by coming to Yale in the first place—I could now stand onstage without my knees shaking. I was most proud that I had accomplished my goal.

Because of the work we'd done at Shakespeare & Company,

Ahren and I were more emotionally available than most of our classmates. They wanted to know where we had learned what we knew about emotions, and we told them. They began to understand the importance of voice class and breath work (you access your emotions through your breath). But once people began to pay attention to me, it opened up a can of worms. And I didn't have the skills and wasn't mature enough to deal effectively and sensitively with people who were impressed with my ability. I didn't know how to navigate my growing success as an actor.

That summer I worked at the Eugene O'Neill Theater Center in Waterford, Connecticut, where Yale's Dean Richards was the artistic director. The theater center was bustling with new playwrights, new plays and actors. My insecurities surfaced. Walking into the lunchroom on the first day felt as nerve-wracking as being back in kindergarten. "Who's going to sit with me? Am I going to have to sit by myself?" And after I performed for the first time up there and people praised my work, I didn't know how to emotionally deal with the attention—especially from the women. I was spinning out of control. I tried to apply my acting techniques to aid me in decision-making. Because some decision-making processes used in acting—such as flipping a coin—are very arbitrary, it was a deadly combination. But I wouldn't learn that until much later in life.

By the second semester of our first year, all of the newness of drama school had rubbed off, and Ahren and I were thrown into the casting pool with the other students. Yale is a production-based drama school. At any given moment, its forty-five students are writing, directing and acting in about forty plays. NYU is more of a studio-based school—they may do two shows a semester. Now that we were also acting, things became more intense. Our second year at Yale was about Shakespeare and we broke down the Shakespearean plays to the word, the sentence, the punctuation and meter. We literally had to beat out the rhythm of the whole play. The rhythm tells you what's happening emotionally. Ba-dum, ba-dum, ba-dum, ba-dum. In Shakespeare the rhythm is the play's heartbeat—it even tells you how to breathe. I found all the detail overwhelming, so I stayed with my head in my notebook. I knew I had to stick with it to get it. Now, putting things in order, I loved it. It spoke to my upbringing. Once we started doing the scene work, it all came together for me—the emotional and the technical. I started flying!

In the meantime, one of the young women in our class had become our class star. From first semester, Earle kept repeating, "This kid's brilliant." She did have extraordinary talent. The rest of us knew she would be very successful. But the second semester of our second year, our acting teacher pushed her and made her bring her scenes back. There was no reason. He was just pushing her buttons—he set her up. She wasn't used to getting corrected, so it took her out of her element. The teacher sensed her fear, proceeded to pick her apart and exposed that her work ethic was weak. It showed me that the warning that my voice teacher had given me was correct—three years *is* a long time to be going to school to get an agent.

That same semester over at Yale Rep, which was once of the most distinguished regional theaters in the country, August Wilson was producing a new play called *Fences*. Lloyd, who was going to direct the play, asked Earle if he could cast a student. Earle suggested me. I didn't know I was being considered for a part, but in the meantime I read the play and thought it was fantastic. One day Ahren told me, "Something big has happened. Go look at the casting board!"

"I'm in a hurry, Ahren. Just tell me. What is it?"

"Go look at the casting board."

When I saw my name I almost fell down. This was not an ordinary student production—it was an August Wilson play! *Ma*

Rainey's Black Bottom had just played on Broadway and been nominated for all sorts of Tony Awards. I was in shock! But I knew this was a direct relation to the hard work I was doing in my classes with Earle.

Now I was in an August Wilson play but I didn't know upstage from downstage. Lloyd didn't give me a lot of direction; he assumed everyone was well qualified to perform their role. He treated me like Cory, my seventeen-year-old character. I was so mad at him! I wanted to be treated like James Earl Jones and Mary Alice and Charlie Brown and Frankie Faison, Ray Aranha and the other adults—I wanted to be in the group. On breaks they'd be talkin' and laughin', and I'd be off to the side by myself. Every now and then I'd try to chip in. Lloyd would look at me as if saying, "Did somebody ask you something, boy?" I hated feeling like a little boy—seen and not heard. What I didn't know at the time was that he was teaching me.

We spent an entire week sitting around the table reading the play over and over, stopping and starting, asking about this moment and that moment. Inside I was thinking, "What are we doing? Can't we just get on our feet?" I didn't realize we were charting the emotional course of the play. By the time we got up on our feet to begin blocking, I realized I didn't know anything about my character because I had been wasting time. Now I had to do the emotional and physical work at the same time, which is very difficult. Lloyd had been waiting for me to ask some questions so he could actually direct me. Now we had finally gotten to the part of the play where we were blocking my entrance, and August's stage directions read, simply: Cory enters.

But how? I wondered. What was he doing? What did he have on? What does he say? How does he enter? And when is somebody going to tell me what to do? Because I was too insecure—yet acting like a know-it-all—to ask any questions, Lloyd pulled me aside after I had upstaged James Earl.

"Courtney," he told me gently, "if James was any other star, he would tell you himself, but I'm going to tell you. The way you're positioning yourself when you're talking to James, you're upstaging him," he explained.

"Oh, that's what upstaging is!" He was teaching me stagecraft.

At one point it dawned on me that, like Cory, I had played football when I was younger. I had been a quarterback; quarterbacks have cadences. I should apply what I knew. So I stood off to the side before my next entrance and said quietly, "Blue fifteen. Blue fifteen," then entered the scene.

"What did you say?" Lloyd asked me.

"Nothing."

"No, Courtney. What did you say? Just say it louder, Court."

"Say it louder?"

I took off from there. Now when I entered I had a whole thing.

"Blue fifteen. Blue forty-two." I ran onstage, dropped my book bag and stuff, and dropped back like I was throwing the ball. "The quarterback fades back…." I threw the ball to myself way up in the air like it was a long bomb then caught it. "Touchdown! WE BAD! YEAH, WE BAD!" Then I did an end-zone dance.

I had finally started to click onstage, but personally I was completely discombobulated. In addition to learning the play, I still had classroom work, a work-study job, a girlfriend, a dog/child and classmates who wanted to know everything that was going on and not only envied the opportunities I was experiencing, but my relationship with Ahren. I was overwhelmed. I couldn't talk to anyone about what I was going through; it didn't feel safe. I couldn't talk to Ahren because I felt guilty that the woman who I loved and who had gotten me started in this part of my life wasn't a part of what I was doing. I couldn't talk to my parents because they didn't know anything about this world. And I couldn't talk to anyone in the play because they were treating me like a child. (I didn't realize they were intentionally treating me like my seventeen-year-old character.) I had no place to put my fears and insecurities, which were considerable and overwhelming. I hid behind a facade of competence, which worked well—onstage.

By third year I'd come into my own. My outlook shifted inside and I began to think more about my own interests. My classmates resented me. I didn't know how to deal with it. There were times when I wasn't very sensitive to them, other times I tried to ignore them and times when I tried to divert the attention by diminishing myself. None of the approaches worked. In my defense, I was dealing with an incredible amount of success in a very short span of time. None of my classmates had to deal with the pressures I was under. On the outside I looked and behaved—acted!—like I was incredibly happy. But on the inside there were times when I was a wreck.

Now that, as a class, we had turned the corner and were on the "back nine," educationally, we were no longer little young bucks. As a class we'd been through a lot. There were several cliques, several camps. We weren't close. Now we had to come together to develop our scenes for the Leagues. While that was going on, I learned that *Fences* would be performed in Chicago at the Goodman Theater and Lloyd wanted me to reprise my role as Cory. Talk about an uproar among my classmates! But it was no big deal to me. I was a student; I knew I couldn't be in it. No outside professional work—that was the rule. As far as I was concerned, that was all there was to it.

What I didn't know was that Lloyd had a very specific vision for the school. For years he had been developing playwrights at Yale, the O'Neill Theater Center and elsewhere, and perfecting a process by which their work would travel to Broadway by way of the regional-theater circuit—Yale Rep being foremost among them. At each stop on the regional circuit, the play would be deepened and perfected, and the regional theaters would be credited and compensated as producers once the play reached Broadway. Although playwrights from Athol Fugard to Lee Blessing would eventually journey this road Lloyd was paving, Lloyd began the process with August Wilson, who was black. Unlike most other playwrights of his caliber, August had a large enough body of work that the process Lloyd had envisioned could be repeated and perfected. In fact, August would eventually make that journey ten times with ten different plays to great acclaim (*Fences* was second). But it was Lloyd's vision that August stepped into. So Lloyd—the play's director and Yale drama school dean—made an exception: I would be able to perform in Chicago! Now my opportunity became not just a big thing at school but a big and openly divisive thing for Lloyd's entire tenure. White students already resented the fact that because of Lloyd, black students were getting many opportunities at the Yale Rep, O'Neill Theater Center and in all of these new August Wilson plays—opportunities that hadn't been open to them in the past. They were also envious because Lloyd was a master teacher but only performed administrative duties on campus, so none of them could be taught acting by him; yet a few black students were getting to perform in plays under his direction. And now the final salt in the wound was that this black student would be allowed to tour as a professional in a play in violation of school policy. The script had been flipped. People were hot—students and alumni alike! Ahren and I were caught in the middle.

The *Fences* cast rehearsed in New Haven for about a month then traveled to Chicago, where I performed in the play for about a month. It was emotionally draining and difficult for me; I was working harder than I had ever worked in my life. At the same time I was having the time of my life. Chicago's a great town, and by that time the cast and I had grown close and were like family. I was also learning life lessons from the play. When my character, Cory, was seventeen and about to graduate from high school, he got in a big fight with his father, Troy, played by James Earl, who kicked him out of the house. Cory then joined the marines, where he worked his way up to the rank of captain. He didn't return home until seven years later, when he received news that his father had died. Cory returned home to tell his mother, Rose, played by Mary Alice, that he wasn't going to attend his father's funeral.

"Son, you've got to go to his funeral," she told him.

"I'm not going," Cory told her and ran down a list of his father's shortcomings and how they had hurt him.

"Your father wasn't always right," Mary Alice told Cory before acknowledging how hurtful some of Troy's actions had been. "But that's all you got to make a life with. You gotta find the good in him and take it then move on and make a life with it."

In the next scene Cory's little sister, Raynell, who was seven years old and barely knew Cory, comes onstage. She asks, "You know that song Papa used to sing?"

Cory starts singing, *Had an old dog, his name was Blue / Ol' Blue was mighty true / You know Blue was a good ol' dog…* Then she joined in and they sang a stanza together.

"You know the song, too—he taught it to you, too?" Cory said. And though Raynell and Cory barely knew each other, that song became their connection. Through it, their father's spirit lived on. And through singing the song with Raynell, Cory realized how much he missed his father and that he had to go to the funeral.

Behind the scenes there was an ongoing disagreement about how to finish the play. The producer thought the play should end with Cory singing the song; August thought that the play should end, as written, with Gabe, Troy's mentally ill brother, blowing his horn and opening up the gates of heaven so Troy can enter. They wouldn't resolve the issue for a year or so. Yet the idea of looking for the good in someone and building upon it and letting the bad go, resonated with me and would remain with me for the rest of my life.

Meanwhile back at the ranch, poor Ahren was getting whipped. She was completely in the middle. She caught all the drama from my classmates and had to hear about how much fun I was having. Plus, she had to do all her class work and walk Bottom morning, noon and night by herself. "Courtney, when are you coming back?" she'd ask me.

On top of everything else, in my infinite wisdom, I decided to audition for a movie just to "stay sharp." Richard Wright's *Native Son* was being cast and they'd been looking all over the country for the actor to portray Bigger Thomas, whose character was a mixture of innocence and manliness. I walked in, did the audition and was told by the producer, "We have been auditioning all over the country for this role and, baby, it's yours!" I was shocked! I went from being Bigger to being a baby again. "No, I'm not really even doing this. I'm in school," I told the producer and director.

"Well, this role is yours," they told me. "You'd better call somebody so you can do it."

"Well, I gotta call my dean."

"Well, you better call him then."

My head was spinning.

"Hey, Lloyd, guess what just happened?" I said to Dean Richards. "I just auditioned and I got this part. I mean, I was just auditioning to be auditioning. I didn't think I'd get the role. I gotta go back to school."

He said, "Well, I think you know what to do. I'll see you in a week back at school."

"Yeah, I know that's what I gotta do. But since I don't have an agent I just wanted to check in with you."

"Okay, see you Tuesday."

Then I called the casting director and said, "I can't do it because I've gotta go back to school."

"You *what?*"

"Yeah, I'm in school and as soon as *Fences* is over, I gotta go back and finish my third year."

"But this is *your* role! You can't turn it down."

"Well, sir, I just did. I can't do it. I gotta go back to school."

"If you turn down this role, you'll never work again. Do you hear me! You'll never work again in this town and you'll never work in New York!"

The man scared me real bad. I am so thankful that I had the presence of mind to tell him, "Talk to me in five years." I hung up the phone. Then I ran over to Frankie's apartment and told him what had happened.

"Man, that was scary!" I told him.

"But whoever gets that role, it's gonna be good, Court!"

"I know, but I'm going back to school."

"I know, so let's go out and celebrate your decision!"

I think that was on a Tuesday and *Fences* was closing on Sunday. In between I got a call from someone in the film (I don't remember who) saying, "You'd better call your dean. There's a way to work it out if you want to do the film."

"What!"

I called Lloyd.

"Courtney, go ahead and do the film," he told me.

"Huh?"

"Sometimes there are difficult choices we have to make in life," he told me. "This is one of them."

We talked a bit more and then we hung up. I didn't know that the movie people had called many of the drama school alumni and given them the impression that Lloyd was pressuring me to return to school and not allowing me to do the role. In turn he hadn't heard back from me, so he assumed I wanted to do the movie. Now I was back in limbo. Since my moral compass was shaky and I didn't have the greatest problem-solving skills, I depended on other people. I depended on

Ahren. I depended on Lloyd. I couldn't depend on my parents because they didn't know this arena. They said, "Court, this is what you want, isn't it? You got a film!"

"But, no, Mommy; I'm in school! I went there to finish and I'm half a semester away. That is what my dream was."

"What do you mean? I don't understand...."

At three in the morning, as I was in the middle of packing for the return trip to New Haven, I dialed up Frankie.

"What should I do?"

"Court, man, this is up to you. I can't call it, brotha."

I sat in the middle of my hotel room floor with tears rolling down my face. I called Ahren not realizing my classmates were still hounding her: "When is he coming back? When is he coming back? The show is closing on Sunday. He'll be back Tuesday, right?" Some of this was their resentment, but some of it was justified. They needed me to prepare for the Leagues scenes, where we partner up, choose scenes and then put a show together based on the scenes. It was the culmination of all our work, and for those folks who had gone to the drama school to get an agent, it was the most important acting opportunity of their lives. However, none of the scenes they were preparing could proceed without me.

"Courtney, what do you mean 'you don't know what to do'? You've got to come back!"

"But Lloyd told me—"

"I don't know what's going on, Courtney. I can't take this! I'm in the middle of all these people asking me what you're going to do. These people are driving me crazy!"

"Well, he's telling me to do the movie. I'm going to do it."

"I can't believe you, Courtney! I can't believe you've done this."

I returned to New Haven a couple of days later. Ahren was a mess because she couldn't take the pressure anymore. I tried to talk to her but she was in tears. "I don't know you anymore...."

That broke my heart—it broke my heart. I was struggling

with the same question and didn't have the emotional tools or support I needed to figure it out.

"Ahren, I'm going to talk to Earle and work it out. There's got to be a way to work it out."

"Okay, Court...."

So I went to talk to Earle and explained the situation.

"How am I going to deal with this? How can I work it out so I can do the movie and come back in the summer finish up my last semester? How can I do it?"

He said, "Courtney, you can't. You're out."

"Whaat!" My lip trembled. My jaw shook. "I thought there was a way to work it out."

"Courtney, you can't do a movie and come back. If you do the movie, you're out."

"But what if I don't do the movie?"

"Did you sign anything?"

"No."

"Well, if you didn't sign anything then just call 'em and tell 'em you don't want to do it."

"Can you call them as my representative? Somebody's got to represent me. Somebody's got to speak for me."

"All right," he said, then turned around and picked up the phone.

When someone on the other end answered, Earle identified himself and the situation and said, "He doesn't want to do it," then hung up the phone.

"Finally, somebody has got my back," I said, then broke down in tears.

Earle took the flack for me for three days as a variety of people in the movie industry caused the phones in the dean's office to ring off the hook. There were thirty to forty nasty messages left on our answering machine. They called my parents and threatened them. My mother took to her bed. Ahren and I had to get out of New Haven. We escaped to New

York. After several days the furor died down. We returned home and by then they had recast the part. The movie, which starred Elizabeth McGovern, Matt Dillon and Oprah Winfrey, did poorly and disappeared.

What Earle did in that moment was one of the greatest things anyone has ever done for me. I'll never ever forget what he did in speaking up for me. Shortly after he stood up for me, Earle lost his voice. A lifetime smoker and a drinker, he developed cancer of the larynx and they took out his voice box and installed a mechanical device.

When I returned to school the following week, everyone knew everything that had happened. Our voice teacher called a special meeting. She was the emotional center of our class. She said, "People need to say what they want to say and air out their feelings." She moderated, but the whole class lit into me.

"I just think that it's unfair that…"

"You just think that you're better than everyone else."

"You're getting special treatment because you're black."

I just sat there and let them vent. Eventually I was given the chance to speak.

"I was just auditioning to stay sharp. I didn't think I would get the part."

"Oh, that's what happened?"

"Yeah, they gave it to me on the spot!"

Why did I say that?

"Everything you do just comes out right."

"Well, I don't think it's right that you're just getting so much."

"Blah, blah, blah, blah…"

Ahren came to my defense. "He just did what any of you would do. He merely went on an audition."

Eventually everyone hugged and cried and as a class we came back together. We came out of the experience energized and ready to prepare for the Leagues. And in spite of my public humiliation, I was glad to be back with my classmates.

The Leagues didn't go well for many of our classmates. On the train ride to New York everyone was very excited. The ride back was painful. Many people were devastated, knowing they'd never work again. Ahren and I had done well, however. We both got agents and were poised to go.

Graduation from drama school was a blur. Shortly before the ceremony, Ahren stumbled across a long list of 1-900 phone calls on our phone bill.

"What are these, Courtney?"

At my birthday party a few months earlier, one of my friends had given me a present.

"Here, Court," he said, handing me a slip of paper.

"What is it?"

"Your birthday present."

I looked at it. It was only a number.

"What is it?"

"1-900-blah, blah, blah."

"But what *is* it?"

"Call it up and see!"

Later, I called.

"*Whaaat?* This is *crazy!*"

I started calling it all the time. I was on that telephone ten times a day. It was impersonal and it was safe. I had been calling them whenever I was feeling down. Now I was exposed. It was embarrassing. Everything I knew about pornography was that it was secret.

"What are you *doing?*" she demanded. "You're spinning *out of control!*"

I knew it was wrong. But with my father hiding *Playboys* at home and telling me nothing about sex or relationships, I'd had no mooring on these issues. It was nothing, I told her. Just something a friend had told me about. I promised not to call them again.

Making things worse, our moving-to-New-York money was almost gone because Bottom had developed bad skin and he needed expensive veterinary treatments. And the *Native Son* fiasco had put a serious strain on our fragile relationship. We were used to sharing each other with other people. But in the process we might have lost each other. In front of our parents we acted our way through it. They were just so happy. Their children were graduating from Yale. We were not just actors, we were Yale drama school graduates! But we were just hoping we could make it through the day. Behind the scenes we were asking: Should we stay together? Should we break up? Should we move to New York together? "I don't know if it's the right thing, but I don't know what to do if I don't go with you."

Chapter 5

It's C.P. Time

Charles and I moved into the one-bedroom, fourth-floor walk-up apartment across from Central Park on 105th Street between Central Park West and Manhattan Avenue. Compared to where we lived in New Haven, the apartment was small. In the bedroom, there was only about one foot around the perimeter of the bed. The kitchen looked like an old Italian farmer's kitchen with a big industrial sink. Roaches came out of the faucet—little baby roaches, not big palmetto bugs. I could deal with them; they weren't big or as bad as the bugs I was used to in Florida. They just aggravated the hell out of me because they came out when company was over. Across the street was a raggedy, run-down, abandoned building. It had bats in the belfry. Now I think it's a beautiful condo.

At the time, I was twenty-four years old. I wasn't looking to marry Charles, but we did have a relationship. Needless to say, my mother wasn't happy about it. "Oh, you're shackin' up now," she said about our living arrangements. I knew what I was doing fell outside the Bible and what I'd learned in church. But I was growing and exploring and figuring things out, so I lived with him anyway.

As soon as we moved in, I scoured the *New York Times* and

started talking to my friends from Yale and Negro Ensemble about what jobs were available. I got my first job out of the *Times,* booking spa services at Georgette Klinger Salon on Madison Avenue. Back then, Georgette Klinger was a big name in facials, salons and spas. There are a whole lot more salons and spas now, but back then she was *it* in New York City. For five days a week and one weekend a month, I worked in this little hallway with phone banks and huge schedule boards. We couldn't wear pants even though we weren't seen by the clientele. Folks would call and request a treatment from Ms. Galeana, Ms. Ivanca, Ms. This, Ms. That. The women were all from these European countries with one sister from Jamaica. To get to work I had to take two subway lines to get to the East Side, then walk a few blocks. I would start early in the morning and worked until six. In between, I'd get forty-five minutes for lunch and one ten-minute break. For that I got paid $225 a week, every other week. It was like slavery, but compared to some of the other women, I was doing well. I made more because I was an American. The Iranian girl who trained me made $200 a week for doing the same thing.

I would go to auditions on my forty-five-minute lunch break. Oh, Lord, the stress! Oh, the tears! I'd come in and my agent would call and say, "You have an audition at 3:20 p.m." Then I'd ask Ms. Whoever was the head of the phone bank—she was always well coiffed, white-blond hair, little glasses, very sophisticated-looking—I'd say, "I would like to take lunch at three today." It would usually take around twenty minutes to get to the audition. Going downtown was one thing, but if I had to walk crosstown about two or three avenues, that's where the stress came in. And you'd get there and, of course, your audition would be running behind. If I was lucky, it would only be five or ten minutes behind. Sometimes it would be a half hour. There were so many times when I was late returning to work.

"You are late! You're late. Coming back late is unacceptable.

Blah, blah, blah," Ms. Coiffed would scold me. But she knew what I was doing; nobody else who worked there was trying to be an actress. They knew this was my survival gig—a means to an end. Later that day the same Ms. Coiffed would tell me, "Oh, Angela, you are going to be a big star!" It was very schizoid. She'd chastise me on the one hand then praise me on the other. It was too much stress—all this trying to get to the audition, get back in time, missing the audition because I got there late, having to leave the audition early or rush through it so I could get back to work without getting reprimanded, then later that day get applauded because "one day, you're going to be a star!" Depending how I was feeling that day, I would fuss under my breath or go into the bathroom and cry. Sometimes I'd feel very discouraged. I'd wonder, Is it ever going to happen? Am I ever going to get a chance to be an actress? Will I remember what to do if I finally get a job?

Meanwhile, Roc wasn't working; he was auditioning. He just didn't have that sort of coordination where he could focus on more than one thing. Even though he's a people person, I don't think he would have been any good at waiting tables or anything like that. He'd be talking and you'd still be waiting for your food. He was good at what he was good at, and that was acting. So he and another buddy, Reggie, put together a cabaret show at the West Bank Café. On weekends at 11:00 p.m. or later, they would perform scenes they'd made up then split the door—whatever the door was—with the establishment. He'd give me about twelve dollars a week. Well, that was the electric bill—at least it was something. But the rent still had to be paid. For a while all that responsibility fell on my shoulders.

One day someone told me that *U.S. News* and *World Report* was looking for an assistant. I was hired on the spot. At *U.S. News* I had one boss and one little desk. My job was to pull *Associated Press, United Press International* or *Sigma* photos to accompany the articles. I'd present a selection to my boss, he'd identify which ones would run and I'd compile them and send them by FedEx to the main office in Washington, D.C. Sometimes we'd run late and I'd have to take a plane to D.C. to hand them in. That was kind of exciting. And now when I'd get calls for, say, an eleven-thirty audition at ten, I could tell my boss and he'd say, "Oh, leave now and prepare." He understood that I was an actress and this job was just a stop on the way. I did my work. He let me go. It wasn't like a pressure thing. I was so happy.

One month after starting at *U.S. News*—it was the spring of 1984—I got my first job, as the understudy for *Colored People's Time* performed by the Negro Ensemble Company. *C.P. Time,* as I called it because I didn't like to say "colored people," was a series of vignettes throughout history strung together, ranging from slavery to a Billie Holiday-ish character singing to the troops. When I called my mom to tell her I'd gotten this role, she was excited. She then told me what came to be the signature advice for every role I won: "Work hard and be nice!" At first I was trying to do both *U.S. News* and Negro Ensemble, but before long my boss told me, "Angela, it's not going to work out with the rehearsal schedule and working." I started crying. In that short period of time the company had been so good to me, allowing me to prepare and go into auditions confident enough to get the job. Then I shook myself—Isn't this what you went to drama school for?—thanked everyone and headed out the door. Being selected to join the theater company I'd written my thesis about—a theatrical group with such an important legacy in the black community—was a tremendous honor I didn't take lightly. I was very aware that I was following in the footsteps of Ensemble alumni like Lorraine Hansberry, who wrote *A Raisin in the Sun,* which I performed a monologue from when I was a child, as well as people like LeRoi Jones, Louis Gossett Jr. and Phylicia Rashad. I knew God had given me a gift. I intended to care for it.

As understudy for *C.P. Time,* I had to learn all three women's parts. That included singing, which I was not happy about. Singing always made me nervous. I consider mine an average voice; I don't think I can carry a tune all the way through. Of course, I grew up in the choir and was in gospel choir at Yale as a young adult. But to sing solo, no accompaniment, no choir—just you and your voice? I had never done that. In drama school I took a singing class and had to sing one song. I chose "Love for Sale" and never sung it to my teacher's or my satisfaction. I should have picked an easier song and worked on it and worked on it and worked on it. But I like to complete things and move on. So my confidence in that area was nil.

One girl I was covering was a real singer—Carol Maillard, one of the original members of Sweet Honey in the Rock, the Grammy Award-winning black, female a cappella ensemble. She was real encouraging and worked with me and taught me how to sing-talk a little bit. That worked out. You're playing a character and maybe the character doesn't have a voice like a canary. She sings okay but she's playing it, she's entertaining the troops. I also understudied L. Scott Colwell, one of the original members of Home, and Ahren Staunton, who came out of Julliard the year before me. Samuel L. Jackson and Charles Weldon were also in the play. I knew each of the women's parts "off book"—I knew them by heart. I didn't mess around. I studied the women, the inflections, their tones, their ways, how they played the scene. I was able to go on for any one of them at a moment's notice. Of course, none of them missed a beat. They might be late to the theater and I'd think, "Yeah!" ready to go on, but then they'd show up. Except Carol. Once she got sick and couldn't go on for two performances. I would get weak in the knees, play the part, then come off the stage and fall onto my knees.

After we ended our run in New York, we traveled around New England, Pennsylvania, New York State, New Jersey and Ohio on what they call a "bus and truck" tour. We'd ride on the bus, get to the place, do the show, finish at ten-thirty, get a bite to eat, maybe see the town, get in bed and check out at 9:00 a.m. Sam called me the "rack queen" because I could curl up and make the bus seats look like a queen-size bed. One of the guys in the cast was always giving me the eye. "Hey, girl, why don't you come over here and sit on my lap." I played it off for weeks. Then one day I couldn't take it. I shouted, "I am not a piece of meat!" in front of everyone else. He was stunned. I mean, I wasn't trying to hurt anyone's feelings, but I wasn't interested—he was married! After that he stopped talking to me completely. At some point during our trip L. Scott schooled me, "The code of the road is silence"—meaning, that for the two or three months that you're doing regional theater, you're gone, you do things, you see things and then you come back home to your life. "Oh!" Today they say, "What happens in Vegas, stays in Vegas."

One day I approached the guy who had been hitting on me and said, "I'm just a mean ol' heifer, ain't I?"

"Well, I dunno. You know, you kinda, you know…I don't wanna mess with you…"

"I'm not really mad at you. I was just, like, getting tired of you pressin' me with that song."

After that we were real cool.

While we were on the road, Charles was back in New York and had been offered a role in *Ma Rainey's Black Bottom,* a play by an up-and-coming black playwright named August Wilson. Although we weren't aware of it at the time, opportunities for black actors were about to open up. We would ride the crest. *Ma Rainey* had premiered at Yale Rep while we were in school. Now that it would be hitting the regional circuit, Charles was cast in it. To prepare himself, he had to travel up to Yale for rehearsals. After it toured, the play made it to Broadway, which was a pretty incredible experience for someone a year out of drama school. *Ma Rainey* was phenomenal and Charles was phenomenal in it. Now, Charles didn't play the trumpet, he wasn't a musician. But his character, Levee, played the trumpet, so the boy learned to play the trumpet and brought it to life. He was really amazing! I have to give it to him—Charles was undeniable!

Once *Ma Rainey* hit Broadway, Charles had officially been introduced to the theatrical community. He isn't waiting tables or working at Georgette Klinger's; he's doing the play and life is lovely! After the performance, admirers would invite him out for dinner or drinks. And let me tell you, when folks who can afford to pay for dinner and a ticket to go to the theater are feting you, it can get very heady. It was a wonderful time, a very attractive time. I'd laugh and tell him, "Oh, you're just a fat rat in a cheese factory." It was also the time when our relationship started to get *strange.*

On Broadway a play typically starts at 8:00 p.m. You get there early, you're finished by 10:30 p.m., you may grab dinner or a drink or meet some admirers afterward, and then you're done. While Charles worked, I'd be up in the roach-infested apartment waiting for him to get home. At first he'd come in at maybe two in the morning. That was okay 'til it got to be night after night after night. After a while I would tell him, "What the heck is going on here? I ain't your roommate, I ain't your secretary, I ain't your mama and I ain't your sister." Of course, Charles always had an excuse—this person or that person wanted to take him out. He had always been good at making something sound halfway believable and leaving you questioning yourself—of making you think that ol' jelly jar was a Ming dynasty vase. But it got to be where he said he had to be gone at odd times during the day and night. Or he'd come in at four in the morning. Or he'd be gone for two days at a time. He'd tell me stories, like he had to go up to Yale. Or he was using his producer Fred Zollo's apartment because he was writing a play about the life of Ira Aldridge, the African tragedian. Now, he really was into Ira

Aldridge at the time; he was reading his biography. But I wasn't sure that I bought his story that he was working at Fred's because our little funky, too-small, fourth-floor, roach-infested apartment wasn't conducive to writing. Especially when he couldn't give me Fred Zollo's number or tell me where his apartment was. Things were sounding mighty unusual.

There were many times I wanted to break up with Charles, beginning at around that year-and-a-half mark. Instead, I allowed our relationship to stretch on for something like three years. When it was good, it was really good. We'd go to plays together, the movies or his mom's house in Baltimore, and she'd make crab boil and we'd hang out. We had a lot of fun, and I have to admit it felt nice to be connected with someone people held in such high regard, and to be part of this held-in-high-regard team. But I wasn't as strong as I could have been in insisting upon my standards. I spent a lot of time wondering, Hmm…is he telling the truth? I'm not sure. Is this the truth? Is that the truth? Is it a lie? A lie mixed with some truth? Let me suss it out. I also thought I could fix him and that he needed me to take care of him. I'd think, Oh, this poor thing. He can't even wash his clothes without turning everything pink. Or, Poor thing, he can't cook. Or, Poor thing, he can't pay the bills. I'd tell myself, I guess I have to put up with this unsavory part of it. Other times I just wanted company. I was new to New York City, working in a tenuous profession. I needed someone familiar.

One of our major problems was that Roc could be insanely jealous. He couldn't stand the friendship I had with a guy named Bill, who'd been my friend since freshman year. He wanted me to end it.

"What are you seeing Bill for—are you fucking him?"

"Hey, you'd better back up," I'd tell him. "Bill is my friend, and I ain't never letting him go. Now you? You can go. But I am not letting my friend go."

Then he would back off and wouldn't mess with me about

Bill. But if I met a guy I wanted to have a friendship with, I'd have to call him; I didn't want him calling the apartment. Though Charles was jealous of Bill, who wasn't a threat, he failed to detect the threat of a fellow actor I did some work with in New York. Then again, maybe he wasn't much of a threat— the man was about eighty! I really liked him as a person. But one day when I was at his apartment for some reason, he said, "Angela, let's take advantage of each other." I didn't want to hurt his feelings, but I thought *You'd* be taking advantage of *me*. I don't see what advantage *I'd* have. His hair was as white as snow. I knew there would be gray hair—oh, never mind! I thought it was funny. I got out of there as quickly as I could. He died shortly thereafter. Thankfully it wasn't in my arms.

After a while, my relationship with Charles became habit, just habit. I got used to it even though it was dysfunctional. At one point things became so bad I would tell myself, "If I just mark an X on the calendar on every day we have a fight, the whole month would be blacked out; there would be more black days than clear days." I developed a way of working within it. We fussed, we fought, we made up and were happy. Then it started all over again. The highs were high and the lows were low. This is my boyfriend, I thought. This is how it is for now. It's not going to last forever.

In the spring of 1985 Charles got nominated as Best Featured Actor for a Tony, the annual award celebrating achievements in theater. We were all excited. I asked, "I should go get a dress, right?"

"I dunno, I dunno. I don't know what I'm going to do. I might take my mama."

"Oh, you're going to take your mom. Oh, okay…" I figured I'd watch the ceremony on TV.

The night of the Tonys, one of my dear friends, Michael Knight, a director in drama school, and his mentee, James, came and watched the show with me. When the nomination for best actor came, we were all psyched up. The camera panned to Roc wearing his white ascot and suit. I thought he'd have been smiling, but for some reason he was looking real tight, tense—it looked to me like he had a hot poker up his ass. I wondered why. Then the camera panned over some more. I saw this really pretty woman in a gold dress sitting next to him. *She* was smiling. *She* looked happy and proud. *She* seemed to be excited. But she *darn* sure wasn't his mama! Behind them, Jim Simpson, our director friend from school, was also smiling. But Roc wasn't smiling. I guess he was saying to himself, "This obviously ain't my mama, so I guess she knows now."

I was just stunned. *"Ohmygosh!"*

There it was as plain as the nose on my face. My intuition had been right.

"And the winner for Best Featured Actor is…Barry Miller for *Biloxi Blues!*"

"Yeah! Uh-huh. See!" I hollered at Charles through the TV. "God don't like ugly and he ain't too fond of cute!"

I felt terrible, I felt so embarrassed. Everyone in New York's black acting community knew we were together. And now he had humiliated me.

"I don't believe it—on *national TV!*"

Fortunately, I had my boys there to comfort me. I collected myself and called up his mama; she liked me. I was the girl who had put the money in the Bible and who had paid the rent and who was making sure the roof was over our heads and the lights were on. Now it was payback time.

"Hey…"

"Oh, my God!" she said and started crying. "Aw, my God, Angela. You're just so nice and you've always been so good."

"Look," I said, getting right to the point. "The rent is due and I don't know where he is. Where is he?"

"Here is her phone number."

"Okay."

So I waited until about 8:30 a.m. the following morning. He picked up the phone half-asleep.

"Hullo…"

"Hey!" I put on my nice "Julia" voice.

"How'd you get this number?"

"Oh, don't worry about it. I've had it for a while. Anyhow, the rent is due."

"Okay, I'll bring you a check."

"All right, have a great day. Bye!"

Click.

And he gave me the check, too, for about three months rent or something. He's always been generous—that's one good thing I can say. But then everyone was walking around looking at me, staring at me. And people I hardly knew were saying to me, "Oh, God, it was terrible, terrible, terrible." That was the worst part of it.

Now, you would think that would have ended our relationship, but we still kept dealing with each other in some kind of way—him going back and forth. He ain't really gone, but he ain't really with me.

He would ask me, "You wanna break up?" probably hoping I'd say yes.

I'd say, "Y-y-y…no…." Then we'd go on a little longer, then a little bit longer than that.

I remember praying, "Lord, if it ain't meant to be, please kill it—and end it in such a way that I won't go back, 'cause I ain't strong enough. So, Lord, really end it good. Let me know." By then I was getting regular work and starting to think I could make it on my own. I remember appearing on a couple of episodes of *Cosby*, which was a big deal at that time.

Then one day we were in the apartment having another blow-up argument, when Charles claimed an agent only agreed to meet me because I was in a relationship with him.

"Awww, shit!"

Shoomp! In that split second the window came down, the drapes were pulled, the hatches battened, the shutters closed, the door was slammed *and* locked. I only got something because of him. Hmmph! That was complete and utter bullshit. After receiving standing ovations at age sixteen, four years of college, three years of grad school and a year of performing in New York, I was certain of my acting abilities. People have different gifts and I was fortunate enough to discover mine early on. It is a gift from God. It has nothing to do with anyone else. In other areas I might have to compromise and negotiate about many things in my life, but I never had to compromise about acting. So trying to mess with me about acting was intentionally messing with my self-esteem. It was like you don't want to whup my ass, but you do want to sabotage me emotionally to try to make me your slave.

"Oh, I see what you doin'," I said to him. "You got an ego and you tryin' to con somebody. Well, you know what? I may not know everything, I may not know a lot. But I can act my *ass* off! You can mess with me about some other stuff, but 'bout some actin' you'd better step back—you can't do it. 'Cause this is what I do and it's not something I chose to do, it's from God. *He* gave it to me, not you."

That was absolutely the end of our relationship—it was sho' 'nuff over. I may have been weakened in some ways because I didn't have a father, but on the other side of that, I had my mother's take-no-prisoners, no-bullshit "get out!" as an example. That strengthened me, so I used it. I gathered up all his things, addressed them to him in care of the woman in the gold dress and sent the package off. Honestly, a part of me was kind of glad he had somebody because I knew he would be all right. After that I said R.I.P.! "Thank you, Lord!" I lit some candles and gave myself seven days—oh, yeah, I gave myself some time. It had been three years; I had never dated anybody that long; you gotta mourn the death of something. If I wanted to cry, blubber, fall out, feel sorry for myself, what the heck. But at the end of seven days, that was it; it was over. I'd wash my face and blow out the candles.

After that, folks tried their best to drag me back through my shit. "Oh, you must have been so embarrassed!"

"Yeah, yeah, yeah, it was embarrassing," and this, that and the other. But, I said, "Moving on!" I'm sorry, that was yesterday. Ain't nothin' hap'nin today. "What? Who? Huh? What's wrong with you? Please! I'm over it. What you talkin' 'bout? Girl, please, put some music on! Come on, what club we goin' to? Oooh, ain't he cute!"

By now I was in the second half of my twenties. I wasn't sure about marriage—when or how it would happen—but I did entertain the notion of having a baby. I had gotten the idea in my head that I should do that when I was twenty-nine. But when I mentioned it to Mama, she put an end to that notion by reminding me about the opportunities I had, what her life had been like and that the Bible said things should occur in "decency and in order". Marriage came before babies. "Oh, Angela," she told me. "I hope you'll get married first."

That same spring of '85 Lloyd Richards, the former Yale drama school dean, called me. Aleta Mitchell, an alum from the year behind me, would be leaving *Ma Rainey* to get married. He offered me the opportunity to play the role of Dussie Mae. I was excited! I had actually played Dussie Mae one summer during grad school when I had worked at the Eugene O'Neill Theater in New York. But by the time the play came to the Yale Repertory Theater, I had already graduated. Now something good, exciting, that I'd always dreamed of, was finally about to happen. Of course, you-know-who was also in the play. Yet I knew this would be my pièce de résistance. The fact that I would be performing with Charles didn't even matter.

My character, Dussie Mae, was the friend of Ma Rainey played by the late great actress Theresa Merritt. Charles's character, Levee, likes her, but one of the other characters tells him to watch out.

You better get your eyes off Ma's girl.

Ma ain't got that girl. That girl got a mind of her own, Levee answers. He flirts with Dussie Mae, and she tries to get what she can get. There are scenes in the play where Dussie puts on her stocking in front of him, leans over him, sits on his lap. I worked those scenes.

Do you want some of this lemonade?

Charles and I were on the outs, but all our scenes were *hot!* We treated each other nicely behind the scenes, but when we were onstage we were battling out our personal life on a Broadway stage. Our performance was infused with all the drama that was going on in life. This lasted for about two weeks, until the play's eight-month run ended.

About a year and a half later, Lloyd asked me to come to Yale Rep to play the character Martha Pentacost in August Wilson's third play, *Joe Turner's Come and Gone.* In the play, set in Pittsburgh in 1910, Martha had lost her husband, Herald Loomis, after Joe Turner, a notorious Tennessee plantation owner who existed in real life, had enslaved him illegally on a chain gang for preaching and trying to save some black men's souls. Martha and Herald had a child together. When their love was ripped apart by these circumstances, Martha dealt with it by leaving her daughter with a relative, migrating north to Pittsburgh and pouring herself into the church—in essence, by marrying the Lord. In the meantime, locked up, Herald turned away from God. Once he was released, he set off to find his family. But they weren't where he had left them. He searched for them, eventually finding his daughter and, finally, Martha. The play is over two hours long and you hear about Martha the whole time, but she doesn't come onstage until the last twenty minutes, during which she goes into something like an apostolic trance. Her only scene is with Herald, who was played by— who else?—Charles.

Well, we were up at Yale rehearsing and working on the play. I was doing my thing, kind of marking and learning it, when one day Lloyd says to me in his proper, professorial kind of way, "Angela, you and Charles used to date, right?"

"Yeah…."

"Well, use it."

"Oh, shoot! He done called me out," I remember saying to myself. "Now, that's a low blow." Of course, he didn't mean it that way. I hold Lloyd in the highest regard. Back then he was like Papa San—"Dean Richards, sir." It's only recently that I started using his first name. I guess he knew Charles and I had a little history, a little drama, volatility or whatever.

"Use it!"

That's all he had to say. When I came back and did my scene after that, I started speaking in tongues.

TheLordismyshepardIshallnotwant….YeathoughIwalkthroughthe-valleyoftheshadowofdeath, Iwillfearnoevil.

I was levitating off the stage.

You weren't there, you weren't there. I didn't know what I was supposed to do. Here I am nineteen and have this baby. I needed you, I needed you.

Charles came right back at me with tears coming out of his eyes.

Blood? Blood make you clean?

You really sensed that Martha and Herald loved each other. People were mesmerized. I learned to put all my experiences— be they happy or be they not—into the work.

So we did *Joe Turner* at Yale Rep, then we toured several cities. My cast member Ahren Moore had this cute, skinny, athletic little boyfriend, Courtney B. Vance, the same prospective student Charles, John Turturro and I had taken out when I was just leaving Yale. They had both gotten into Yale though the odds were so against them. They had also set up house and were doin' it. They were so young, yet they were such a team. I admired that. I remember thinking that they were just amazing. They bad! They *bad!* Courtney followed Ahren from town to town to see her perform as we traveled the regional theater circuit. We never really said much more than hi and bye, but I could see he was a wonderful guy. Around the time we hit the road, Charles left to do a movie, which paid more, I'm sure, and was very prestigious. So he left the play and Delroy Lindo came in.

Delroy was my buddy around New York. He's a great actor, strikes an imposing figure and has a very powerful voice. But we had never worked together. Once we got started, we kind of worked differently. With Charles, I had, "Y'all used to date? Just use it." With Delroy, we had to find something else. I was hoping to be able to work our roles out together—to affect him and be affected by him as an actor. You say it, and it makes me feel, and I react. That's what I was used to doing. But I imagine he felt like he was behind and had to learn all these lines in a vacuum. He seemed to do an awful lot of work off to himself. Some nights I felt that he was really hearing me. Those nights were really sweet. Other nights, I felt that he was trying to beat me down with his size, his physicality, the power of his voice, his anger. I felt like we weren't in sync, that we were missing so many subtleties. I wanted Herald Loomis to hear Martha Pentacost and Martha to hear Herald. Instead, it felt like, "I got my point and my point is more important!" "Well, I've got my point and *my* point is more important!" Who knows, maybe it was all in my head. But that's what I complained about. I complained to anyone who would listen. I complained, complained, complained so much that I got sick of hearing myself. At one point I dropped out of the show. Then Lloyd called up and asked me back. At that point I decided, I love this role, I love this play and it's a phenomenal opportunity. I'm gonna freakin' stop bellyachin' and complaining and trying to be right. I worked on looking at Delroy differently. I started picking out things I liked about him personally that could make me love Herald Loomis. The fact that he was kind, that he would cook all sorts of healthy foods for me and invite me to dinner, the crook of his neck or whatever. It worked.

While *Joe Turner* was playing in San Diego, a young man named Wren T. Brown came backstage and introduced himself to me. Wren was a Los Angeles actor. He had heard about me from Ahren Staunton, my castmate from *Colored People's Time*, whom he'd met while they were each working in the Philippines. Wren and I became fast friends. While in California, I also auditioned for my first movie, *Dessa Rose*. I tried out for the role of Dessa, one of the female leads and a slave. I borrowed a long skirt and blouse from a friend, rented a car and drove to L.A. for the audition, then continued with the show.

In late March of 1988, *Joe Turner* reached Broadway, where we played at the Ethel Barrymore Theater. This time—at not quite thirty years old—I was on Broadway for real, in a role that I originated, as opposed to a show I'd joined. Opening night was incredibly exciting. My mom, D'nette and my New York aunts and uncles came to see me. As I sat in the dressing room for two hours while I waited for my entrance, I could hear the audience buzzing and feel its electricity. We had been traveling and honing the show for months. This night everyone was finding their perfect pitch!

At the play's climax, Martha tries to bring Herald back to the church.

He'll give you peace. The blood of Jesus will make you clean.

Herald says, *Blood make you clean?* Then reaches into his pocket to pull out a knife, which he then drags across his chest in a symbolic bloodletting, a letting out of the poison that's gotten into his heart. The prop knife is filled with blood, so as he touches his skin it looks like he's cutting himself.

But this night Delroy reached into his pocket to get his knife and his knife wasn't there! The play had been going along splendidly, on all six cylinders. Poppin'! It was like the roof was going to blow off. But now his knife wasn't there.

If you had seen the look in his eyes—I mean, it was like someone had grabbed his heart, like someone had died. And for a split second, he was no good, just no good—"Oh, no! What the hell do I do?" When that happened, me, L. Scott Caldwell, the little girl—everybody in the scene—we were scared, scared for him. There was nothing we could do; we couldn't help him. The moment didn't lend itself to improvisation. He was a drowning man and none of us could save him. Though we were standing there, at that point there was a part of us that was gone—out of the scene. Actor to actor, we had that look. Our bodies were still there but our faces said, "Holy moly." Hopefully, we were professional enough that our faces didn't show it. Delroy was scared as hell. Now, what was he going to do?

Fortunately for him, for us, for everybody, we're standing in the kitchen in front of a table. He thinks quick and grabs the butter knife on the table and he scratches across his chest with it.

Blood, blood. You want blood?

Of course there's no blood. So he covers his chest then runs offstage, which is what Herald Loomis does—runs off into the world. I grabbed our little girl and we cried and we finished the scene. Then we did our curtain call. Following our final bow, Delroy sat on the steps and cried, sobbed, he was racked with grief. To be perfectly honest, I felt smug—an actor always checks his props. Even if your prop person hands it to you, you always check it. So he cried and I stepped over him and went on downstairs. Fortunately D'nette had a lot more compassion. She consoled him. "It's okay. It was still good, it was still really good tonight." And she was right. Even with the mistake, it was a phenomenal evening. The play had been soaring up to that point. He had done a phenomenal job—that mistake didn't ruin it. We knew we were going to get a good review.

After we changed, we attended the cast party. It was very festive, there was a lot of music and everyone was in a celebratory mood. Charles showed up, accompanied by the same woman who had been wearing the gold dress, but who was not his mama. While she was sitting on one side of the room, he worked his way over to me.

He said, "Ang, girl, you were wonderful!"

"Yeah? Well, thank you. It was a pretty good night."

"Girl, you were *great!*"

Charles and I had a friendly conversation, but I noticed he was giving me very close body language—very face-to-face, leaning in, laughing. From the outside looking in, I'm sure we looked very buddy-buddy, conspiratorial, maybe even like something's going on between us—like something that *ain't* going on *is* going on. Now, I'd been in the position of the woman on the other side of the room before, feeling uncomfortable, looking and wondering if something was happening between Charles and another woman. And our breakup had already been ugly, it had already been embarrassing. At that point I didn't want a lot of confusion. So I leaned in and said, "Hey, Roc, let's draw the curtain on all this drama. Why don't you take me over and introduce me to your lady."

"Huh?"

"Yeah, you know," I continued. "It's been a whole lot of drama. Let's just draw the curtain. Because I'm sure this conversation we're having—to her—is keeping something going. So why don't you take me over and introduce me."

Needless to say, the laughter stopped. He took me over to meet her.

"Debbi, this is Angela. Angela, this is Debbi."

"Hey," I said. "It's nice to meet you."

"It's nice to meet you, too."

I sat down, Debbi and I chitchatted for a few minutes, then she took the conversation a little bit deeper. Charles's friend Reggie, from the midnight cabaret, had this girlfriend named Irene whom I knew.

Debbi said, "Irene told me I would like you if I knew you."

"Oh, really?"

I guess that was, in a way, her admission. (The "other woman" always knows about the first woman, right?) But how in the world would we have gotten to know each other with all this stuff going on? So we talked cordially. In the meantime my sister kept flitting around the table, because she knew—and everyone else in the room knew—our history, and they were all kinda lookin'. I don't know if they thought a fight was gonna break out or what. At one point Charles came over to the table and said, "How y'all doing?"

"Oh, we're good. Real good. How are *you* doin'?"

I guess he could handle it when he had one woman over here and the other over there. But once we were talking to each other, he must have wondered, What in the hell are they telling each other?

D'nette came by the table yet again—this time with her camera—and took a picture of us together that opening night: Debbi and me. I still have it today. The whole interaction was nice. It was very empowering. Once again, I was no longer mad at a woman—this time, a sistah—over a man. I didn't feel insecure anymore. I wasn't having a conversation with him and by default making her feel insecure. I wasn't giving him more power and her less power. Instead, let's settle stuff. And that evening that's what happened. In that moment we fell in like with each other, and all of the nonsense was over. Eventually Charles married Debbi Morgan, the actress and soap opera star (they've since divorced). You know her as the first Dr. Angela "Angie" Baxter Hubbard Harrison Foster on *All My Children,* the first Dr. Ellen Burgess on *General Hospital* and *Port Charles,*

Mozelle Batiste Delacroix in *Eve's Bayou* and Twana in *Woman Thou Art Loosed.* To this day, when Debbi and I are in each other's company we're genuinely happy to see each other.

That era—the mid to late '80s—marked the rise of August Wilson as a great American playwright. All told, ten of his plays made it to Broadway, the most of any other American playwright and certainly more than any African-American. His death from liver cancer in 2005, at age sixty, brought his life to an early end. Lloyd Richards directed five of Wilson's plays. This great director/playwrighting team garnered many of the theater's highest honors, including Tony Awards and Pulitzer Prizes for their work together. Although the two ultimately chose to go their separate ways, the mark they left on the stage was indelible. Lloyd passed away on his birthday in 2006 at the age of 87.

But back in 1988, August Wilson was *it!* Like *Ma Rainey* and Tony Award-winner *Fences, Joe Turner* was nominated for a Tony Award for Best Play. Delroy snapped back from his opening-night snafu and was nominated for Best Featured Actor. Today you know him for his fabulous acting in *Get Shorty, The Cider House Rules* or *Lackawanna Blues,* among others. L. Scott Caldwell, Ahren Moore and Kimberly Scott were all nominated for Best Actress (L. Scott won). And August Wilson, the play and cast were nominated for all sorts of Drama Desk awards. As a performer it was exciting to see black faces on Broadway and to receive such wonderful acknowledgment and recognition. It was finally "C.P. time" in the best sense of the term—a time for black actors to shine! The door to the world of theatrical acting opportunities that had been all but slammed shut to black actors of earlier generations was beginning to crack open, in large part because August Wilson's genius couldn't be denied. A whole new generation of black actors was getting ready to step through it. I didn't know it yet, but I would be one of them.

Chapter 6

When Life Was Grand

In the summer of 1986 Ahren and I moved to New York together. We got an apartment in the Fort Greene section of Brooklyn. There were mice running all up the house. Thank goodness Bottom was there, so they didn't come into our room. But every now and then a baby mouse would sneak in and Bottom would bat it around and play with it. Bottom weighed ninety pounds. We'd say, "Bottom, let the little mouse go!"

Bottom was still totally untrained. And it was his nature to howl when he heard sirens. He could hear a siren five miles away. But if your dog howls when you live in an apartment, they will put you out. So every time we heard a siren we grabbed his snout to keep him from opening his mouth. He became such a part of our rhythm we would wake up out of a dead sleep when we'd hear him starting to howl. I'd reach down onto the floor, grab his snout and keep him from opening his mouth until the noise went out of range and he'd go back to sleep.

The first summer we lived there we tried to get our relationship back to square one. We put one foot in front of the other. We lived off our savings. With the money I had earned from *Fences*, we knew we could go nine months out if we scraped our pennies together. Ahren got a temp job and was auditioning.

I also started auditioning right away. We were poor as could be, and that summer was hot as blazes! We were hot and miserable and scared and hopin' and prayin' and countin' pennies.

We still hadn't figured out our relationship. We probably should have been thinking about marriage. But neither of us knew how to talk about commitment, much less about marriage. That July I was offered a role in the movie *Hamburger Hill,* the story of one of the bloodiest battles of the Vietnam War. I was shocked. My agent promised, "This is going to launch you…." Ahren was gracious, as always. "I'm so happy for you, Courtney. It's going to be wonderful." But beneath her kindness and love, the troubles in our relationship had not been fully mended.

Right before I left for the Philippines, where *Hamburger* was filmed, we learned that *Fences* would be heading to Broadway via San Francisco. Between these two roles, for me, it was confirmation that I'd made the right choice when I'd decided to turn down *Native Son* to return to school.

"Wow! You did the right thing, Court!" my parents affirmed.

"I knew what I wanted to do in my heart," I told them. "I just got confused."

I was in the Philippines for about two months. Being outside the country for the first time in my life was amazing. The first thing I noticed when I got off the plane was *whoosh!*—the humidity. The second was that every person who came up to me asked, "Are you Magic Johnson?" The country was a political hotbed. The United States had just decided to pull all of its troops off the bases where they had been stationed for years. Corazón Aquino was president and bombs seemed to be going off everywhere. The black people who lived there, who people called "negritos," were physically very small in stature and treated worse than poor black folks in the States. It was very painful to see.

All of us in the *Hamburger* cast were unknowns: Don Cheadle, Dylan McDermott, myself.... They hardly paid us anything so they could spend the money elsewhere, like on blowing a lot of things up to make the movie seem realistic. One of the first days they started filming I was sitting with the director thinking out the next shot, when I heard a commotion. A man was down and they were performing CPR on him. We learned shortly that it was one of the electricians on the set. He had gotten electrocuted. He was dead before he hit the ground. We were all in a state of disbelief. This was supposed to be a movie—it was supposed to be fun. But after that I felt, "Can we go home now?" The cast and crew voted to stay. It was not pleasant. We were traumatized. On top of that, there were no trailers and it rained constantly, so the filming was grueling and uncomfortable. I made lifelong friends, but it wasn't a pleasant experience.

In the meantime Ahren and I were just trying to keep our relationship going. We wrote a lot of letters back and forth because we couldn't afford phone calls. In the back of my head I was wondering if Ahren and I would still be a couple when I got back.

Some of the guys were losing their natural minds with all the sex trade over there. You could just pick out a twelve-year-old and have sex with her—you could walk into a room and they had young girls lined up along the walls and up the stairs. I thought, "This is too much for me. I'm getting out of here. I'm not hangin' out and doin' a whole bunch of mess. I can't take this, it's too much for my spirit." Some of the other guys said, "Oh, Courtney, come hang out and have some fun." But I didn't care. I was on triple overload. I couldn't take anything that was painful to my spirit. I would come home, do my work, write in my journal and go to bed.

Boy, was I ever happy to get home! Ahren and I celebrated my return and had a wonderful Christmas. We had struggled, but we broke through to the other side. We'd been through thick and thin and decided we were going to make a go of it. We thought, "This is going to work. We're going to make this work. How it's going to work, I don't know. But we're going to work on it." Once again, we probably should have started talking about marriage but didn't.

I had a couple of weeks of downtime then began rehearsals for the pre-Broadway run of the play. Life was grand. I was on top of the world. Everything was new, but I still had the same types of personal issues. My father was a people pleaser, and now I had become one, too. And people liked me, so I could get away with things. I was prone to tell folks what they wanted to hear whether or not it was quite accurate. And even though my parents had taught me right from wrong, I wanted and needed attention and affirmation. I knew the business of entertainment was cutthroat. When no one was watching, whose morals were going to win out? I didn't have enough of my own moorings and moral center to maintain my integrity in the gray zones. I began to play the good boy, but when I thought I could, I'd try to get away with little stuff. I'd tell little white lies to people—I'd tell one person one thing and another person another. In my mind my intention was to fix it later. Until then, the ends justified the means. I still looked at myself as a good person. I was getting all these accolades, and I had people around me who believed in me, were confident and on my side, to lean on. People were amazed by my accomplishments. The experiences I was having were amazing! "Will you look at this boy—just graduated from Yale, got a film and about to go to Broadway!"

In retrospect, I find it very interesting that the same kinds of personality problems I was having were reflected in Bottom's behavior. Bottom was a really good dog at heart but had gotten big, was misbehaving and was generally out of control. Ahren couldn't handle him. I decided to hire a dog trainer.

"Tell the dog to come, Courtney," the trainer told me.

"Come here, Bottom!" As usual, Bottom took a good five minutes to come to me. He looked at me; he walked around; he sniffed at this and that; he played little games.

"Oh, I've got it," he said. "You've confused your dog. The dog is fine, I've gotta train you!"

"What do you mean?"

"You've got to tell the dog exactly what to do—how to please you. If you don't tell him how to please you, he doesn't know. He'll do what he wants to do."

"Oh, wow…"

"Whatever side of the sidewalk you want Bottom to walk on, tell him that's his side. He'll gradually know that that's his side."

I thought about what we'd been doing. Sometimes I'd tell Bottom what side I wanted him on and sometimes I wouldn't. No wonder he'd look at me like, "You didn't tell me that last night when it was dark and no one was looking out those big windows—you let me take a dump on those people's lawns then. Now when they're lookin', you want me at the curb? Hmmph!"

When he didn't do what I wanted, I'd call him to me and would spank him or hit him on the nose. But he was a very intelligent dog. The next time I'd call him he wouldn't come.

"Courtney, who wants to come when they know they're going to get a spanking?"

"Good point. No one, I guess."

"Whenever your dog comes to you, it should feel like home. Good or bad, it's home. So praise him, then take him over to what he did and reprimand him. But do it with love so that your dog can't get enough of you."

We rehearsed for *Fences* in New Haven then performed at the Curran Theatre in San Francisco. When we returned to New York there was major drama behind the scenes. August Wilson and the producer Carol Shorenstein Hays couldn't come to an agreement about how the play should end, and Lloyd was caught in the middle. Who has the power—the producer because she has the money, the director because he's directing the thing, the playwright because he wrote it or the star, James Earl Jones, because he's onstage? Two days before we opened, Lloyd announced they had reached an impasse. Lloyd wasn't going against his playwright, so he was stepping down. We were not going to open. We all stood up and begged for a compromise but left that evening not knowing what was going to happen. We were called in the following day and August announced to the cast that he and Ms. Hays had come to an understanding about the ending of the play, Lloyd agreed to stage it, and the play opened. It was an instant hit!

In spite of the demands it placed on everyone, *Fences* became one of the biggest hits in Broadway history. The play opened March 27, 1987. In May it was nominated for six Tony Awards. In addition to doing the show, there was a monthful of luncheons, when the nominated actors and actresses got to meet the Tony Award voters. So my days were taken up and the shows were pressure-packed because the Tony voters were in the audience. I was stressed out wondering if I was good enough. There was too much personal pressure and life pressure. And to perform well, I can't eat too much. I lost about fifteen pounds—I almost wasted away. It was a grueling experience.

Now, all of a sudden I had to figure out how to maintain my energy for eight performances a week, night after night for ten straight months. I had two shows on Wednesdays, two on Saturdays, and Monday was my day off. Even though my training at Yale involved long days and many all-nighters, I hadn't worked as hard as I'd have to work in the play. It was exhausting! And nobody can tell you how to do it; you have to figure it out yourself. Plus, my role was very emotional. Every night Corey had to cry and mourn his father's death. Some nights I was as dry as a bone. But if I got my B.A. from Harvard and my M.F.A. from Yale, *Fences* earned me my Ph.D. I had to learn how much energy to use—to expend the exact amount of energy I needed: no less, no more.

Fences won every major award that year: Best Play, Best Director, Best Actor, Best Featured Actor, Best Featured Actress, Best Script, the New York Drama Critics Circle Award, the Pulitzer Prize for Drama, a bunch of other awards—everything. Frankie and I were both nominated for Best Featured Actor. It was great but the process was stressful. Frankie would ask me, "Gosh, Courtney, you're on top. What are you so worried about?" Unfortunately, Frankie and my votes canceled each other out. But I won the Clarence Derwent Award, which recognizes outstanding debuts in a Broadway play.

With all the attention, my immaturity became a bigger issue. Everyone was saying, "Oh, Courtney, you're so wonderful," and I would believe them. People would recognize me as I took the subway back and forth to Brooklyn; they'd recognize me when I was on my bike. I wasn't seeking out the attention and I was out and about among the folk. That early–August Wilson era was the first time black folks had any reason to come see a play in a long time. I was new at dealing with my "celebrity quotient."

"Didn't I run into you the other day? Oh, at *Fences!* You were in *Fences!*"

"Yeah, I'm in *Fences*."

"Oh, maan!"

By August, I had hit my stride and onstage I knew how to give people their money's worth without overextending myself. My time management and emotional management were no longer major issues. That month also marked contract renegotiations, which occur five months into any Broadway play. We had to decide if we were going to re-up for another six months. I was excited because I thought it meant I'd be making more money; we were making the Broadway minimum, which Ahren and I were banking. In the meantime, the producer had made back her investment five months into the run (and about thirteen million dollars overall). Now, the producer relies on the general manager to tell her how to deal with the actors. The general manager makes his money by keeping the show running tight in every area, including financially. James Earl earned a percentage and rightly so; he was the star. The GM told the rest of us, "There's no increase. Take it or leave it!" He knew there was no place else for black theater actors to go. Our understudies were talented and would be happy to take our places. I was outraged.

"Ahren, I want to leave the play. This is ridiculous!"

She encouraged me to do some soul-searching and talk to the other actors. I spoke with Frankie, Ray, Charlie—the other members of our "family." Everyone encouraged me, "Stick with it, brother, you can't leave."

"But it's not right!"

"Just bite the bullet. Just hang. It's wrong but there will come another day."

It was a big business lesson for me. *Fences* taught me acting lessons, business lessons and life lessons. Sometime in the midst of the run, *Hamburger Hill* opened. I couldn't attend the premiere because I was doing the show—what an amazing time!

While all this was going on, Ahren auditioned and was cast for August Wilson's third play, *Joe Turner's Come and Gone,* which I consider his masterwork—it was a very difficult play, which is why it's so rarely done. It's slippery. When Lloyd wasn't present (he'd often have to travel back to Yale), the cast would sometimes lose hold of it. Nevertheless, I was so happy for Ahren. She deserved it. Once again, I felt like we were doing this "acting thing" together. Wherever *Joe Turner* played I traveled to see her. I ended up seeing the play about twenty different times. Ahren was fabulous—she was outstanding onstage. Many people describe August Wilson plays as similar to the musical style the blues. His characters are people we all know in life. He infuses them with so much veracity that the actor has to be very closely cast. If the actor isn't able to flesh out the character—if she doesn't hit her exact right note at the exact right time—the audience will know it. Ahren was pure honesty in the play. She sang her note to perfection! The rest of the *Joe Turner* family was fabulous as well. I particularly remember noting how Charles Dutton was just energy personified—he's unlike anyone else. And Angela Bassett was a force of nature coming onstage two hours into the play and totally changing its direction. Her role was very difficult, and I told her as much. I liked traveling to see Ahren. It made me feel good. As supportive as she had been to me, it was the least I could do.

Joe Turner reached Broadway in March 1988. It, too, was nominated for a bunch of Tony Awards. Three of the women in the cast were nominated for Best Featured Actress. Ahren was one of them. We had both become Tony Award nominees. It was amazing! We came along at an incredible time to be a black theater actor (or theatergoer). August Wilson plays became a chance for black folks to gather on Broadway. That had never happened before—at least not in recent history for straight drama. (Musicals like *Sophisticated Ladies*, *Dreamgirls* and *Tap Dance Kid* had done well.) But at the opening of *Fences*, *Ma Rainey*—and, over a total of twenty years at *Joe Turner's Come and Gone*, *The Piano Lesson*, *Two Trains Running*, *Seven Guitars*, *King Hedley II*, the revival of *Ma Rainey* and *Gem of the Ocean*—black actors would gather. Each premiere became a de facto reunion of August Wilson alumni. We had spent two or three years working together and touring the country before our play arrived on Broadway. These openings became a chance to reconnect. They were characterized by shrieks of joy, hugs, kisses, lipstick on cheeks and soulful hugs and handshakes. "What's up! How are you? How's your life? I miss you. You're getting married? I admired your performance! Are you finding work as an actor? Did you hear so-and-so is expecting a baby?" We laughed, we cried, we ran lines together. Each "family" was very, very tight. Other actors would show up to enjoy amazing theater and celebrate. Black actors may have competed against each other as we vied for the few theater, television and movie roles offered us, yet we shared in each other's triumphs and tragedies. Over the miles we supported and encouraged and rooted for each other.

This system that Lloyd set up and August delivered on became a testament to family—most visibly a testament to black family since our sudden presence on Broadway became glaringly obvious. But over the years, many, many regional theaters and community and equity actors of all races and around the nation became part of Lloyd's system and, therefore, our extended clan. Lloyd and August have since passed and the world has lost one of the greatest director and playwright teams. But what he and Lloyd set in motion will reverberate for generations.

Fences' Broadway run closed in 1988. After that we performed in some regional theaters. I'll always remember that when the play was in L.A., I experienced my first earthquake. Ahren, Bottom and I were in bed asleep when it happened. The tremor woke us up. Ahren called out and reached for both of us. We were literally shaken up but there for each other. In 1989, I auditioned and got a role in Athol Fugard's *My Children! My Africa! My Children* got a mixed review, but the review I got from Frank Rich, the *New York Times* theater critic, was absolutely stunning. I don't read reviews, but Ahren told me to read this one after she read it. It waxed on for about a column and a half.

Next I got a role in Václav Havel's *Temptation*. My agent told me she had negotiated a handshake deal for the part with the general manager of the Public Theater since I was up for a role in *The Hunt for Red October.* I was naive at the time. A handshake means nothing, and the agent knew it. Obviously neither the

GM nor my agent thought the issue would come up. When I actually got the role in *Red October* my agent told me, "The general manager's saying he doesn't know anything about a handshake deal."

"Whaat! Well you'd better go and remind him. You'd better do your job."

"I don't know," she told me. "You may have to talk to Joe Papp." Papp was the theater's famous producer.

"Why do I have to go see Joe? You're the agent. He's just going to yell at me."

"You gotta talk to Joe."

I was *so* mad at having been placed in this position!

So I went to see Joe, who was sitting behind his desk with a yellow legal pad in front of him.

"Okay, Courtney, you tell me the reasons why you think you should go do the movie, and I'm going to tell you reasons why you're not going to go."

In my head I was thinking, Um… Because I've made up my mind. If they're going to sue me, they're going to have to sue me. But I kept that to myself.

"Well, Mr. Papp, your general manager told my agent that if this role came up, I'd be allowed to go. That's all I know."

We talked for a good half hour about how it really was not going to work out for me to go. I thanked him for his time, left in a gentlemanly fashion and went downstairs to continue my prep to do the show. On my way downstairs, someone from his office caught me. "Mr. Papp wants to talk to you."

I went upstairs. Apparently the East Coast and West Coast offices of my agency had been talking. The head of the firm in New York called Joe. They were old friends. Joe got the general manager in his office and pushed him to the wall. "Did you make a handshake agreement with the agent?" The GM finally admitted he had.

"You can go," Joe told me.

* * *

Acting in *The Hunt for Red October* was a dream come true. Sean Connery and Alec Baldwin were starring in it. (So was James Earl though I never saw him.) It was big studio film, filmed on the Paramount lot—I had never been on a studio lot before. I had my own little trailer. I was really well prepared but still in some ways an innocent. When an actor finishes the last scene for the day, the first assistant director shouts, "Last scene for Courtney B. Vance. Courtney B. Vance, last scene," and everybody applauds. It's a tradition. I was so naive, I thought they were applauding for me. Right about that time, Sam Neill, who later starred in *Jurassic Park*, took me under his wing and explained how things worked on the set…including the last-scene-of-the-day tradition.

Hunt came out in early 1990 and did well at the box office. The premiere was a huge deal—it was a big, big function. My parents, Ahren, Cecilie and I went. My folks had been to all of my openings and, as always, we had a lot of fun. They were just ecstatic that this "acting thing" that they hadn't understood was turning out so well. They kept asking when Ahren and I were going to get married. I didn't know how to answer because I'd never been given any guidance on what a healthy male-female relationship leading to marriage looked like.

My father got to meet Tom Clancy. Even though he was having a lot of fun, I remember thinking Dad looked a little tired.

Between theater and movies my momentum was strong. I wanted to ride it as far as I could. I went back to New York and auditioned for *The Last Black Man in the Entire World* by Suzan Lori Parks, a black female playwright who would eventually win the Pulitzer Prize for *Topdog/Underdog*, starring Mos Def and Jeffrey Wright, as well as a MacArthur Foundation "Genius" Award. I loved the piece. I wanted to do it. But at the same time I auditioned for *The Last Black Man*, I also auditioned for a John Guare play called *Six Degrees of Separation*, which was based on the true story of a lost young black man who bluffed his way into white high society by pretending he was the son of Sidney Poitier, an idea which was equally enticing. It was a grueling audition process with James McDaniel, Andre Braugher and myself as finalists. Then we all had to go through a huge callback where they worked with us individually. Mine went really well, but they chose James to play the role opposite Stockard Channing and John Cunningham. I was really disappointed.

Chapter 7

Room to Shine

Shortly before *Joe Turner* opened I learned I had won the lead role in *Dessa Rose,* the movie I'd auditioned for when we were playing in Los Angeles. After only two months onstage in my first real Broadway show—and a critically acclaimed one, at that—I had to give notice. "Whoa, look who's having a fabulous year!" Although *The Color Purple* had happened a few years earlier, few roles in film had opened up. There just weren't that many roles for black actresses, and I had won one of them!

Dessa Rose was based on the novel of the same name written by Sherley Anne Williams. The movie was being filmed in Charleston. I arrived there a week or two early to prepare. They put me up in a Holiday Inn. It was my first time away by myself and I liked it. Charleston was quaint; I got a bicycle and rode around a bit. In the meantime I reread and reread the book, taking every little jewel, every little pearl and every little tidbit I could use to inform the work. I also researched my character's back history. I just lived it, breathed it, consumed it. I was living in the period and very excited about it. I was prepared for the role, ready!

Soon my castmates—Laurence Fishburne, Tony Todd and Natasha Richardson—and I started rehearsing together. Then in came Cicely Tyson. "Oh, my gosh!" As a black child growing up in the '60s and '70s, you'd watch television and not see a soul who looked like you. If you were lucky you might catch *Sounder*. And now here's Cicely Tyson, who starred in *Sounder, The Autobiography of Miss Jane Pitman* and *Roots*—one of the few faces I'd seen on TV during my childhood that actually looked like me. I couldn't believe it. It was an honor.

"Hello, Ms. Tyson," I said, bowing and genuflecting. "I'm Angela. It's *such* a pleasure to meet you."

She received me very graciously, and we got the preliminary niceties out of the way. Then we went into the rehearsal hall and got to work. I just couldn't believe it. If I had had any sense, I would have been intimidated. Instead, I was excited to have the opportunity to show her what I could do—to do what I loved doing with a person who I loved watching, with a woman who had inspired me as an actor. "Let's throw down!" We improvised some scenes between her character, this mother figure, and mine. We were giving it back and forth. I'm in Cicely's face, she's back in mine and I'm right back in hers—we're firing hot! It all went very, very well. I had to be dreaming.

Between our scenes I would go to my trailer and be surprised to find people asking me if I wanted anything. "Huh? What can I have?" I felt like I had gone to sleep a pauper and awakened a princess. I didn't know what to ask for. "Water? Diet Coke?" About forty-eight hours before we started shooting, Laurence and I rehearsed a scene in which we were both sitting on a horse. As we tried to maneuver and change positions, the horse reared up, threw me and took off with Laurence on its back. I hit the ground on my hip, like *pi-yow!* Understandably, they were concerned because their star has fallen off a horse. But I was young, so when I hit the ground I bounced. But next thing I knew, I heard a knock at my trailer door.

"Who is it?"

"Hello, masseuses!"

I thought, Oh, my gosh! This is so incredible! I'm a princess, but a nice princess.

Right after shooting began, our director, Irwin Winkler, left unexpectedly to fly out to L.A. When he returned a few days later his arm was in a cast. Rumor had it he had thrown his fist through a wall. *Dessa Rose* was to have been his directorial debut; however, the studio had suddenly pulled the money. Apparently he offered to pay the ten million dollars it cost to produce it from out of his own pocket. But something happened with the insurance bond, so the plug was pulled completely. I wouldn't have the opportunity to play this leading role—my first role on the big screen—after all. I was disappointed but had lived in the moment and enjoyed the fullness of it. I was to learn from my agent this lovely term "pay or play," which meant that I was to be paid my fifty-thousand-dollar salary—they had to pay me anyhow. So I went from having about fifty dollars in the bank to fifty thousand. *Fifty thousand dollars!* I was *rich!* Before we all departed, Cicely pulled together a fabulous catered farewell party at the house where she was staying. I remember her saying something like, "She was going to be so wonderful!" about me. I glowed. As a parting gift she bought me the baby doll from the prop department that we used in our rehearsals. In the movie his name was to have been Mony, so I named him Mony Tyson. He's sitting in my living room today. After the party everyone cried and we all said goodbye to each other.

When I returned to New York, the word was already out. Every black New York actress was saying, "Oh, you must be devastated!" That was the word—*devastated!* I said, "Nooo, I'm disappointed." I had left Broadway to play the lead in this film, and now the movie hadn't happened and I couldn't go back to the play without the other girl getting replaced, fired or something. So I was back in New York and back at square one. At least I had fifty thousand dollars; that made me feel better. Now I could go into an audition with some confidence.

* * *

Well, I wasn't into shoes or anything like that, so what was a girl to do with fifty thousand dollars? See what was happening out in L.A.! People had begun to go to L.A. to get work, and Los Angeles casting folks had been coming to New York to look for talent. My agency, Ambrosio Mortimer, had even opened up an L.A. office. But it seemed that when it came to black characters, casting directors might audition New York actors but they cast actors who already lived in L.A. Wren had been encouraging me to come out there, so I thought I might as well go and try my hand at television. Well, TV or movies—it really didn't matter. I would work with whoever would cast me.

So I called my girlfriend Andi Chapman, whom I knew from drama school and had helped find an apartment in my building in New Haven.

"Andi, I'm coming out there. Can I stay with you?"

"You can stay with me for thirty days."

At the time I thought, *whaat*—thirty days? Today, I realize she was very smart; she had boundaries. That was very wise of her. I stayed with Andi for about two weeks, then lived with another friend, Joy, who had said, "Come crash—whatever." Not wise in the end.

I arrived in Los Angeles on October 10, 1988. I was thirty years old. My intention was to stay for six months, which was the standard amount of time people were giving themselves to find work or go home. I would go out for pilot season, intending to return to my life in New York. A television pilot is the one episode people use to pitch sitcoms or one-hour drama series to studio executives. During pilot season, actors come to Los Angeles to audition for the pilot episodes. If the pilot gets picked up, you're hired for the series.

I figured that maybe I'd go back the following year for six months, then maybe go back and forth—six months in New York and six months in L.A. But little did I know, when I got there, they'd canceled pilot season that year. The new thought was to cast things throughout the year. I was just sitting and waiting.

Since Ambrosio Mortimer was new to Los Angeles, too, the casting directors didn't know them so they were struggling to get their clients into auditions. I was used to auditioning frequently in New York. Now I was starting all over again; it was probably a month before I got my first audition. Fortunately I had money in my pocket and wasn't hungry.

Before I arrived in L.A., California seemed halfway around the world. Every picture or postcard I had seen of it had been palm trees, sunshine, Venice Beach. But compared to Florida, it was cold when I got here. I didn't know that Los Angeles is located on a desert, and it can get really cold at night. I had only brought one suitcase filled with my little sleeveless and short-sleeved things. I needed sweaters and coats.

In addition to needing clothes, I also needed a car. L.A. is big and spread out. You can't just hop on the subway and get wherever you want to go like you can in New York. The hustle of trying to find a job is very much the same, except in New York you're on foot and in L.A. you're in your car. I didn't have that many auditions, so I would take the bus or catch a ride. I missed walking down the street and getting bumped and jostled by other people.

As I got around, I remember thinking the people were so beautiful. Everyone was tanned and fit. In L.A., people went to the gym and it was actually affordable; whereas back in New York you'd pay about twelve hundred dollars a year to join a gym that was nowhere near you.

Joy was very generous with her car. Lots of times she let me drop her off at her job at the Hard Rock Café and borrow it; otherwise, it would just sit there while she was working. I remember thinking that I needed to buy a car of my own, but it was confusing; I didn't really live there. I lived in New York and all my stuff was there. I was looking for work here, yet I wasn't thinking of relocating. In L.A. there were lots and lots of parties. But I felt lonely without all my family and friends from back East.

After about thirty days I got cast in a new television show with Avery Brooks called *A Man Called Hawk*. I was his pseudo, cryptic, clandestine love interest—Avery didn't want his character to show vulnerability, but he had a relationship with this woman; you just didn't see it. The show was filmed on the East Coast, so I flew back and forth between L.A., Boston, New York and D.C. I think the show lasted thirteen episodes; I did two. Afterward, I returned to L.A. and auditioned for every one-hour episodic drama on TV. Finally, I started to get cast. Every few weeks I was getting a job, so I felt good. In this incredibly competitive field, I was fulfilling my dream of becoming a working actress! But there were a finite number of roles available to black actresses—there ain't but so many prime-time hours on TV. I began to expand my sights—I started auditioning for movies of the week. I got roles in movies like *Fire! Trapped on the 37th Floor* and *The Morris Dees Story,* about the famous civil rights attorney at the Southern Poverty Law Center. I even got to meet Dees himself. I also began to notice little parts were opening up for black folks in feature films like *What's Going On?* and *The Mighty Quinn.* I started to set my sights on them. I got small roles in films like *Kindergarten Cop* and *Critters 4*—the kind where you might miss me if you arrive at the theater late. In the meantime, a lot of my classmates had been auditioning for films. But guess what they wanted? Television! You know how it goes: what they want, you're getting; what they're getting, you want....

After about a year, my living situation with Joy started getting old. She was an actress, too, but she wasn't working as an actor; she was working at the Hard Rock. I was working as an actor, yet was always using her car. On top of that, we hadn't entered into the apartment as roommates. It was her place, so I moved into it. I didn't want to pay rent and not have a room of my own. I also got tired of people asking, "You're working—why are you living with her?" So I found a place out in the Valley. I lived in a little one-bedroom bungalow in North Hollywood. There were four apartments in the complex, all connected. It was like a little commune, a little family. There were three actresses—Jennifer Lewis, Roxanne Reese, me—and two gay guys. I was by myself but around other people. That was nice. That worked. Before long, I joined the local church—First Southern Baptist—which was small and family oriented like back at home.

Once I was working and had a place of my own, I kind of tried to start dating. Unlike in New York, where you run into people on the street, it was hard to meet people in L.A., especially if you didn't go out a lot, which I didn't. I remember feeling as if I kept meeting the same people over and over at all these parties I went to. I felt like there wasn't much good boyfriend material out here. And I seemed to pick po' folk, people who ain't going up; I'd catch them on their downside. I dated one guy who was living with his mama. One day I woke up and realized that was a dead end; it was going nowhere fast. Then I dated another paramour I thought was really pretty special. Things started out nicely. It was polka dots and moonbeams, dessert every day. Everything was lovely. But I obviously wasn't paying attention. First of all, his mama cooked for him daily like it was Thanksgiving. And every now and then he'd mention an ex-girlfriend—but I didn't want to believe he hadn't gotten over her. In passing, he would mention the way she looked. I knew I didn't look like that. I don't think anyone would call me dark-skinned, but I knew I wasn't fair enough for his tastes. I'm not lighter than a paper bag—that whole sickness that comes out of slavery and Jim Crowism that still seems to plague so many people. I didn't have that long, luxurious, silky black hair he seemed to like so much.

Still, after we had been dating for a little bit he told me he had done a wonderful thing. "I've broken up with five girl-friends over you," he proudly announced.

I hadn't even known he had five girlfriends. But instead of going *"Whaaat!"* or *"Huh?"* I remember feeling very proud. Like I must be a pretty incredible person to knock five other girls out the box, to be the last one standing, to be standing at the top of the heap, on top of it all. To be the one who was going to walk into the sunset on his arm. Now, I told myself, I was going to get all the attention rather than it being divvied up in sixths. In hindsight, that was pretty dumb. I should have shown him the door.

Well, a couple of months later, he asked me what I thought he should do about someone he'd gotten pregnant. I guess he hadn't really broken up with all of the five—or maybe there was a sixth who had climbed on board at some point. He tried to elicit my sympathies and my help, which I naively offered.

"How do you know it's yours for sure?" I remember asking him.

According to him, the woman decided to have an abortion. Yet one evening shortly thereafter, he came by and told me that I just wasn't his ideal woman. It just wasn't going to work out, he told me. I guess he was trying to let me down easy; while he was breaking up with me, he was almost crying. But by then I had decided he had a Casanova complex. We were still spending time, but I detached myself emotionally as I had done somewhat with Charles.

"Can we still be friends?"

"Oh, sure!" Anything to get him to go home. Silly me! I should have heeded the warning signs. At least I didn't pine over him.

Whether the relationship was romantic or platonic, other than Wren, whom I grew very close to and hung out with often as just a guy friend, I found it hard to find a man who had my best interests at heart. I like people for people, but out here I never knew what folks were looking for. Even with women I felt a little out of my element.

"Hey, whatchu up to?"—that was the question I remember getting asked. Or "Whatcha doing? Working on anything?" If you work in the arts, people ask you those kinds of questions. They don't ask you that if you work for Morgan Stanley or some insurance company, but when you're in the arts: "Sooo, whatcha working on?"

I never knew—and still don't know—how to answer that question. I might not have been working on anything at the time, but maybe something was getting ready to come out, then they'd see what I'd been doing. But the work had been done a year ago. Did they want to hear about that? Or I was doing this, I was doing that, I was doing a lot of different things, but none of them was a feature film. Was working on an animation project as important as working on a feature film, and was that what they wanted to hear about? I didn't know. Or maybe I'd be trying to get a movie made or was working on a documentary about AIDS in Africa. Do you really wanna hear about *everything* I'm working on? I hated the idea of defining my worth based on my work. And though some people's motives were very nice, others were only trying to ascertain if I was up to something prestigious. So a lot of times I might say, "I'm working on being the best me I can be." Or "I'm working on being happy." Sometimes what I really wanted to say was, "I know what *I'm* doing. How are *you* doing?"

Around 1990 I was offered the opportunity to audition for a role in a movie called *Boyz N the Hood,* written and directed by John Singleton, a recent University of Southern California film school graduate. John was going to cast it, and had producers and executives who were making the way smooth for him. I met him off Crenshaw Boulevard at Marla Gibbs's Vision Complex. (She was way ahead of her time and had bought a theater, a jazz club and other buildings long before folks were thinking like that about that area of town.) John is about ten years younger than me. I remember thinking he was cordial and nice, and had these big puppy-dog eyes—real sweet, like he was enamored of you. I remember thinking he was just a baby.

John and I talked about a lot of different things.

"Who is your favorite poet?" he asked me.

"Langston Hughes."

John liked Langston, too. We talked about him, and I believe I recited some poetry. He told me that Laurence Fishburne had already agreed to be in the film as the dad. I shared that Laurence was supposed to have been my love interest in *Dessa Rose*—until *filmus interruptus*. John and I got on well, and he cast me as the mom. Maybe something about me reminded him of his mom; the movie was semi-autobiographical. Once I got cast it was, "Here we go, Laurence! We didn't get to make our last film, but here we are again." In *Boyz*, we were playing love interests again—this time the estranged husband and wife with this son, this man-child, to raise.

Knowing as much as I do about black folks' struggles, sacrifices and accomplishments, I've always been extremely aware of the images put out there about us. I'm particularly conscious of images on film. Celluloid is permanent, the pictures are forever; they travel the globe and become the first depictions many see of black people. So I'm conscious of what I put out there about black folks. In the first place, there are too few images of black people, black women and people of color, in general. And some of the ones we see—have seen—are outlandish and hurtful. Sometimes that's been because people did what they could with the opportunities they had at the time. Other times it seems it's been because for some folks the entertainment industry is all about the dollar. It's more important to make the money than to be dignified. The way I look at it, there needs to be a balance between laughter and dignity. There's been enough of that other stuff; I want my portrayals to be positive. I want people to be uplifted by my work, to feel empowered, just as the images of black people I saw portrayed by James Earl Jones, Cicely Tyson, Rosalind Cash, Lonette McKee, Vonetta McGee, Sidney Poitier and others touched, inspired and represented possibility for me.

I've also wanted my female characters to demonstrate their love of the black man. Our characters may not always get along, and our relationships may not work out, but, ultimately, I don't want the characters I portray to ever malign or tear down a black man's dignity or castrate him. So, as Laurence and I performed our scenes, I chose to add a little something in the moment—a little flavor—to my lines. Something like, "Oh, yeah, you fine but…"—admitting his character was undeniably attractive but that my character wasn't going to allow that to come into play in the circumstances that faced us. Our relationship ain't gonna work, but I ain't blind, I do see you. Another actress might interpret those same lines like, "You ain't shit." I tried to lean toward, "This is not right, but let's make it right." I was glad John allowed me that opportunity— both to perform the role and to improvise. *Boyz N the Hood* did well at the box office and has become a cult classic. It was one of the first of what would later sometimes be referred to as the *Boyz N the Hood* genre.

Similar issues about black images arose when I was cast in the role of Kathleen Jackson in the made-for-TV movie *The Jacksons: An American Dream*. After they sent me on the audition, my agents tried to talk me out of playing the role. People had begun to disparage Michael Jackson. They were saying that he seemed to be kind of off center, and his sister La Toya was crazy.

"Oh, it's just going to be a joke," they said of the movie. "You shouldn't be a part of it."

"Then why did you call me with an audition time?"

I didn't care what they said; I *loved* the Jacksons growing up and knew other black folks did, too. Plus, I wasn't playing La Toya or Michael. "I'm playing they mama—Katherine Jackson—

whom they love and revere. I think that's a good thing to say in the world about mamas and they children," I told my agent before accepting the part.

While we were filming, I remember watching the kids who played the Jacksons as children. They were singing, dancing and acting and they had to go to school. They really had a lot to do. One young man, Wylie Draper, played the older Michael Jackson. Afterward, he developed leukemia and passed on. He lived his dream. He came to do what he was supposed to do. He was phenomenal to watch. *The Jacksons* aired in 1992 and got a forty share in the ratings, which is extremely good. My instinct about the role had been right!

My next big movie I auditioned for was Spike Lee's *Malcolm X,* where I tried out for the role of Malcolm's wife, Betty Shabazz. Denzel Washington was playing Malcolm. Before the audition I remember reading everything I could about Malcolm and the Nation of Islam, trying to sop it all up. I slept in Malcolm X T-shirts that I'd bought on 125th Street in Harlem. I slept with the script under the mattress just to absorb by osmosis anything that would help me play the role and play it with respect and humanity for everyone to understand. This was not a character I was making up in my head from scratch, from the ground up. This was a real human being who was courageous and fragile and heroic and idiosyncratic. He and his family went through such a sacrifice. He sacrificed his family to the Muslims. Betty sacrificed her man to the world. They had done more than most of the rest of us would have done. I felt a responsibility to bring my best self and not cheat them, and so did everybody else. Denzel was very protective of Malcolm. He had played him before in the stage play *When Chickens Come Home to Roost,* which was taped and shown on PBS. And now Denzel was playing Malcolm in the movie. He had come full circle with playing this character.

A great deal of pride was demonstrated during the filming of that movie. Spike had done an incredible amount of research, and we were telling this story "by any means necessary," as Malcolm would say. The making of the film included all sorts of tribulations. It had been hard to get it made in the first place, then at one point the money fell apart. Spike couldn't get it from the studios, so he reached out to the black community and got it from people like Magic Johnson, Janet Jackson and other folk who had resources and wanted to make sure the movie was made. Until he got the infusion of funds, you didn't hear anyone asking, "Is the check going to cash?" It was more, "We gotta tell this story." It was a story we wanted to tell about ourselves, for ourselves. It was gonna get made. Nobody was going to discourage us or keep us from making it.

On the set everyone was ready and organized and prepared. People were minding their p's and q's, working at their highest level and giving their best self. They might act like "crabs in a barrel" on other occasions, but not at that moment. A lot of time is wasted on a movie set. There is a lot of joking and fooling around. This time we had fun, but nobody "skated" or gave less than two hundred percent on anything. We spoke to each other differently—"Brother This" and "Sister That"—out of respect and love. It felt like I would imagine it did during the civil rights movement when black folks had a common cause, a common fight. We carried ourselves with the dignity and poise you see among many members of the Nation. We might as well have been in it—we behaved like it; we read everything we could about it. I remember going to Ferncliff Cemetery, near Hartsdale, New York, where Malcolm is buried. Spike introduced us to this Malcolm aficionado we could spend time talking to; he had so much information about Malcolm and the period. There was even a tape of the moment that Malcolm was shot.

Because we were going to film Malcolm's assassination, I

listened to the recording. It was haunting. I could hear Betty's wail, her cry. After listening, I was able to grab hold of the pain and re-create the scene. I knew that after he was shot she was on her knees behind the podium holding his head in her lap. I remember we rehearsed it once. It was important to me to get this scene right—to know what Betty must have felt while watching her husband killed in front of her eyes. Murdered. Assassinated. With a baby in her stomach and two little babies at her side. They saw it also. Just the idea of that would make me crazy. I could understand if someone didn't want to go on or if they lost their mind. I wondered how she found the strength to keep going, to raise her family, to educate, to sustain them. Without the support of the community that Coretta Scott King had had, since back then so many people viewed the Nation as a cult over on the side.

During that rehearsal in the Audubon Ballroom and Theater in Harlem, I knelt on the ground, in costume, off to the side. Denzel came by. Denzel puts every fiber of his being into his work. He's undeniable. Unquestionable. I asked him, "Would you just put your head in my lap? Will you just let me look at you and take it all in—husband assassinated, wife pregnant— and let whatever emotions wash over me? Will you let me see what it does to my senses, to my body, to my spirit, to my emotions?" And with all that he had to do—with everything he had on him to carry that movie, Denzel was very gracious and agreed. The environment was so loving and open and professional—above and beyond.

At one point while we were filming, the issue came up again of how I was going to handle conflict between a black woman and a black man. Betty says something like "hush" or "shh"— "shut up"—to Malcolm. And I remember Denzel asking, "How are you going to say that?" He wanted to know my character's intentions. Was I going to have Betty dog him out? "SHH!"— "Shut the hell up!" I could have said if I, as an actress, chose to take it there. Or was I going to choose a sweet way of saying the line, like there's a sweet way of saying nigger? Of course I chose sweet.

On the personal side it was nice to be back in New York while we were filming. I got to see my family, go to the theater at night, reconnect with old friends, walk places and take the subway. My aunt Lorraine (my mother's sister) introduced me to a guy named Joe, who served on some board with her up in Harlem. We started dating. Joe was really nice, bright, well educated and came from a good family. I thought he was a great catch. He was a lawyer and had an easygoing personality, though practicing law didn't really seem to be his thing; he was more entrepreneurial—opening a restaurant, a travel agency, an ice-cream parlor. He also had strong ideas about what he thought was important. He liked to fast once a week and one weekend a month, and wanted me to do it with him. In the beginning of our relationship, I would think, "Okay, but damn, I'm hungry." By the time the weekend was over, I would be eating cookies, drinking soda, orange juice—anything I could get my hands on. Later on, I would tell him, "But I don't *want* to fast." He tried to twist my arm, but I wasn't into it. Still, he was a good guy, and after the filming of *Malcolm* ended and I returned to L.A., we continued to date long distance. That meant I would return to New York periodically. On one trip it seemed like everyone on the subway was reading Terry McMillan's novel *Waiting to Exhale* at the same time.

Shortly after I returned to Los Angeles, I got a call for an audition for a movie based on *I, Tina,* the memoir of Tina Turner, which had been published about a year earlier. I had not read the book but I certainly knew Tina Turner. Everyone knew Ike and Tina, just like we knew Nancy Wilson, Diana Washington, Lou Rawls and the people who sang all the other classic music your parents played on the stereo. I could sho' 'nuff sing some "I'd rather sleep in a hollow log...." My audition was with casting director Ruben Cannon. Ruben had his own business, Ruben Cannon & Associates. In a sense he had had to audition for his job just like I had to audition for *I, Tina*. Ruben's role was to keep up with the talent pool, to know who was dependable, who was most right for a given role, to find the talent that would make the director happy. He didn't have the power to say, "Yes, you have the job," but he could say, "No, you can't meet the director."

I went to Ruben's office and presented myself as a fresh, clean face—a blank canvas—not a lot of makeup. I wanted him to see me as Tina; I have eyes shaped like hers, I have full lips like her, I have brown skin like her, I have hair... Well, you can make hair look like anything; I chose to pull mine back into a ponytail. I wore a simple shift—a spaghetti-strapped, knee-length, A-line dress with an abstract yellow, tan and beige design. You could see my arms, my legs, my calves. You could see that I was fit—not big, not small.

When I walked into the room, there was Ruben, the desk and me. And there were résumés everywhere, just boxes and boxes of pictures on the floor. I had the definite feeling that everyone—even if they didn't have an agent—wanted to be part of this film. After I entered the room, Ruben opened the blinds and window. Then he picked up a CD of Tina—one with her wearing an Afro. He held the CD out in front of him, sort of looked at it, then he looked me. He looked at it. He looked at me. Then he said, "You can audition. I'm going to let you audition for the director." That was it. I guess my strategy worked. I resembled her in a way and he could see from my résumé that I was working. I had done quite a bit of television movies and episodic dramas. I had also done *Boyz N the Hood* and that had done well. I had just played Katherine Jackson. That had done very well. And I had a Yale drama degree. I was hopeful that it would help me in this weeding-out process, and it did.

For the audition with the director, I was not able to read the whole script beforehand. At some point I did, though, and I knew it needed a lot of work. It opened on the banks of the Nile River with a cloudy-eyed old lady doing a fortune-teller, guru, all-knowing kind of thing, reading baby Tina's fortune. When I read it, I thought, "What the heck is this?" I'm certain I was given several sides, individual scenes a couple of pages long. When you get sides you try to imagine the context: Who am I? Where am I? What's going on in my world? Sometimes it's clear from what's written; other times it's not, but you have to make perfect sense of whatever you're given. If you're lucky you hit it on the nose, but you could also be way off the mark.

This situation seemed pretty clear: Ike and Tina had a relationship. In one scene she tells him that maybe they should do another kind of music. Her comment gets his ire up. She starts backpedaling and apologizing, then a fight breaks out. The scenes weren't long but they were intensely emotional. You know how a car might go from zero to sixty in ten seconds? Well, these scenes went from zero to sixty in what felt like three seconds. You had to turn on a dime, from peaceful and serene, everything's okay to—*Pow!*—getting the crap beat out of you. From calm to where you're fighting, scared for your life. Fortunately, I knew how to do that from my role as Martha Pentacost. I called on that experience as I prepared.

I came to the audition with my same blank-canvas look. I couldn't look like her any more than I did. Maybe I could have done my hair like hers, but that would be trying too hard. Even then, I needed to lose a few pounds, I wasn't a dancer, I couldn't sing. (Fortunately, there was no singing in the sides and she was going to redub the songs, do fresh recordings.) What was called for was acting. I sat alone in the anteroom. That was good. Most times when you arrive at an audition, you usually have to wait in a waiting room with other actors. "Hi, how are you? What have you been doing lately?" Ugh! Or maybe one of the actors is talking to the receptionist. "How's so and so been?"—the insider thing—and your insecurities kick in. She knows them. You're thinking, They like her; she's a shoo-in. Or maybe someone starts talking to you and engaging you—perhaps they haven't seen you in a long time or they're gregarious or giving you nervous, mindless conversation. Maybe how you relax is by going over your lines or sitting quietly—but you can't because someone is giving you conversation, conversation, conversation. You can't step outside to get away from them because you don't want to miss your turn.

The walls in this office were paper thin. Sometimes when this happens you get a little preview, you hear what happens. "That doesn't sound believable," or "Hmm…she really put her foot in it." You can get a little intimidated or feel more confident. I didn't know who the person auditioning was—I was certain she would be better than me. Yet I was hoping I could put my own twist on the lines. Like we were all wearing the same blue pin-striped suit, but maybe I'd made the lining of mine shocking red or canary yellow. It's still a little pinstriped blue suit but—it's got a little flare. But as the woman started acting and I listened to how she performed the role, I felt like there was room for me to shine.

When I was called into the audition room, I again met Ruben, who was very nice, along with Doug Chapin, one of the producers who had bought the rights to the book and shepherded it along to this point. I read with Ruben. Ruben is a great casting director but he's not an actor; he didn't have an actor's instincts. Regardless, I had to read as if he did. I had to imagine that he was an actor, I had to imagine that he was Ike. We did about three or four scenes. The last one was very hard and required emotional volatility. There was no lead-up time; it was just turn on a dime. The scene changed in a nanosecond—lightning split, quick, emotional changes, transitions! If Ruben had been an actor, he might have done some things with his voice or perhaps with gestures to threaten me. He was just the reader, but in my mind, in my imagination, I invested Ruben with every bit of violence and intimidation that I could muster. Tina had been afraid and in love and fighting for her life and making up and backpedaling. I reacted to Ruben's—Ike's—words as if he was about to *kill* me! I fell on the floor. Tears shot out of my eyes. In that moment I was there—not outside, not looking in, not removed from it. Ike was real.

"Whatchu say? Whatchu gonna do?"

The scene may have been one page long or one page and a quarter. *Boom!* It was quick. *Quick!* But when we finished I had to get up and wipe the tears off my face. I knew I had "put my foot in it!" as they say—I had performed incredibly well. I thought, "Oh, girl, I surprised myself. Oh, my gosh, I showed up for that one! Aww, that take was sweet. Give me another helping, please!" It doesn't get any better than that. They should have been filming. I wish I were in costume. Any lights, camera, *action!*

Later I would learn that that was the moment when everyone in the room said, "We found her!" At the time, all I knew was that I was satisfied but that other people still had to audition and were scheduled to come in. The gossip on the grapevine was asking, "Is Tina going to do it?" The director was married to Lynn Whitfield. In my mind, that made her a shoo-in for the role; I didn't know they had broken up. I remember thinking that Robin Givens still hadn't auditioned. She was doing lots of movies back then; she was the black "it" girl. Women my age still had to audition and the young Tinas still had to audition. All were wonderful actors. The production team may have felt I was the one, but they still had to be sure, they had to be fair. Like everyone else I waited until the auditions were finished.

But when I got the call that they liked me, it wasn't because I had been awarded the part. I was told that the people I had auditioned in front of didn't have the final authority to hire me.

Disney execs would have the final say. I would have to participate in a screen test. Unlike an audition where there's no scenery or props, for a screen test they try to give the actors and the audience evaluating the actors a fair approximation of what's going on so there's much less left to the imagination. They construct a set and light it properly. The actors wear costumes, act and are actually filmed.

When I was asked to screen-test, I had a good feeling that some established player had not already been cast, as is sometimes the case. The role was really available; however, being screen-tested was new to me. I didn't know how it worked. They had offered Ike to Laurence Fishburne. He had turned it down—it was Tina Turner's story and he didn't know who was going to play Tina. He eventually did. From Disney's perspective, who was I? I was somebody coming up, but not a household name. I might have been fine playing roles on television, but now I would have to carry a feature film. Whether I was a household name or not, did I have enough presence to carry Tina's story? The folks in the audition room thought so, but what about the folks who were putting up the money? What about Touchstone? What about the legion of Ike and Tina fans? They didn't know who I was. Sheryl Lee Ralph, who starred in *Dreamgirls,* was also invited to screen-test. They knew she could actually act, sing *and* dance.

In between the audition and the screen test, I worked with Michael Peters, the movie's choreographer, to learn dance steps, and dialect coach Jessica Drake to learn Tina's accent. I also had to learn my lines for the screen test with Keith David and Samuel L. Jackson, the two guys who were up for the role of Ike after Laurence decided to pass. For about two weeks straight, I worked about fourteen hours a day learning a role I hadn't been cast in and wasn't being paid for. I had a *major* attitude!

"I don't have this job, yet I'm working like I've got this job."

"Oh, Angela, how many hours would you like to work?" Brian Gibson, the director, would ask.

"Ten hours, doggone it—ten hours a day!"

But ten hours was not enough to accomplish everything we needed to get done, which was to learn lines, act and dance for five or six long scenes. We were going to perform "Proud Mary"—you know, "rollin' on the river." We were going to perform Ike and Tina's first meeting. We were going to perform the scene when Ike got upset with Tina for talking about the new music she thought they ought to play, then beat and raped her.

"Just feel confident. You're really wonderful," everyone would reassure me. "It's just got to go through what it's got to go through. Disney needs the screen test to put their stamp of approval on it. We want you to be the best you can be." I was ticked off but kept on going. I was trying to come up in my field and was willing to put up with whatever was necessary to get there. I wasn't in shape. I was constantly tired. My body was sore and achy.

On the day of the film test, they placed me in one trailer and Sheryl in another. I heard that she had only gotten about three days to prepare. I had gotten two weeks with Michael Peters. Knowing that made me feel more confident since I was competing against a real pro. We each spent an hour or two in hair and makeup. Then for about twelve or fourteen hours we'd perform the scenes. I'd do my scene; she'd do her scene. Then I'd do a scene and she'd perform the same scene. In between scenes, the crew would change the set. We were in the house, so they made it look like a house, with a sofa, a vacuum cleaner and whatever. We were in a diner, so they made it look like a diner. We did "Proud Mary," with the hair, yellow dress, lip-synching and klieg lights. We did the young Anna Mae Bullock, the older Anna Mae, the beat-up Anna Mae, Tina in all her glory—the Proud Mary "rollin' on the river" Tina. During the rape scene, Sam Jackson accidentally fractured my hand dragging me across the room. By the time we were done, it felt like we had performed the whole movie. The studio executives told us they'd let us know in thirty days and we would start filming one week later.

Thirty days? And then a week to prepare to play this lead role? That was outrageous. Fortunately, it didn't happen. Later that weekend I learned I had gotten the part. I would have thirty days to prepare. A month was a lot better than a week, but still just *awful!* It wasn't enough time. But you know what? Black folks have been asked to do so much with so little for so long. And here's the grandness and the shame of it: We do it—it gets done! So what does that perpetuate? More of the same; more doing much with little in a very little amount of time.

At this point, I had been cast as the female lead but there was still no word about the male. Around that time, I traveled to New York to attend the movie premiere of *Malcom X* and saw Laurence while I was on an escalator. I knew they wanted him to play Ike. The director had told me, "I had this dream and I saw the marquis. Laurence Fishburne and Angela Bassett were starring in this movie." Even though Laurence had already said no, they kept asking him anyway. So when he saw me, he had a look on his face like he expected me to bug him about something his mind was already made up about—like he expected me to say, "Man, why don't you want to come do this with me? It's going to be fabulous. Come on!" But I figured everybody's got a dream, something they want to do, and some people are really good at getting everyone to help them make their dreams come true. But what about *their* desires, *their* aspirations? Don't pressure folk and don't get your feelings hurt if other people don't catch your fever, too. You've got to consider, What do they want to do?

So I shouted from the escalator, "Hey! They keep talking about you, but I told them to leave you alone. You're grown. You know what you want and don't want to do. They should just leave you alone about it!"

It wasn't like I had some reverse-psychology ulterior motive. I'm not that smart. I just didn't want to pressure him. I figure if folks don't want to do something, move on; you've gotta give them an easy way out.

But a couple of days later the telephone rang, and a deep resonant voice asked, "So you want to get married?"

"Whaat? *Yeah!*" I shouted. "This is gonna be fun! I'm gonna get a chance to work with you again. We're really going to work together on this one!"

Who knows what convinced Laurence to take the role. Maybe he had seen a more recent revision of the script, so he knew it was gonna be all right. Maybe he thought, Angela's doing it. She's good. She's cool. Let me come support her. He had been acting since he was ten or so and had been in a number of different movies—*Cornbread, Earl and Me, Apocalypse Now, School Daze, Cadence.* But he was still looking for a starring role. As he said, back then people couldn't put his face and his name together, which is what, as an actor, you want them to be able to do. This movie wasn't starring the man— and people were going to be talking bad about Ike. But the script was really a two-hander. It needed someone who could do it all in the span of a two-hour movie. You had to be attracted to him—his charisma—yet he had to inspire fear. You had to be drawn in and repelled by him. Laurence just embodied that. He had it all.

Once Laurence accepted, I'm sure they paid him *waay* more than I got, though that's neither here nor there. Their first offer to me was fifty thousand dollars. I knew that wasn't fair. I had gotten that playing in *Dessa Rose.* My righteous indignation sprang up. We settled on two hundred and fifty thousand dollars, which was pretty standard for a newer, up-and-coming actor asked to carry the load.

"This is going to be a breakout role for her," the movie executives said.

I was happy. I had a lead in an important movie and I had never made that kind of money before. I thought, "Let's do this thing, let's make it happen."

Chapter 8

Making a Life With It

I continued auditioning for other roles, and *Six Degrees* opened to rave reviews. Before long, I got a phone call. James had decided to leave the play to do a television series. I was in shock! Could it be possible?

"They're offering it to me?" I asked my agent.

"No, it's between you and Andre Braugher."

"Oh, not again!"

"Yeah, you guys have to audition again. The director, Jerry Zaks, was feeling nervous because he and James had not gotten along well during the rehearsal. Their personalities didn't mix." Since I knew Andre would be fierce competition, my agent thought it would be a good idea to leverage a film I was up for to help me get the role.

"Don't you dare!" I told her. "Jerry's already skittish—he's already had one bad experience. Don't make him think that I'd try to force him to do something."

"Courtney, I think—"

"Take me out of the film! I want to do the play." I knew *Six Degrees* was a masterwork. I knew if I got seen in it, my performance would bring me movies.

"But, Courtney…"

"Take me out and tell Jerry I'd like to sit down and talk." I felt that if I could talk to him, he'd like me and see that I'm very easy to get along with.

"Okaay…"

So she set up the meeting and as I expected, we loved each other. He said, "Okay, Courtney, go see the play and if you like it, then let's do this thing."

A few nights later I sat backstage in the Mitzi Newhouse Theater at Lincoln Center, watching the play with the stage manager from his perch near the lights directly above the stage.

This is amazing! I thought. I wondered what exactly I was seeing that made it so superb: Was it the acting? The directing? I asked Jerry soon thereafter and he let me know that it was a very tightly directed play. I was hooked!

But there seemed to be something missing in how James approached the way the character Paul drew in the family into his web of lies. I thought Paul was completely improvising, as he was living life on the edge, and this should have manifested itself in a slightly higher energy level than James exhibited as he played him. I thought his performance left unanswered the question "Why didn't the family kick him out?" So for five weeks beginning sometime in July 1990, Jerry and I began to explore that fine line of possibility. The role was very slippery to me. Sometimes I'd have my arms around it then it would slide right out of my grasp. But that slipperiness fit the character. He was on edge. He was lost and unmoored and making things up as he went along. "Will you be my family? Will you be my mom and dad?"

John Guare plays are very difficult to do. They have a very specific rhythm and he does not allow you to improvise. During rehearsals, sometimes I'd be saying my lines and lose my place. Sometimes the words would slip my mind. And in performance I'd remember the rhythm but not the lines, so I'd say gibberish until the words came back to me. My cast members, who during the performance would sit in the first row, would laugh and howl. "Oh, Courtney, you're so funny!" They didn't understand how shy I was, that I was completely frightened, how much work it takes me to stand onstage in front of over 1,400 people—or how close I was to walking off the stage. For I, too, was on edge. I was playing the role of a man on a tightrope, and I felt I was walking a tightrope, as well. The entire play hinged on my performance, but the role was so complex it hadn't yet taken up residence in my body and spirit. An acting role will eventually settle into my body's muscle memory so I no longer have to think my way through it. When that happens nothing can throw me. But I wasn't there, and wouldn't be for seven or eight months. The smallest thing—my costar missing a line, someone's cough, an audience member arriving late—could cause me to lose my rhythm. The play was being moved to a larger theater—the Vivian Beaumont—also in the Lincoln Center, and also on Broadway.

The night the play reopened with me in it, it was rereviewed. We got a good review, which basically focused on me since I was the element that had changed. In the meantime, the young man that the story was based on was walking around town telling people that *Six Degrees* was his play—that he had written it. So when I'd come onstage the audience members would be asking each other if this wasn't a masterwork but a rip-off. From the first time I came in, my focus had to be strong enough not to be defeated by what people were thinking—not to mention, my own fear.

Six Degrees became a tremendous success, but for a long time playing Paul took everything I had. Even though the show didn't start until about eight o'clock at night, I'd start getting anxious about it at about one in the afternoon. At about four I'd leave home to catch the subway so I could get there by five. For the next three hours I would read my notes—things I needed to tweak, change or improve—then I'd walk through every moment, every word, every beat of the show in my dressing room, by myself. I had to do that to integrate the changes and build up my self-confidence each night. If I didn't do that, I was so shy and insecure, I'd never have been able to go onstage. After the show, I'd either leave the theater at about ten and go straight home, or call Ahren and invite her to join me for dinner or drinks with friends who had come to the show. The next day I'd be up at six-thirty to walk Bottom. Physically and emotionally, my life was totally exhausting.

Around Thanksgiving of 1990 I learned that something was seriously wrong with my parents' relationship. I knew Dad had been stressed out. He had worked his way up through the ranks at Chrysler, and when the company had financial problems during the late 1970s, he thought he saw a way out. He hoped that Chrysler would go under so he could leave with his benefits and start all over. I don't know what he had in mind, but knowing my dad I'm sure he had a plan. But when Lee Iacocca was brought in and saved the company, my father was crushed. He felt trapped—like he couldn't move on. He had bills to pay, and I was at Harvard. Of course, neither he nor my mother told me this at the time. Back then, Dad worked in the benefits department. The plant he worked at was retooling, so he was responsible for firing and rehiring three thousand employees. Later I'd learn that my mother's sister Lois Ann had been talking to him and had encouraged him to leave for years.

"The kids will understand, Conroy. Everything will be fine."

"No, I can't do that to them," my dad would tell her.

"They'll roll with it, Conroy. If they have to come out of those schools, they'll get over it and be fine. You've gotta do what you've gotta do."

"No, I can't do that to them."

I don't know how my dad's troubles affected my parents' marriage. Dad and I didn't talk like that, and Mom confided to Cec about that kind of stuff. She and I didn't have that kind of relationship. As much as we loved each other, in our family everyone was an island. But it was obvious to me that "all was not well in Denmark." In a marriage it takes two to tango, and it was clear that after thirty-five years, there had been a lot of pain, disappointment and "dreams deferred." My father and mother had been quietly struggling for a number of years.

Ahren and I were struggling, too. I'd started calling 1-900 numbers again. These days things have progressed to Internet porn, but back then a lot of men were into these porn "talk lines." Whenever I felt lonely, I'd pick up the phone. Between the images I'd seen in my father's magazines and what the women on the other end of the phone would say, it created a gulf in our relationship. She had started to go to therapy and wanted me to go, too.

"I don't need to see nobody. I'm fine," I'd say. "What do *you* need a therapist for?"

And she kept wanting us to talk about our relationship and my problem with pornography.

"What do you mean?" I'd ask her. "Things are fine."

"But, Courtney, what are we doing? Where are we going?"

"What are you talking about? We're good. Let's keep going like we are."

"There are a lot of things we need to discuss and figure out."

"Ahren, I'm tired," I'd tell her. I didn't know what to say. I didn't know how to connect with her. I didn't know what it was that she wanted. We were thirty now—we weren't kids anymore—but how we dealt with each other hadn't changed. I didn't have the tools to talk about stuff that mattered or deal with difficult conversations, like "When are we getting married?" which everyone seemed to ask us. We never, ever discussed the subject. I wouldn't allow it. I didn't have the tools to deal with either Ahren's or my parents' emotions. What I did have the tools to deal with was work. There was safety in work.

So I focused on it. I needed to; I hadn't mastered my role yet and being onstage was very stressful for me. I had lost my usual ten to fifteen pounds, I was always tired, constantly tired.

One day in December 1990, I was still in bed trying to get as much sleep as possible in order to deal with my two-show Wednesday, when my mom called.

"Your dad—he's not waking up!"

"Ma, what's wrong?"

"Your dad—he just…"

She was hysterical. Absolutely hysterical!

"He's dead, Courtney. He's dead. He shot himself!"

"WHAT?"

I didn't know what to do or say. There are five stages of grieving. I was in the "shock" stage. Everything became a blur. I remember telling Ahren. She was a mess. We had been together for a long time and it was like she was part of my family—my parents were like her parents.

"Go home, Courtney," she told me.

I also remember thinking, "I gotta call Stockard and tell her." Until that point I had taken no days off. A part of me was afraid to leave the show. It had been hard to get the role in the first place, and it had been such a difficult part for me to learn. Stockard, John and I had this rhythm together. Any one of us stepping out would throw all the others off. But I knew I had to go home. Stockard was very supportive. "Go home. We're gonna be fine. You take care of yourself."

Now, after thirty years of successfully avoiding emotional issues in my personal life, I had to deal with the most intense emotions a person can have—and all at once. Throughout my whole life there was a door my father wouldn't open; consequently, we didn't try to go in there. But now the issues were front and center. There was no way to avoid it. There was no escaping.

I flew home to Detroit. When I arrived, Mom told me that Dad had been violently depressed. His mood swings, she said, had been incredible—a lot of highs and a lot of lows. I believe she knew he was on Prozac. I'm not sure how much else she knew. Later, we would discover he had been working with five or six different therapists, leaving one to go to another. Not going when he was supposed to. Maybe trying to find the right one. Maybe feeling that none of them were right for him. To get coverage he had to stay in his HMO. He was so secretive he probably resisted the emotional sharing that counseling involves. Being a black man in the 1980s. And proud. And ashamed of the stigma. And depressed.

According to my Mom, Dad's foster father had kept guns in his home. My father had inherited them back in 1984 when he had settled his father's estate. Mom had told my father, "Get those guns out of here. Get those guns out of my house!" But later she discovered one or two still lying around. It was like he had been gathering up the courage for a long time—he'd been gearing up.

The funeral. It was held at a funeral home. I was kind of out of my body. Our folks came in from all over. My family is full of really intelligent people—Harvard, Brandeis Yale—very educated, and at the same time silly, funny and goofy. They played the "dirty dozens," cracking on each other all the time. They'd tell jokes close to the bone, up on each other, but with love behind it. My dad had been the life of the party. The center of it all. Everybody was ripped. This was the last thing folks would have expected. Nobody knew what to do or say.

My grandfather pulled me aside. "People gonna try to tell you that what he did was a terrible thing. That he's a coward. Don't you believe none of that. Your daddy was very unhappy and it's a blessing you had him as long as you did. Your daddy was a great man."

"Thank you, Granddad." I appreciated what he said. But I wasn't quite sure what he was talking about. I wasn't churched.

I didn't realize there is a biblical prohibition against killing oneself. It didn't occur to me to be embarrassed.

Everybody spoke. Emotionally, my sister was just gone. Everybody waited for me—"Baby Boy."

"You gotta say something, Court."

When I got up to speak, I said, "I don't care. I don't know what people will say about him. I don't know what they'll think about him. All I know is, that man was my father!" Then I broke. It was all I had to say. Later I would hear the same line— "All I know is that man was my father"—recited in the movie *The Road to Perdition*. My father was the greatest man I'll ever know. A mixture of all the things I want to be. During this time I would remember the advice Rose gave to Cory in *Fences*. "You have to take the best of what was in your father and move on. That's all you have to make a life with." While he was here, my father was the best father any son could ever have. He was always there, always teaching, always there to support me. Although he wrestled and eventually succumbed to his demons, through the way I walk this earth, I'm attempting to "take the best he was able to give me and go on and make a life." If I could do that, I would honor him and the vision he had for me, Cecilie and our mother.

Our family bent hard. We didn't break. But we sunk all the way down to the bottom of the well. After the funeral I stayed home for a month. The weeks after were a blur. Where's Daddy? Why did he do it? Was he mad? Was he mad at Mommy? What will I do without him? So many emotions were swirling within me I didn't know where to place them. I was mad. I was so upset. How could he do this to us? How could he do this to Mom? She is such an innocent person. All she does is love. All she wants to do is help. "Can I help? What can I do, Court? Let me help." She's one of those kinds of people. That's where I get it from.

One of my most vivid memories of those days after Daddy's

death is of my mother trying to put a video in the VCR. My parents followed very traditional gender roles. Dad did the VCR. Mom wanted to watch a tape, but realized that she couldn't figure out how to work the machine. She broke down in tears and crumpled onto the ground.

"I don't even know how to work the VCR…."

"Oh, Mom…"

"Why would he do this? How could he do this to me?"

Seeing my mother broken like that was just devastating. She was at rock bottom. I had never seen her like that before.

My mother, sister and I came together during those painful weeks. We cried, we got angry, we laughed and remembered the good times. Everyone was very emotional and in a fit of misdirected rage, Cecilie and I almost came to blows.

"Cecilie, what are you going to do? I'm bigger than you now. You gonna hit me?"

We were entering the second stage of grieving: anger. Since Daddy wasn't around, we directed it at each other.

"Okay, now we're going to fight? You wanna fight? Oh, Lord…"

"What are you two doing?" my mother shouted. "You only have each other. Eventually, I won't be here. You'll be all you have left. You have to learn to get along!"

At that point we broke down and we all started sniffling and crying and hugging. It was a defining moment. No one wanted to fight. We were just hurt and lashing out. Together, we got in there together and dealt with our feelings. We've been tight ever since.

While we were home, Cec and I went down and cleaned out the basement. One part of us felt, "Let's get this stuff out of here," because we were mad. Another part thought, "We're only going to be home for three weeks. We've got to do this before we go. We can't leave it for Mom." My mother said, "Go ahead and do it. If something comes up you think he might have wanted me to keep, you let me know."

We went through my dad's things together. He was so secretive, we wondered, "What are we going to find?" After knowing so little about my father's personal life, now to have to go through his belongings and to possibly learn what he thought—it was too much! I didn't want to know whatever we might find. I definitely didn't want to stumble across a suicide note. It was just too personal. These things were him; they were her. Fortunately, we didn't find anything like that. I did stumble across a letter my father had written to his foster father, describing the scenario when I had the presence of mind to go racing home when Cecilie's head had gotten caught between the jungle-gym bars. "I've never been prouder of my son than I was today," the note said. It filled my heart to know that that was a defining moment for him. But most of what Daddy had was on his computer, which was so intricately password protected, it was locked up. We never really got in there.

We did discover one thing that broke our hearts. Daddy had ten credit cards that were charged up to the max. He'd been pulling from this one to pay that one. He was financially out of control. He couldn't handle it by himself; however, the last thing he did was pay off my ten-thousand-dollar Harvard student loan. When I saw that, I broke down. That action captured the essence of who he was. Personally, he was lost and didn't know how to ask for help; yet he was thinking about helping me. Ahren came out to Detroit about three weeks into my stay. We were cleaning up in the basement.

"This is it for us, isn't it, Court?"

"What?"

"This is it. This is the end, isn't it?"

"What are you talking about? What are you saying? Where did that come from?" I started thinking about what lies I might have told. Who had she spoken to? What might she have found out?

Ahren didn't say anything else. But the writing was on the wall. She knew this was going to totally unmoor me; that I would never be the same; that *we* would never be the same. She knew I was going to run.

In between all this I would practice my lines to myself. I had to keep the show in the back of my mind. I had to keep my rhythms going—every now and then say the words, just to keep the rhythms in my body.

Right before Cec and I left Detroit to return to our respective lives, our mother made us make a promise to her and each other.

"I want the whole family to go to therapy."

I didn't know anything about therapy except that until this point I had resisted it. I didn't know how to deal with this. I felt like my head was going to explode. I knew I desperately needed help. I thought, "I don't know about you, but I *gotta* see somebody. I'm definitely losing my mind!"

I packed some stuff up into a little U-Haul I rented and drove home alone. I listened to Oleta Adams's "Get Here" and Bonnie Raitt's "I Can't Make You Love Me," which was like Ahren crying out to me.

I wept all the way back to New York. Somehow, I had known that my dad needed me. I felt that somehow he had been calling out to someone his whole life. Somehow I knew that but could never find a way to bridge the gap while I was home. I was always escaping back to school, escaping back to my life in New York and leaving him to his demons. It was a very long drive back East.

I was destroyed. And even though I was returning to my home, I didn't know what I was heading into. Things wouldn't be the same.

Chapter 9

Lightning in a Bottle

Now that I was "Tina Turner," I had thirty days to get in shape, learn the movements, work my behind off. I was a regular person—I wasn't fit, I didn't go to the gym. Since Tina is known for having this incredible body, and dancing is cardiovascular, I decided I'd better get a trainer. I'd get up at about 5:00 a.m. and go work out for two hours. He put me on a diet of chicken, broccoli or string beans and white potatoes—chicken for protein, green beans for carbohydrates, white potatoes for energy. And I drank a lot of black coffee for the caffeine, and water. Every now and then he'd make me some ol' tofu cheese-cake or something for a little sweetness, though it wasn't as sweet as we know it. I didn't have time to go to a restaurant and order, so every week or so I'd cook in bulk. I'd get twenty potatoes, twenty-five chicken breasts and a bunch of green beans. Each day I'd put some in a container, maybe I could heat it up, then stand up and eat. Michael Peters would tell me to sit down and eat, but I couldn't. I only had a certain amount of time and there was so much I needed to cram into my brain, into my body, into my feet. I felt like I was under the gun.

After my morning workout we danced for about twelve hours a day. Michael had a spirit of excellence and an incredible work dynamic. We didn't know it at the time, but he also had AIDS; he didn't have a lot of energy. He would lie on the couch napping while his assistant, Eartha Robinson, and I would work in the studio. Eartha and I would watch Tina's videotapes together and do the exact thing. I had to learn all the steps to all the songs, every nuance, every movement of Tina's. She didn't sit on a stool and she didn't dance easy. It was all very, very physical. I had to learn complete routines so they could be filmed straight through from beginning to end, from top to bottom, nonstop. It wasn't like how we shoot movies—in portions—or how you hear singers sing one line and get that right, then sing another, and the producers put it all together at the end. You had to have stamina. You had to know the routine. You had to make it believable in five-inch stilettos. So Eartha and I would work, then at the end of the evening we'd wait for Michael to get up, then we'd show him what we had accomplished. Eartha was the nurturer, Michael would crack the whip. "This isn't right, that isn't right, tweak this, tweak that. Put on those heels and do it." He worked me. I went, I danced, I stood, I ate a little something, I danced some more. Somehow I got through it. Needless to say, my body was *achin'!* Absolutely everything hurt—*ooh-aah-eee-aah* hurt! The more I danced, the more my body shrank. Every week I'd go to a costume fitting and every week they'd take in another inch.

While I was learning the dances, I also had to learn my lines and get the dialect right. I was trying to approximate her dramatic style of speaking, as well as that particular sound of hers—the "ah's" she spoke, being from the South but living in Europe. I also had to develop the character. Who was this woman? And how could I portray her in a way that you'd believe it and be touched by the power of her accomplishments? I read everything I could about Tina and Ike. I examined the personality of one and then the other. I tried to read between the lines of her biography, tried to put myself in each situation and figure out what my choices would be. I tried to imagine what their interpersonal dynamics were. When it came to experiencing abuse, I couldn't draw much upon personal experience, but I did know what it was like to have allowed myself to be convinced by a man that his way is the right way. I did know what it was like to let a man convince me to stay longer than I really wanted to. I did know what it was like to do something and say afterward, "Why wasn't I strong enough to say no?" Or, "Why didn't I chance to hurt his feelings? Because I felt in my soul—I knew in my spirit, to my core—that it wasn't good for me."

Many times we stand on the outside of another person's life, looking in, judging them. We ask ourselves, Now, why would they allow that? Why would they let someone treat them badly? We think, It doesn't make any sense. The abuse is consistent and it continues. Why can't she say "enough is enough"? I think I have a particular capacity for mercy—for feeling, for relating to, for empathizing with others—especially those who are sad, going through it, put upon, subjugated or oppressed, whether by their own choosing or by someone else's. I don't think that experiencing such circumstances makes a person less worthy of love, compassion, care, sympathy or aid. I had heard talk of my mother going through it that time with Teddy Slaughter. That was just a week, just one occurrence. Still, I could imagine what it must be like when you have no money and someone else controls the purse strings. When you really feel that you're at the mercy of another person for food, shelter and clothing, when you receive the basic human necessities through them. You must feel very vulnerable. You might believe you have to stay there. Or maybe you believe no one else would want you— you let the question "Who would want you?" sink in. I was certain that question could damage a woman if she bought into it, if she believed any part of it. If she didn't believe, for instance, in the Bible verse "If God be for you, who can be against you?" That would play into her fear, which is a very powerful emotion.

At the same time I knew from my own experience of being encouraged by great film and theater personalities that those who have gone through the fire can inspire the rest of us. People can come out stronger on the other end. Or perhaps they just barely come through it, but if they regain their strength or choose not to perpetuate that kind of behavior, they can infuse the rest of us with their spirit. I knew Tina's story had that power and I wanted to make the audience feel it.

Once we started filming, we worked for seventeen to eighteen hours each day. According to my union contract, I was supposed to get twelve hours off between tapings. But it was nothing to have eight, maybe ten, hours before I had to be back on the set. I was asked to waive my twelve-hour turnaround about thirty-five times in fifty-three days. They asked and because there was so much to do, I couldn't say no; the movie had to be made in three months so its release would coincide with Tina's world tour. Most movies don't go from principal photography to on-screen in front of a paying audience that quickly and look like anything of substance. It just doesn't happen.

In spite of these challenging working conditions, making *What's Love Got to Do With It?* was an incredible experience. One amazing scene took place immediately after Laurence, as Ike, disrespected me and called me sorry, backstage, immediately before a concert.

"I'm sorry, Ike."

"Yeah, you sorry."

Now we stood onstage about to perform in front of all the extras who were playing the concert audience. I was looking out at them. Laurence was behind me, standing in front of the band, his back to the audience. Suddenly I sensed him at my side. At this point we were totally unscripted and in the moment I turned and looked at him. I was in the emotional place where he just told me I was the sorriest bitch he'd ever known. I thought he was going to say something like, "Sing. Don't you embarrass me." But he, as an actor, made the opposite choice and he did something really sweet and tender—he kissed me on the cheek. At that point something just surged through me. One tear flowed down my cheek. Right at that point the music came on and she sang that primal *"Ohhhh, there's somethin' on my mind...."* You couldn't have planned or scripted that. The acting, the sound and the music and the lights were all perfect in that moment. That became one of my favorite scenes. We did it in one take, and that photo of us with that one tear rolling down my cheek eventually became part of the poster for the movie.

But few scenes happened that easily. I remember filming the scene where Ike dragged Tina to the bedroom and the little baby boy watches him beating his mama. That day, I cried—I screamed—at the top of my lungs for seventeen straight hours. I thought my head would burst open from the pain. We performed "Proud Mary" so many times I lost count. Each time we'd finish, the director would say, "Let's do it again." There were four or five cameras, each filming from different angles, yet we had to do it over and over. That was the one time I spoke out. From the outside looking in, the dance looked easy. But when you're dancing and singing in five-inch heels, you feel like you've caught a wool sweater in the back of your throat. You can't breathe or swallow. Your feet ache. You're sore at the top of your sternum. It wasn't that simple to just do it over and over again.

"Can an actor have a moment? Can we take one minute— just sixty seconds—to rest?" The production schedule was so tight that I literally meant one minute.

Another time during a bathroom break, I plopped down on the toilet and started doing my business but noticed there was no sound of pee meeting the water in the toilet. Why is this taking so long? I wondered. Then I realized that I, a grown woman, had forgotten to pull my underwear down. I was that fried in the brain. "Isn't that funny! I haven't done this since I was a toddler." I got up, threw my panties in the trash, went out and filmed the scene again. Our last day on the set was twenty-five hours long. We were filming the argument in the limo when Tina finally strikes back physically.

While all this was going on, my friends were telling me, "Oh, no, that's too much! You should go to your trailer and not come out until such-and-such a thing has been handled." I didn't have time for all that. I didn't have time to be upset, to play those games. This was a war and I wanted to win it. Little slings, arrows, hurt feelings—the trivialities—weren't very important. For once, I saw the finish line—my dream: a starring role in a major motion picture. I had to make it. I couldn't stumble with personal hurts, aches, pains, tears and frailties. This was going to be on celluloid and last forever. I was trying to do good work. I was trying to be somebody. There was no way I was going to stumble.

I survived filming *What's Love* on fear. I was afraid that I would fail, afraid the movie wouldn't turn out well, afraid I wouldn't be believable, afraid I wouldn't do Ms. Turner's story justice, afraid I wouldn't have what it took to accomplish the job, afraid I might not have the strength and energy to finish. I was afraid that if the movie lacked in any way, it would in some measure—large or small—be my fault. The fact that movies are filmed out of sequence made me question myself even more. When you make a movie, you film every scene that happens in one location, then you tear that location down, leave and move to the next set. It doesn't matter if it happens at the beginning, the middle or the end of the movie; if it happens at that location it's going to get shot while you're there. You do a scene, cut and move on to the next one. But since you're not performing sequentially, in an emotionally explosive movie it's especially hard to chart where you are. Each scene has to fit with the scene that came before, which you may have filmed days or even weeks earlier or may not have filmed yet at all. I wondered, Is it going to flow when we put it all together?

But rather than collapsing under the weight of my fear, I tried to work it to my advantage. I would constantly self-talk to motivate myself. I'd look into the mirror and give myself a talking-to like a parent or girlfriend would. Sometimes I would be gentle and kind; other times I would be rough with myself. I might not have been able to take tough talk from somebody else unless they softened it with love. But I knew I loved myself, so I could tell myself whatever I had to.

"I can't do this," one part of me would cry.

Then the strong part would answer, "What are you going to do—quit?"

"I really want to…"

"You know you're not going to do that. You are going to *do* it."

"But I can't—I don't know if I can do it. What if I'm not good enough? What if I mess everything up?"

"You tried out and you got the job. You got it fair and square. You got it on your own merit, so hush."

"But it's just too much…"

"Yes, it's hard—and it ain't as hard now as it's going to get. But this is the hardest thing you will ever have to do, Angela. The next time you do something this hard you'll be birthing a child. Just think—anything you do from this point on will be easy. It will be a breeze."

"But I'm so tired…"

"So what do you want to do now—sit down?"

"I just need some time to rest."

"Well, I'll tell you what—you've got five minutes, ten minutes. Why don't you sit down for ten minutes, then get up and hit it again."

Or when my throat would tighten and my eyes would brim with tears, "What do you want to do—cry? That's not going to do anything, but if it makes you feel better, go ahead and have a good cry. Then after ten minutes, get up and let's get started again. Is that all right by you?"

"Okay."

In addition to my self-doubt, I also had to fend off the naysayers. Few black women had had the opportunity to star in a major motion picture before, and their roles were not this visible or of this magnitude. A lot of people worried that I wasn't the woman for the job. I'd hear that folks were whispering, "Well, they got what they got, she ain't no dancer." Others couldn't imagine I'd do justice to this larger-than-life person with whom so many people had had wonderful entertainment experiences. I wondered whether an inadequate portrayal of her might cause her to lose this higher-than-life status in people's imaginations and hearts. I worried that my performance might not satisfy. How could you possibly capture her life and put it on film? How can you capture lightning and put it in a bottle?

One day I read an article in one of the trade papers that said something like, "Well, the word is out. It's not going very well. We don't know what's worst—the script or the dailies" (the scenes that have been filmed that day). Shortly thereafter, I gathered enough strength and nerve to ask to take a peek at the dailies. I waited several weeks—until I thought I had proven myself. The director didn't have to let me see them at all. After all, who was I but a newcomer on the block? But Doug, the movie producer, was very accommodating and kind (at the time I had no way of knowing that directors usually try to accommodate leading performers). I asked for dailies of the "Proud Mary" sequence, since it's quintessential, trademark Tina. I went back to my trailer to watch them alone. I knew that if I bought my performance, everything would be okay. If I could make that scene work, then I wouldn't have to look at any more dailies. I inserted the tape and watched. I was pleased. I was relieved.

"Oh, wow! The work is paying off. They can say whatever they want to say. I won't say anything. I'll just keep doing it."

I didn't have the time to indulge myself anyhow. I had work to do. At least now I knew I was on the right track. For the next six weeks, I continued singing, dancing, crying, running, getting a cake smashed in my face, my butt beat and raped. Every day it was physically and emotionally something. And it wasn't boop, boop—day's over and I can go do whatever. No, I gotta go home and lie down and think about what I have to do tomorrow. I had to get the song together for the next day. I had to hit my marks, make sure I was lip-synching right, inhaling and exhaling at the right place. I had to look like I was performing and delivering each song. I would just lie in the bed and try to get the rhythm in my body and the breathing so I'd be right in synch with her—not lagging behind the sound track and not coming before it. Then I had to sleep 'cause I had to get up tomorrow and do the same thing all over again.

I gave *What's Love* everything I had. At the end of the three months, I was whipped. I was a wet rag of noodles, a brain-dead body hurting from the throat on down. I had sciatica up both thighs and into my butt. My rotator cuff was sprained and torn. My hand had been fractured. I was broke down—to' up from the flo' up. I couldn't even get out of bed to go the best spa in the world, where the producer wanted to send me to be rubbed and scrubbed. Eventually, I rolled myself into my Jeep and drove myself out to the spa in Palm Desert. They pampered me, but it wasn't enough. I needed about four months to decompress and come down—a month to sleep and just not have to do anything. And after all that screaming and fighting and crying, I felt old emotionally.

In the meantime, Joe was probably feeling more than a little neglected. He was dedicated to the relationship and had put up with the way it was falling. Because I didn't want to have to come up with excuses at the end of the day, for basically four months I had totally immersed myself in *What's Love*. Another kind of woman might have said, "He's feeling bad, he's feeling neglected. Maybe I don't have to learn all these steps." Not me. I followed the advice my mama gave me when I was a child: "Get your work done first then play."

While I was filming, it was hard to keep up and massage the relationship. We still communicated and saw each other, but much less than usual. I didn't have a cell phone back then. One time he came to visit me on the set. "Okay…" when he brought the idea up (I admit that sometimes I expect people to read my mind), but once he arrived I was really thinking, Please don't get in the way, I'm working here. It might not have been the library, the hospital or the fire department, but it might as well have been the operating room as far as I was concerned. When filming ended, Joe called me up and asked if I wanted to get together, where—East Coast, West Coast or in the middle—and what I wanted to do when we got there. But thinking about what I wanted moment to moment—much less the logistics of getting together—was just too draining; it took me too much effort to answer a yes-or-no question. I was just too exhausted. I tried to explain.

"My adrenaline is gone and I'm left with what I'm left with," I told him. "I can't even feed myself right now."

"Relationships are very important and you have to nurture them," he chastised.

"I know, Joe, but I just need to lie in bed and sleep like a bear and hibernate. I don't even need the phone to ring."

"Well, relationships need to be nurtured."

"I'm trying to tell you that I'm worn out, Joe. I can't even think. I don't need this conversation."

"Do you want to break up?"

"Yeah, sure. Bye." Unlike the times when Charles had asked, this time I said it: "Yes."

In a way, my response was one of self-preservation. I felt like my back was against the wall. I didn't have the ability to make nice, I didn't have any defenses, I had nothing left. My tank was at zero and I needed to fill it up. In my bed. Alone. I was smart enough to know that. "Don't ask me nothin'!"

Of course, that conversation wasn't the end of it. He had to call back and tell me how selfish I was, how he had invested so much in our relationship, how he had lowered himself to date a gypsy actor. How he had seen our relationship going to the altar but now it would never make it.

Now, I had been fine with the first hang-up; I had been in my power. "Yeah, whatever. It's over." But when we hung up that second time, he felt better and I felt bad. I cried. But I done cried and broken up from relationships before. I knew it wasn't gonna kill me. I knew you move on.

In spite of my total exhaustion and our breakup, I felt good about myself. I realized that I was much stronger than I had ever known, physically and emotionally. There wasn't an ounce of fat on my body. I had marshaled all my strength, all my reserves and all my nerve to get through it. I learned that I'm not a quitter. From a technical standpoint as an actor, I had taken something terribly difficult and made it look easy. While a fellow actor could look at my performance technically and imagine how difficult the requirements were to perform the role, a regular person in the audience would just get transported. To them the performance looked easy. I felt an incredible sense of personal satisfaction. I felt proud—not an ego pride, but a pride in myself as a human being that I had accomplished something so difficult. I hoped I had done it gracefully and with an open heart. I felt that my character had stood the test. When you answer the call, you feel really good.

Three months passed between the time *What's Love* finished

filming and the date the movie was to be released. I was still anonymous, going to the store, running my errands, doing my thing. I remember thinking, It's quiet now, but I knew that was about to change; I'd be getting a lot of attention soon. As our opening date drew near, I remember sneaking into a screening in Pasadena. I sat in the back so I wouldn't be seen. During the rape scene the guy in front of me said, "Nooo! Oh, God!" When the movie ended, that audience applauded. I could tell people were really affected by the film. I ran out quickly so I wouldn't be seen, but I felt, *"Amazing!"* It had turned out better than I could ever imagine.

For some reason, I don't remember the movie's premiere. What I do remember is receiving an incredible amount of recognition from people in the industry and the public. I got a telegram from Kim Basinger, saying she liked me in the movie, a little card from Norman Jewison, roses from Winona Ryder. Flowers—so many flowers! Flowers, flowers everywhere! "Where should I put these?" "Put them in the bathroom!" I remember wishing I could call the florist and have them deliver one bouquet a week. That way I would enjoy fresh flowers for at least a year! And the phone kept ringing, ringing, ringing. *"Congratulations!"* Eventually, the phone rang so much that I had to turn the ringer off. It drove me to distraction. It has been my quest to find the softest ring possible.

Now when I went to the grocery store or to run errands, people would say, "Hi!" or want to touch me. That's what I remember most: people grabbing my arms and being entranced with my physicality. "All those muscles!" or "You still got those muscles?" Men, especially, would touch and feel on my body without asking. That was strange. I didn't want to snap, "Don't touch me. I don't like that. I don't even know you. *Mister,* you're *feeling* on me!" I didn't want to appear ungracious, but that kind of stuff really unnerved me and made me feel kind of skittish sometimes. And every now and then I'd get approached by someone who looked like they had been lonely in a room with my picture or fifteen hundred index cards containing celebrity autographs. At times I'd get the feeling that I needed to watch myself.

But most of the time people were really nice. The movie touched them. I was told countless tearful stories of, "I was in that situation. When I saw your movie, I got out of it," or "My mother was in that situation." Those interactions always touched my heart. They made me know that all the sacrifice and work was worth it; my work had touched, even helped improve, someone's life.

In the meantime there was all this Oscar talk. It started soon after the movie came out—though before big Oscar campaigns were mounted as they are today the process was a lot more subtle. However, there was interest in my performance. It had gone very, very well. And the movie was a hit, it was positive and people loved it. *What's Love* contained memorable performances and mine was one of them. As people began to talk, I would look around and ask myself, Is there anything more memorable? Is there anything that touched me more? I wasn't sure that there was, but I didn't know what other people thought.

Early in the award season I won a Golden Globe from the international film correspondents for Best Actress in a Musical or Comedy. That was just sweet! In my acceptance speech I got to say, "Tina, I thank you, wherever you are in the world!" Afterward, Dick Clark interviewed me backstage. That was surreal; I'd grown up watching him on *American Bandstand.*

"Angela, congratulations! How does it feel?"

"Thank you, Mr. Clark..."—I remember he was so tickled that I referred to him as "Mr. Clark." I guess it was like a breath of fresh air. But I didn't know how I could just meet someone older than me and say, "Well, Dick..."—maybe after years and years. While he and I were talking, Pierce Brosnan walked up to me, kissed me on the hand, congratulated me and told me how good my acting was. Shortly thereafter he became the face of James Bond for about the next decade. But that didn't change him; he's still a gentleman—always the same.

After I won the Golden Globe, I started to think, Maybe I can win an Oscar, too. I didn't know how Oscar campaigning went—I have a bit more insight today, years after the fact—but at the time I didn't know what was involved and no one was telling me. I wasn't into all the campaigning. I was just into doing good work. I thought, "My performance ought to speak for itself." I didn't know that for an Oscar, some people would run an ad in a trade publication. At some point I started receiving *Variety* magazine and the *Hollywood Reporter* and noticed that the studios were placing ads: Nominate so and so; remember such and such a performance. I also didn't realize how significant it is that the Golden Globes has two categories: a category for musicals and comedies and a separate category for drama. The Globes had categorized *What's Love* as a musical. In the Oscars there's only drama.

The night before the Oscar nominations were announced, I hung out with Wren and his wife, Ann, at their home. Wren had grown up in Los Angeles. Acting was his whole thing. His grandfather, Troy Brown, had been in the movies with folks like Hattie McDaniel, the first black woman to win an Academy Award (for Best Supporting Actress for her performance as Mammy in *Gone With the Wind*). Ann and the children went to sleep, but he and I stayed up all night waiting for the announcements, which are made at 5:00 a.m. Pacific time, 8:00 a.m. out East. I remember they announced Best Supporting Actor first. Wren and I almost woke up the whole house when they called Laurence's name. And when they got to Best Actress and announced my name, "OH, MY GOSH!" Wren was so excited for me—he's such a good friend! I just couldn't believe it. All I could think of was how far I'd come in my life. The recognition was overwhelming and humbling. Then the phone started ringing—I mean it just rings and rings! This person and that person is calling to congratulate you. They're happy for you and ecstatic and you just can't believe it's happening. I had never even dreamt of winning an Oscar. All the recognition made me feel like I'd climbed Mount Everest or something.

So I jumped onto this train and took the ride all the way to Oscarville! I wanted to experience what this whole Oscar thing was about. I was just overwhelmed with emotion. And there were so many decisions: people want to dress you, you've got to decide what you want to look like, what dress and jewelry you're going to wear, what makeup, you've gotta figure out who in the press you're going to talk to. You have to think about the people you want to thank if you win. It's so much but it's great fun! All the activity goes on for about a month, then you fall over dead! Along the way I got to meet all sorts of people I admired: Rosa Parks, James Brown, Sidney Poitier, Diahann Carroll. I had the opportunity to attend the Oscar luncheon, held shortly before the ceremony, where you are awarded a certificate to commemorate your nomination, and all the nominees take a picture together alongside an oversized fabrication of the Oscar. Of course, I'd never been at the luncheon before. I remember running a little late. The publicist and I got out of the car—and, oh, the paparazzi! Until very recently they had never been interested in me. Now I had to walk through a phalanx of photographers. They all want you to stop and take a picture in front of them.

"Angela, Angela, right here! Look over here!"

"Oh, okay, okay!"

Click, click, click.

I took as many pictures as I thought I could without being too late—I mean, they can take over fifty pictures of you in less than a minute. But after a certain point I started saying, "I'm late, I have to get in there! Okay, I gotta go now...." Right before I went inside, I remember walking in front of this one photographer—a woman with short black hair who was missing her front teeth. She always seems to be standing up front on the red carpet. I stopped for a moment for her to photograph me, but apparently it wasn't long enough. "BOO! BOO!" she shouted. I mean, she booed me at the top of her lungs. I was green to all that stuff—and Southern, all accommodating, in terms of my upbringing. I wasn't cold like some people are. I was the type of person who cared what others thought of me. Seeing her face as she booed me like that was like looking at the devil! Her derision pierced me like an arrow. It was an ugly sight, and ugly piece of humanity. I started crying. Later the *National Enquirer* ran a picture of me wiping my tears on my little hot pink Donna Karan jacket, the best piece of clothing I had.

While I was trying to blot my eyes, I walked through the door into the hotel. I immediately bumped into Anthony Hopkins and started crying again. I admired Anthony Hopkins for all of his roles—for portraying Hannibal Lecter in *Silence of the Lambs* and Jack Lewis in *Shadowlands,* for instance—but I had no idea I felt strongly enough about him that I would start crying. I was just "Wow!"—he'd just popped right off the movie screen and now was standing right next to me. The whole thing was just emotional—I was a raw emotional wreck. I stood behind Anthony while we posed for the official paparazzi—the photographers who were allowed on the inside. I guess the people outside were trying to get whatever pictures they could to support their livelihood. For all I know, the people who knew better may have rushed by them so they could get inside. But on the inside, everyone walked graciously in front of the photographers and we were treated well.

The Oscar luncheon was great—it was a lot of fun! At one point Stephen Spielberg walked up to me and asked, "Where have you been?"

"Oh, I've been here acting all along," I told him. "I was aware of you, you just weren't aware of me." We laughed. It was a very exciting time. For the first time people could associate the face and the names of both Laurence and me. Having people associate your face with your name is every actor's dream.

I invited my mother to be my date to the Academy Awards themselves. I thought it was only appropriate that I bring my mom. She raised me. That's who put values and work ethic in me. She was the person who had always told me, "Don't settle for average," and "Work hard and be nice!" I wanted to make my mother happy. I wanted her to be proud of me. When we were seated, I sat there on the aisle wearing my big, poofy Escada dress—feeling all princessy. Her seat was right next to Anthony Hopkins, which was nice since he and I now had a little history. I got to say, "Mr. Hopkins, this is my mom, Betty Bassett. Mom, this is Anthony Hopkins!" She was thrilled and impressed with him. Wren escorted my sister to the ceremony and they sat elsewhere in the auditorium.

When the presenters started reading the names for Best Actress, the category for which I'd been nominated, I remember Mom squeezing my hand. She was squeezing it so tight she almost cut off my circulation.

"And the Oscar goes to…"

And in that moment before they called the name, it was so exciting. It was like time sped up and slowed down at the same time. Although I definitely wanted to win, I had the thought in my mind that whoever's name they called, whatever happened, I knew I would be okay with it. I felt Mom keep squeezin' my hand. Then I could see the presenter form the first letter of the winner's name. "Holly Hunter!" And it's like, "Ahh!" and you exhale. And you know that with that television camera focused on you, you want to be strong and be a lady. And you saw the movie and she was very good in it. But part of you can't believe it because you know it could have gone either way. And your mother is still squeezing your hand.

Yes, Holly Hunter won the Oscar that year. But in the years

from then until now, if I haven't heard, "You should have won the Oscar," a thousand times, I haven't heard it at all. For a long time every day of the year, I must have heard it twice a day. All these years later I still hear it often. Consistently. But it was as it was for whatever reason—whether Holly's fabulous performance as a mute woman in *The Piano* or the Academy not being ready to give an Oscar to a black woman. I'll never know. I would have loved to win that Oscar, but as I said, I focus more on the work. There are some awards that are important to me, but by and large they are more important to others.

Chapter 10

What Else Can Happen Now?

Back in New York there were two missions I had to accomplish: one was to get back into the show; the other was to find a therapist. I called Stockard right away. Regardless of the other things I had to do, the show would go on, and I was worried about what it was going to be like getting onstage after being away for over a month. I knew I'd have to start all over again. But I figured that once I had the show back in rhythm, I could figure out what the heck I was going to do in the other portions of my life.

I threw myself into my work. From the outside things looked good. *Six Degrees* was the talk of New York. Professionally I was on a roll—*Six Degrees, The Hunt for Red October, My Children! My Africa! Fences, Hamburger Hill*—everything looked wonderful! I was making a decent amount of money, and Ahren and I moved into a nicer apartment. I would eventually earn a Tony nomination for Best Actor for my performance in *Six Degrees*. But personally, I was in crisis mode; on the inside, I was dying. Eight times a week I was playing a character who was lost and trying to find himself, trying to connect with somebody, a black man trying to fit into a white family. At the same time I had lost my father to an incredible tragedy, was feeling adrift and going to work and relating to people in exclusive, predominately white, environments. My character, Paul, was struggling; I was struggling. We were both on the edge. I was barely eating. Every night onstage, I was just "gutting it out." The irony of the role I was playing ripped me apart. I'd go home and just focus on the play. I became obsessed. "Let me read my notebook." I kept working the play over and over, whenever I had an opportunity. I knew I had to get up onstage that night and I wasn't sure how I'd do it. I started to lie more and more to prop up my facade. It became hard to find a place in my mind where there wasn't a lie. The biggest lie was the one I was telling myself: that I was fit to be onstage.

True to her incredible heart and spirit, Ahren was there for me every step of the way. But our relationship was getting more tenuous. I was rarely at home, and when I was, I was focused on the play. I became addicted to 1-900 numbers as a way to alleviate my pain. Pornography is like a drug. It is a sickness and I was in the thick of it. I didn't make time for her. I paid no attention to her or what was going on with us. I didn't know anything about therapists, but Ahren was kind enough to let me see hers. As an actor I had become comfortable with the idea of talking about my emotions. I now knew it was okay to cry and that where the heat of the emotion was, that's where I'd find relief. But I'd never done therapy before. What was I supposed to do? Was I supposed to talk first? How did it work? The first time I went I just held my head in my hands the whole time. The therapist asked, "Do you have a headache?" In my head I responded, "DO I HAVE A HEADACHE! YOU KNOW I DON'T HAVE A HEADACHE! I JUST DON'T KNOW HOW TO BEGIN!" I was upset that she wasn't being helpful.

Initially, I didn't have a good feeling about Ahren's therapist. I knew she was a professional, so I didn't worry that she would judge me. But I needed help and I didn't like the way she sat back and seemed to be waiting for me to do something—I wasn't sure what. Next I met with a black woman. She was the same way. She sat back and waited. I knew I was numb; I knew I was a mess; I knew I needed to find someone who would proactively facilitate my healing process. So I kept getting recommendations from people. I knew I'd eventually identify someone I was comfortable with.

On Wednesdays, between the matinee and the evening show, I started getting massages. One of my cast members told me she had a great Swedish-massage person named Guinila. The first time I laid down on Guinila's table, she asked, "Is there anything I should know about before I begin?"

"My father committed suicide about a month and a half ago," I said. Then I broke down in tears. Guinila worked on my body for about two hours. We talked about a lot of things and I told her that I was looking for a great therapist. At the end of the session she said, "I think I know the perfect person for you."

"Who?"

"Her name is Dr. Margaret Kornfeld."

I decided to make an appointment.

The night before I met her I had a very vivid dream. I was wearing cowboy boots and there were big decorative pillows on the ground to lie on. I remember they felt very comfortable. Later that day when I went to Dr. Kornfeld's office, I knew she was the right person for me as soon as I shook her hand. Her spirit was very gentle.

"Where do you want to sit?" she asked.

There were two sides to her office: the side with the desk and chair seemed a little more formal; the other side was more relaxed. It had a couch with pillows on it. The pattern on the pillows was the same pattern as the pillows in my dream! I knew I was home. By now I understood that therapy involved talking, so I just started pouring everything out, talking a mile a minute.

"Courtney, you don't have to tell me everything at once."

"Oh, I don't know exactly how this works."

"It's okay. We'll take it slowly. A step at a time."

I felt relieved—as though I finally had time and space to devote to just me. I felt excited about having someone to talk to who would understand and help me. Once we got going I found therapy so freeing I wished I had started ten years earlier. There was a lot of stuff I really needed to deal with. In one session she asked me to tell her about my childhood.

"I don't remember it."

"You don't remember your childhood?"

"No, but I used to write down my dreams. I have a book of dreams at home I could show you."

"Bring it in."

I brought it in but it was really too spotty to help in any meaningful way, so I began to look for dream books and workshops. I found a workshop at the New School that looked promising: Breakthrough Dreaming by Gail Delaney. I immediately alerted the stage manager of the show that I would be "sick" in about a month so I could attend the day-long class. It was there that I found the tools to begin what became a life-altering journey into my dreams. Ms. Delaney taught that people, locations and settings of dreams are very important; however, our dreams are encoded in a way that is unique to us. Therefore, no one can interpret our dreams for us—a blue sky means something totally different to me than it does to anyone else—we just need to figure out what our subconscious is uniquely telling us. One way to do that, Ms. Delaney explained, is to train our minds to remember the last thing we were thinking upon awakening.

Eager to try out my new techniques, I got some paper, a pen and a flashlight and put them by my bedside. Each time I woke up I wrote down the first thing that came to my mind. The first three days I tried I got nothing. But on the third night, dreams began coming like a flood! I began by having a couple of dreams a night and ended up with seven or eight a night! Of course, Dr. K. was totally overwhelmed when I brought in fifty dreams that first week. She encouraged me to identify the one dream that had the most emotional heat—intensity—and bring it in so we could discuss it.

I threw myself into recording my dreams each night. I rushed to go to bed; I felt like I was on a mission! During the night I would awaken several times, turn on my flashlight and write down all my dreams, giving them catchy titles based on where I felt the heat—names like "Runnin' in the Attic," "Ketchup," "Peanut Butter Soup." I had dreams about Bottom; dreams about attics and basements; dreams about offenses and defenses in football and basketball; dreams where I was running from something; dreams about race—black and white.

In time Dr. K. began to see patterns.

"Do you know that whenever Bottom's in your dream, that's you?"

"Bottom's me?"

"Yes. In real life you and Bottom are so intertwined that you know what's going on with each other. You know when he's upset, when he isn't feeling well. You can touch his nose, look in his eyes, look at whether his tail is up or down and know what's going on, right?"

"Right…"

"So whatever's happening with Bottom in your dream is actually what's going on with you in your life. How Bottom's feeling in the dream is actually how you're feeling in life."

To someone who wasn't very in touch with his feelings and was just learning how to deal with them, that was a powerful revelation. In time our work with my dreams eventually began to give me a tremendous amount of insight into how I was doing. But my healing took time. The unfolding was slow. The process occurred over three years.

By late spring of 1991, I started getting *Six Degrees's* rhythm down; it took up residence in my bones. Rather than having to start my preparation early in the day and arrive three hours early to do a walk-through in my dressing room, I could come in at seven-thirty, get hyped—I had a ritual similar to that of a professional athlete—and be ready to walk onstage at eight. I knew how to give the part exactly enough energy to play it well without wearing myself out. I gave no more, no less. Still, in addition to the physical rigors, to play such an emotional role in the middle of what I was going through was tremendously taxing.

In the meantime, Ahren was continuing her therapy. She became able to articulate her feelings for me, as well as what she wanted and where she wanted the relationship to go. She wanted us to be closer. She wanted a truthful, honest relationship. It became more and more clear to her that we needed to talk. She kept trying to find ways to bridge the gap and use all the tools she was learning in her sessions. But especially now that my father was gone, I was as numb as could be. She was trying to get clear, but my whole life, while improving, was still in shadows. I was slowly coming to realize that my life was a lie—that I had become an actor in life as well as onstage. Back then, I told people whatever they wanted to hear or whatever I needed to say to get them off my back. I didn't yet know how to have a conversation that might be difficult or unpleasant or require me to be honest about my emotions, so I kept avoiding them.

"What do we need to talk about? Things are fine."

I'm sure at some point Ahren must have wanted to discuss marriage; however, I was only beginning to become aware of how I was feeling, which is essential to telling the truth. I knew what it meant to be boyfriend and girlfriend and "play house." But I was just beginning to learn what it meant to be a man. I didn't know yet what it meant to be committed to someone. What was the next step? How do you get to it? I didn't know. I was a mess. In the meantime, Ahren must have thought, "I can't marry this man!" She didn't know what to do. Even if she had wanted to, she couldn't have afforded her own apartment. I was stuck; she was stuck; we were stuck.

Late that summer, she and I took a big two-week vacation at a five-hundred-acre hay farm in upstate New York. It was harvest time. Warm and beautiful. We needed to get away. Our relationship hadn't improved much, but I was starting to learn to communicate better.

"Ahren, I've gotta get out of the play," I told her. "I'm exhausted."

"Then give your notice, Courtney."

We had a lot of fun and invited a few friends to visit. That farm became our little sanctuary. "It's so nice here, I don't want it to end," I told Ahren. But I don't know what we were thinking; we both had allergies out the wazoo. When they cut the hay, our eyes swelled shut and we had to leave. I got blue at the thought of going back to work and the pressures of the show.

"What are we going back into when we leave here?" Ahren asked me. We cried together. It was like she sensed things between us would disintegrate from there.

When I returned to the city, I gave six-weeks' notice, which was enough time for them to find somebody else. James McDaniel didn't want to come back and they couldn't find anybody else, so they decided to close the show in early January 1992. They wanted me to stick around.

But I was done. I literally could not do it anymore. Something had to change. "I'm tired. I'm exhausted. I can't do no more."

"What will it take to get you to stay?"

"The hardest part is commuting back and forth from Brooklyn and hanging around the city in between shows," I told them. "I'm tired. So give me a car to and from the theater, and double my salary so that when I come back to Broadway I'll come back at a higher rate."

"No!"

"Okay, I'm out!"

"Hold on, Courtney! We'll double your salary and give you the car three times a week."

"No. You can't pay me enough money to continue to do this role. I have loved it but it is time to stop. It's not about the money; it's about the car. Please give me a car or I am fine with ending my run now." We came to an agreement. I got the money and the car and now I could relax the whole way to the theater and finish out my run with the show.

My work life now became more manageable, but that fall my relationship with Ahren deteriorated. I was still emotionally numb on the inside. Even though through my therapy I was becoming more self-aware, I had a lot of issues to deal with that had been years in the making, and I was still reeling from my father's suicide. I hadn't connected the dots enough to match my feelings with my actions. I didn't know how to grow closer to Ahren, like we both wanted. Nor could I figure out what to do after eleven years of being together. I knew I needed to do something, but instead of turning toward her, I ran away. I caused our relationship to fracture. I'm not too ashamed to lay out the details of my behavior; however, I don't want to be insensitive to her by resurrecting painful events. My behavior back then was callous enough.

Suffice it to say, I went through a painful, ugly period during which I caused a great deal of hurt to a number of people. Ahren was foremost among them. I ruined our relationship and caused it to implode. While it was never my intention to hurt Ahren, I did hurt her—and very badly, to the extent that she told me she didn't want to see or ever talk to me again. My family worried about what was going on with me. Several months after we broke up, I came to my senses and I knew I had made a mistake. I reached out to her two or three times to tell her I was becoming a better man. I had hopes of winning her back. But by then she was emotionally healthy enough to know that, as well-meaning as I may have been, she needed to stay away from me for her own sanity. She hired an attorney. He sent me a letter telling me to leave her alone. She needed to protect herself emotionally from me to heal.

When I read the lawyer's letter, I experienced what I call a "King Lear moment." The protagonist of Shakespeare's *King Lear* threw away his entire kingdom. Ahren had been everything I wanted and needed—she was pure gold—yet I had ruined our relationship. I was devastated to know that I had hurt Ahren so much that she felt she needed to use a lawyer to protect herself from me. When I read that letter, I felt like one of my lifelines had been cut off, like a door had been slammed shut—no, not just a door, a door on a dungeon. For eleven years Ahren had been the love of my life. We had grown up together. I'd journeyed through the most important events of my life with her—college, Shakespeare & Company, Yale, *Fences*, *Native Son*, appearing on Broadway, my father's death. Even as a grown man, I relied on her to help me solve problems and make decisions. Clearly at this point in my life, I was no good for Ahren. I didn't know how to talk to her. I didn't know how to handle emotional situations. She could only do her part. She needed somebody who would relate with her—she needed somebody to talk to. I was afraid to be that man because everywhere I looked I found lies. But without her how I would move forward? I wondered.

Every feeling that I'd been avoiding came down on me at once. My emotions crested over the top of me. The pain I was in was palpable. I was unable to eat but I could feel it and taste it. There was no place to escape—no sleep, no workout, no record, no movie, no walk with Bottom. I wasn't suicidal but I was at the end of my rope. I didn't know how I would recover. I knew that if Ahren, of all people, didn't want to talk to me, I had serious, serious work to do on myself. The fact she felt she needed to protect herself from me was a serious indictment of my character. I realized that I had to learn how to behave in a manner consistent with the good person that I imagined I was. I wanted to be a better man—a man who was worthy of talking to her. I wanted to apologize. I went off the porn talk lines cold turkey and did everything I knew to get the numbers out of my head.

I promised God that if he would give me another opportunity, I wouldn't mess it up. I would be prepared the next time God brought me somebody very special. But for that moment, I knew I'd lost her. I tucked my tail between my legs and finally began, in earnest, my journey toward healing.

At age thirty-two, for the first time in my life, I was living on my own. I was alone with myself and my demons. Ahren was gone; I had completely alienated myself from my friends; I had no one to fall back on. My family rallied around me, of course, but they were very disappointed that Ahren and I had broken up. She had been in my life so long she had become one of us. Even my dying grandfather told me, "Courtney, I just thought you and Ahren were like Romeo and Juliet." I was stunned. I hadn't known he felt that way. Everyone had been invested in my relationship with Ahren.

Now it was just me and Bottom. It was truly a case of "man's best friend." He and I began to settle into a rhythm. I had my walks with Bottom and my sessions with Dr. K. to anchor me; otherwise I was by myself. For the next several years I undertook a monstrous effort to become the man of integrity I aspired to be. With Dr. Kornfeld's help I did an incredible amount of soul-searching. I knew that I had drifted onto that broad boulevard to destruction that was paved with good intentions.

"I cannot do this! I *will not* do this!" I told myself about the 1-900 numbers. "I will not be controlled by this." When something sexual came on television, I turned it off. I stayed out of the magazine section.

I hadn't meant to be a bad person, ironically, my ability to act—the very gift that had helped me cast myself beyond my life circumstances—had contributed to my undoing. There wasn't an area of life that didn't involve a performance. There wasn't a place I could go in my mind where I didn't discover a lie of one kind or another. We examined my tendency to tell "white lies," exaggerate or flat out not tell the truth.

"Why is it so important to please people?" Dr. K. would ask me.

"Because I want them to like me," I admitted. I didn't like to upset people or feel that I'd let them down.

"But why? Why can't you just be who you are and let that be enough?"

"Maybe I feel that if I am who I am, that won't be good enough..."

We also began to examine my choices, including the ones that led to the demise of my relationship.

"How do you make decisions?" Dr. Kornfeld asked me.

"I kind of flip a coin."

"You flip a coin?"

"Yeah, like the luck of the draw—fifty-fifty. I just pick one or the other," I told her. In theater, flipping a coin is an acceptable technique for making certain decisions. Sometimes you just pick a character attribute or path and go for it without looking back because in rehearsal you can always change your mind.

"Courtney, that's no way to live your life. You can't make decisions that way. It may be fine for acting, but for life it's a disaster."

"What do you mean? I flip a coin, make a decision, then react off of it."

"Oh, I understand now. You're the king of reaction."

"How do you do it then? Is there another way?"

"Sometimes when you don't know what to do, Courtney, it's best to just sit still."

"I can't be still. When I know that something needs to be done I just want to do it."

"But, Courtney, sometimes there's nothing to do but sit

there and wait. I wonder if you can be patient enough to let the mud settle in the water and the water become clear?"

"What does that mean?"

"You allow yourself to be quiet long enough to allow other options to develop."

I would learn from Dr. K. that as well educated as I was, as accomplished as I was, I was missing some basic life skills. She and I began to meet several times a week. She taught me to construct my life around rhythms and rituals. With her help I began to bring more structure to my life. At the foundation was my relationship with Bottom. I made a full commitment to him and he became the focus of my life. Knowing that I had to walk him at 6:30 a.m., 2:30 p.m. and 9:30 p.m. each day gave me structure and helped me organize my life. In between walks, I would go to the dry cleaners, buy groceries, go to work at the theater (I continued auditioning for roles in plays and movies), cook dinner, go to bed and write in my journal. Those activities provided the framework and the rest of my life happened around them. Having patterns and rhythms simplified my life. They helped me grow more in touch with myself. I started knowing how I was doing by whether I kept up with them. The structure also gave me something to focus on and helped me quiet the conversations in my mind. I'd often second-guess or beat myself up about decisions I'd made.

"Yes, you messed up in the past but it's finally time to deal with the 'why,'" I'd think. "You've got to get started now."

"But, I hurt her so much…"

"You can't go back and change that, so just start where you are, Court. Just start where you are."

"I know but—"

"Just start today, and tomorrow build on what you learned from the previous day. You're going to mess up—that's a given. Just start all over again."

"But—"

"Just begin, Courtney."

And I did. As my life became more orderly, I didn't think as much about how much I had squandered, what I had or hadn't done. I didn't wonder, Why did I do that? as often. I started living methodically, moment by moment by moment, one task at a time. I stopped overcommitting myself. For the first time in my adult life, I was dealing with a manageable number of tasks and activities. Consequently there were fewer people to try to keep happy and less reason to exaggerate, overextend myself or lie. When my mind would wander or I'd slip up, I'd just bring my thoughts back to the task at hand or start all over again.

We also continued to delve deeply into my dreams. As we examined them, Dr. K. was able to know what was going on in both my conscious and subconscious minds without any filtering, censoring or editing on my part. Our work was similar to a type of therapy she'd later inform me was called analysis. By using my dreams she didn't have to try to figure things out or drag them out of me. Everything was right in the dream. My sports dreams were usually about my personal boundaries. When my team's defense was really, really "on," I knew I was being effective with people and my personal boundaries were strong. If my defense got run over by the offense, I was having a hard time navigating relationships and was letting people take advantage of me. If I was on offense and was advancing with the ball, I was being appropriately assertive in life.

Many of my dreams were about race. They helped me uncover that I held deeply suppressed feelings about being a black man living in a world of white privilege. All my life there had been a part of me that felt as though I didn't belong. Even now, whenever I sat on Dr. K.'s stoop waiting for my appointments, I was aware of a bitter irony. In my professional life I was a very successful actor. In fact, while I was Dr. K.'s patient, I had received Tony Award nominations for *Six Degrees* and *Fences* and an Obie Award, which recognizes off-Broadway performances, for my role in Athol Fugard's play *My Children! My Africa!* But when I wasn't onstage, I was the prototypical "invisible man," sitting below street level on Dr. Kornfeld's stoop, watching white people go by and feeling like an outsider.

It was no wonder I didn't feel like I belonged in the all-white world of privilege. I'd been navigating and negotiating it alone for much of my life with no one to translate or run interference for me. I remembered how painful it felt to be ripped out of my all-black neighborhood school, where I had good friends, so I could attend all-white schools. Most of the people at my new schools were nice enough, but starting all over socially was rough. And the kids were different; the culture was different; the activities were different. The way I spoke suddenly didn't feel good enough. I remembered Cecilie's observation that I had started talking "white" and realized that I had changed my manner of speaking in an effort to try to fit in. I realized I had "gutted" my way through some incredibly elite and competitive environments—from Detroit Country Day School to Harvard to Yale to Broadway—without any personal or professional support. I hadn't even known that being supported was possible—I didn't know what it looked like. To survive— actually, I had thrived—I had stuffed down some very intense feelings: fear, anger, sadness, loneliness, isolation. It had worked, but at a price. By becoming numb to how I was feeling, I had cut off an important part of myself. Rather than "feeling" my way through situations, I learned to "perform" my way through them. Ironically, this may have helped contribute to my gift as an actor. Eventually, Dr. K. helped me bring that knowledge full circle. We talked about my father's life—what a pioneer he had been, how many environments he had integrated, how many places he'd had to go alone as a result of being abandoned—I realized how well he'd done with so little emotional support. Though I was appearing in Broadway plays alongside some of the world's greatest thespians, my father may have been the greatest actor I'd ever known. Through my work, I could "complete him."

As my life became ordered and the voices inside my head quieted, I began to notice again my desire to find my way back to the Lord. I had tried to find him while I was still in college, but now my desire to bring together the good man I saw in my mind with the man of my actions led me right back to the search I had begun and abandoned years before. I hadn't realized that God had placed a hedge of protection around me all along and had been trying to get my attention. Unbeknownst to me, everything had to "unravel" so I would slow down enough to listen and "let the mud settle." He had positioned me to embark upon my journey to grow into the man I had always seen in the back of my mind—the man my family would need me to be. I had a long way to go. I was not that man yet. But slowly, ever so slowly, I began to turn my focus toward God.

By participating in therapy diligently, I recovered essential parts of myself—peace of mind, my integrity, my emotional well-being. I'd awakened my spiritual self. By the end of 1993, I was able to accept that the door to Ahren was closed. I knew that I had closed it and took full responsibility. I know I messed up, I told myself. But there will be a next time, and I will be ready! I knew it was really time to make a fresh start.

During the late 1980s and early '90s, there had been an exodus of actors leaving New York and moving to Los Angeles. People were starting to make L.A. their base and travel back to New York. I had done all I could do in New York for now. I needed a change of scenery. Since all my buddies and boys were out on L.A., I decided to move there, too. I flew out there and stayed with some friends while I looked for a place. When I returned, I called the Mayflower Moving Company to come and get my things, packed what would fit into my Honda Civic wagon and asked my good buddy Robert Bristol to drive to the

West Coast with Bottom and me. (I flew Robert back home.) Along the way, we explored the country. That was an incredible road trip, a rite of passage of sorts—just the boys: Rob, Bottom and me.

Chapter 11

Tending to the Rest of Me

What's Love marked an incredible milestone in my life. There was the time in my life before *What's Love,* and there was the time after it. After receiving so much critical acclaim, I suddenly didn't have to audition anymore. People just offered me parts; they thought I was the right person for the role. In a way that was kind of cool. I never had really considered before the idea that my previous work was my audition or proved that I was right. But I have to admit there's some security that comes with auditioning and winning the role. You've proven you're right for the part. You aren't showing up on the first day hoping you're giving them what they want.

Although I was being offered a lot of parts, I wasn't sure that they were right for me; I was looking for roles that were equal or better. I didn't think it was right that after being nominated for an Oscar, I should go back to being a guest star on a sitcom. Before *What's Love,* I would have been happy to play those parts. But after you've performed in a role of that magnitude, exactly what do you do next? I didn't know; I'd never been in this position. Did starring in such a successful film now make me a film actress? There weren't then and still aren't many leading roles for black, female actors. I wanted to do work that would keep me seen in certain ways—as a dramatic actor—in the industry. I knew I couldn't do just anything anymore. But I didn't feel like I had anybody I could bounce my thoughts off of. I had come from a low-income family. No one from my childhood had an entertainment industry background. Other than my management team I didn't have any personal advisers. Even if I did, this was a new situation for a black actress to be in. I'm not sure how much they could have helped me. There are times in this business when you either have to wait for the right opportunity or create the opportunity yourself. I wasn't in a position yet to create opportunities, so I waited. For the first time in my career since graduate school I wasn't working. Fortunately, I was exhausted and needed some downtime anyhow. It was a little unsettling but it didn't freak me out. Plus, it was a good time to immerse myself in and enjoy other parts of my life.

Until this point in my life, I had focused on my work and conducted other things around it. I was trying to work my career and make the most of it. Now I finally felt I had some breathing room in this precarious profession I love, I felt secure enough to breathe a little bit and pay more attention to the rest of me. I began to become involved with causes where my celebrity could help this Ronald McDonald House or that Boys and Girls Club or ACTSO, a major youth program offered by the NAACP, or a pediatric-AIDS initiative. One particularly memorable volunteer experience occurred when Glenn Close called me up during the mid 1990s. Glenn, who has starred in such memorable movies as *Jagged Edge* and *Fatal Attraction,* as well as *101* (and *102) Dalmatians,* was volunteering at a women's prison located in Bedford, New York. At some point she had asked a group of women, who had sought to further their education while confined in prison, who they'd like to speak at their graduation ceremony. They told her,

"Angela Bassett." I assume that they had seen *What's Love* and maybe could relate to it. So Glenn reached out to me and extended the invitation. I accepted, but I thought, "Oh, no, public speaking!" Public speaking is the number-one fear of most folk, even actors. Give me some words that a playwright has written or a screenwriter has penned and I can interpret for you six or seven ways—I'm a character then. If I have to get up and speak to you from my thoughts, it's a whole different story. But there are certain moments when you can't say no. You want to say no but very quickly another part of you says, "You cannot say no! You have to come up out of yourself. This is an opportunity to really help somebody else." You come out of yourself because it's no longer about you; it's about serving others.

So I traveled to Bedford, spent the night with Glenn and stayed up until three or four in the morning trying to get my speech ready. What could I tell these women? I wondered. What did I have worthwhile to say? Then I went to the prison and I ate lunch with them. We sat at the table and said grace together. Then we talked and shared. The women were graduating with degrees ranging from their high school G.E.D to Ph.D. They were delightful and beautiful and brilliant and smart, yet whatever choices they'd made—to protect themselves, for instance—had landed them there. Then I got up and said my speech to try to encourage them. I don't remember what I said. What I really remember is feeling insignificant and being encouraged and buoyed and lifted up by them and all they were going through living in that place—not giving up on their children, furthering their education, being strong and determined in difficult circumstances. I remember meeting a little boy there—the son of one of the women.

"Can I give you *my* autograph?" he asked me.

"Of course," I said. As I left, I watched him standing behind the bars. How could I help but give?

* * *

I was attending the NAACP Image Awards ceremony in 1994 when one of the actors sitting near me happened to mention a small, grassroots program called Artists for a New South Africa, an organization of artists and actors whose goal was to bring attention to apartheid, which was still the law in South Africa all these years after I had first learned about it as an undergraduate. I thought the organization sounded interesting, so I contacted Sharon Gelman who heads it. Sharon told me about an upcoming trip where a group of artists would tour the different townships and states to help get the word out about voting, since 1994 would mark the first time black South Africans would be allowed to participate in the electoral process. We would show black people how to vote and dramatize mock elections so they could see how the process works. It was a chance for us to bring ourselves and our celebrity to a huge humanitarian issue. To shine a little light—our light—on a human tragedy and help counter misinformation that the "powers that be" were spreading to intimidate blacks from voting. I'd never been to Africa before, but as a black woman it was an important place to me. This seemed like a great opportunity to travel there and work for an important cause.

A group of about seven of us—Sharon, Delroy and his wife, Nashormeh; Danny Glover and his former wife, Asake Bomani; Blair Underwood; actress CCH Pounder; and Alexandra Paul, one of the women on *Baywatch*—traveled to New York, where we held a press conference. I remember Alfre Woodard, who participated in the media event but didn't go on the trip, speaking about the problem so eloquently and passionately. She was just so invested and so heartwise. I admired her. Afterward, the rest of us flew for eighteen hours to Johannesburg. I was surprised to find that Johannesburg wasn't at all like the talk I'd heard about Africa being the "dark continent"—not to mention, the Tarzan movies I'd seen during my childhood. It is a bustling cosmopolitan city that put me in mind of New York. I didn't expect to see people getting around on buses just like they did at home. I was surprised when I found out that Alexandra had signed up for a spinning class. There was a mall attached to our hotel. I was curious about what a mall in Africa would look like, so I set out to explore it. There was a Gap, a Victoria's Secret and other stores you'd find back at home, in addition to shops selling local and indigenous items like beautifully painted ostrich eggs. Walking around, you saw faces of sho' 'nuff black people who had no white folk in their lineage. You saw mixed-race people. You saw white people. You saw black people who looked like people in your family yet lived on the other side of the world. You saw human beings. I saw how alike we all are—our commonalities. I felt very proud, I felt excited—like I had finally made it home to the "cradle of civilization."

I quickly learned that one thing we did not have in common with South Africans was the level of danger we lived with. While I was walking around the mall, a bomb alert was broadcast over the intercom. We had to evacuate. My first day in South Africa, I'm in the mall and there's danger of a bomb going off! I don't think there actually ended up being a bomb—if there was, it certainly didn't detonate. But it was a volatile time. So many people didn't want apartheid to end or black people to vote, and they were using scare tactics. I realized that as an American and a black American in the late twentieth century, I certainly took for granted my ability to walk around and go where I wanted to go. Bombs and blatant discrimination were the reality for black and "colored" folks here every day.

We spent a couple of days in Johannesburg, educating people about how the voting process works. Then we made our way to Durban and Cape Town then Soweto, the black township where little children started the revolution that transformed the entire nation! Everywhere we traveled the people made us feel welcome, really welcome. They knew that we were Americans and how far we had traveled to help them. They knew our history—they knew that our ancestors had been snatched away from this continent. That they didn't leave of their own volition. They looked at us African-Americans as prodigal sons and daughters coming home, and to the civil rights movement as the model for how they'd transform their society. The fact that our historic struggle was providing them with the template for their struggle and the knowledge that it could be won made me feel extremely proud.

Physically the trip was exhausting. We hit the ground running after flying over many time zones in the course of that week. You talk about jet lag! But we just had to deny that and any other discomfort we may have experienced, given the importance of our work. I would get up in the morning and put on my skirt (it's the height of disrespect for South African women to wear pants), then we'd all pile into a van and drive across the country. The land was lush and green. We traveled from Cape Town, which was on the water where the Atlantic and Pacific Oceans meet. It was bright and lovely—a lot like Malibu, California. We also passed black townships and villages where people had very modest little homes—we'd call them shacks over here—with tires on top of the tin roof. (I learned the tires were used to ground the houses during electrical storms.) We saw the disparaging difference between the white "haves" and black "have-nots." We saw scores of children living on the street. We had been warned that the people didn't have much, and maybe materially they didn't; they might live in a shanty and their outfits might be mismatched. But the women always had on a skirt and everyone was always clean and dignified. The people took pride in themselves and their appearance. They had a clear sense of what was appropriate and what was not. Out in the bush we would arrive at a village that might be marked by stakes in the ground, say, five inches apart, forming a fence.

There would be an entrance in the fence, but according to protocol we couldn't just walk in; we had to wait to be invited. If the chief wasn't there to invite us in, we had to wait. If it took forty-five minutes for him to get back, we waited forty-five minutes. Wherever we went the women would greet us with a welcoming dance.

Many black South Africans' white employers were telling them, "They're going to tell me who you voted for," implying that the employers would cause black voters harm if the they were to vote for Nelson Mandela of the African National Congress, which is who most of the black folks wanted to win. To say that to someone who doesn't read or spends countless hours working to earn a dollar a day—that kind of story would just break my heart. Our purpose in South Africa was simple: to teach people that their vote was private, that it was between them and God, no matter what people who wanted to intimidate them might threaten. We were trying to squash that fear, that threat. So we would meet people in their community centers, which were often like a big open shed with a floor and a roof but maybe no walls. We taught them "you vote your heart." Then we would perform mock elections. For instance, I would demonstrate how to vote and then we'd give them paper and have them do it. I didn't realize how many black people had been denied the opportunity to learn how to read or write. So we taught those who were illiterate to make their choice with an X, which was what people did back in the day when your X was your signature. I remember watching one man—he must have been in his nineties or something—all bent over and walking with a cane toward the voting box. As he shuffled forward, I imagined the experiences he must have had during his lifetime of living under apartheid. And still he was going to vote; he was determined to be enfranchised for the first time. He reminded me of my great-grandfather Slater. I just sat in a chair and wept. I saw this kind of thing over and over. There were lots of young and middle-class people with energy and enthusiasm, but when you'd see a poor, older person—maybe bent with the years but strong—emotionally it would just take you out. I felt like I was glimpsing what slavery or Reconstruction must have looked like. It made me wonder what kind of slave I would have been. In any case, I was incredibly proud to participate. I was a kid when the civil rights movement took place, but this gave me a sense of what it must have been like to be a part of it.

So we would teach them how to vote, then we would rush off to the next town. No matter how we tried not to, we always offended people because we had to leave so quickly. Whether or not they had many material possessions, they expected us to stay and break bread. They wouldn't dare allow anyone travel so far and not prepare a meal for them. Johnny Clegg, a well-known white South-African musician who was accompanying us on the trip, would always apologize in Zulu for our rudeness. Sometimes it would take him forty minutes to make the situation right so we could leave without offending.

One of the highlights of the trip was meeting Nelson Mandela, who visited with us for a half-hour lunch one day. Since my late teens I'd heard the story of how this lawyer had endured twenty years of imprisonment (he had been given a life sentence) for defying the apartheid government and fighting white domination. Over the years he had been made offers that would have freed him in exchange for compromising his principles. He'd refused. Finally, in 1990 he was released with his integrity intact. I had such a sense of pride in what he—a black man—had accomplished with his sacrifice. Someone who had lived so sacrificially was too much for me to fathom; I certainly couldn't imagine it in my own life. When you meet someone of that importance, of that stature, you never know how you're going to react. Are you going to gravitate toward them? Are you going to hold back but think, *"OH, MY GOD!"*

I didn't know how I'd react, and there was so much anticipation. First we were waiting, waiting and anticipating, anticipating, that he was coming, he's coming, then he's here, he's here. Then he walks through the door! When I saw those eyes, that sweet face, that hair, that stature—that history of all he had done that I had been aware of for so long—my whole body just flew over to him. It was uncontrollable, an impulse. I just threw my arms around him. "Oh, my God." I just hugged him and cried and embraced him. I said, "I love you, I love you…." He hugged me back saying, "Daughter, daughter…." Delroy was kind enough to suggest that I sit next to him at lunch. "Angela, take a seat," he said as he pulled out a chair for me. I will always be grateful for the group's kindness for that; I had wanted to sit next to him but would have been too shy to ask. As we sat eating our bread and butter, Mr. Mandela told a story about two men from different places who sat around a fire and somehow by the time they left they understood each other. "That's what artists do," he told us. "They bring stories and human conditions to the world." He allowed us to take pictures with him. Then he was gone. It was a very memorable interaction. Shortly thereafter he won the election and became the first democratically elected president of South Africa. From all my incredible experiences on that trip, I realized that with everything I had going for me, there was nothing I shouldn't be able to do.

By my midthirties, my work had taken me to Europe, South Africa and Japan. I'd learned that I loved to go places and see how other people live, to actually experience all these places I'd read about, heard about, dreamed about, seen in movies. I was also fascinated by people who would leave their culture and families to move to a completely different place where they don't speak the language. It had been enough for me to move from New York to California! But I loved going to visit and, when possible, trying to get to the nucleus of the place—not to stay on the periphery but to really get a sense of what it must be like to live there. Because I have an appreciation of the differences of people, I like to meet brand-new people. I like to soak up the humanity that exists all over the world. I think it's lovely and amazing. So I started to travel to places like the Virgin Islands with a boyfriend, to St. Martin when the comedian Sinbad did his first comedy thing, and to Paris and Rome. And then I enjoyed coming home.

Back in California I had been renting a nice apartment for all this time but really wanted to buy a house. After growing up in the projects, I had dreamed of living in and owning a house for my entire life. I asked my accountant if he thought I was financially secure enough yet. He told me I had the means to purchase a house, but didn't quite have enough money to maintain it. So I bought my first condo instead!

I also began to pay attention to my love life. I was thirty-five and wanted to get married and have a family.

By now both Jean and Lynn were married. Jean had married Vic, her college sweetheart, who went into the army. Jean and Vic, in turn, introduced Lynn to Al, one of Vic's army buddies. Lynn and Al got married. To this day both my sisters have wonderful marriages—they picked wonderful men! Straight up and down, stable, attentive and warm men. Over the years I would go to visit my sisters on the different military bases where their husbands were stationed and just be in awe of them as women. They are wonderful with their children, who, of course, I think are beautiful. I remember sitting under the beautiful, crystal-clear blue sky in Hawaii or Utah or wherever and just observing what wonderful mothers they were. I'd watch them with their children—telling them what to do in firm but loving voices, how sweet they were, how easily everyone laughed, just how delightful their laughter sounded. How much fun they had with their children; yet the children were well behaved. My heart would feel warm and full. I have so much respect for the strength of their families and marriages. I wanted that for myself.

Before *What's Love* I'd had a degree of anonymity. I hadn't realized that I had anonymity because I was trying to become known so I could get more and better work, but I had the benefit of anonymity just the same. I hadn't thought about how being well known would impact on my life, my relationships or how I met men. Previously I was meeting guys on relatively equal ground: I don't know you and you don't know me, or I have a job and you have a job, or I'm relatively successful and you're relatively successful, too. After starring in a movie that resonated so strongly in popular culture, overnight it became hard to meet somebody where I didn't know them, they didn't know me and we were both starting at square one. Dating suddenly became very strange.

Over the next couple of years I dated a series of men—short-timers, I called them, since none of the relationships lasted more than three to six months—as I tried to find the man who would one day become my husband. Some of it's kind of humorous now, though it was frustrating, disappointing and sometimes painful at the time. I went out with a couple of guys who thought they were starting at square twenty in our relationship because they'd seen my work or heard such-and-such thing about me. They seemed to think that I had the same characteristics—the same strength or compassion or integrity—that a character I had played in a movie may have exhibited. I felt like, "I know this may sound crazy, but please ignore the pink elephant in the middle of the living room. You may know my work, but you don't really know *me*."

A couple of guys wanted me to behave like the characters I'd played or had fantasies about me. I couldn't fulfill them. That wasn't fun for me. It didn't give me any satisfaction.

"Should I pretend to your face that I'm kissing someone other than you?" I asked one suitor who wanted to pretend he was out with a movie character. "How would you like that—when I kiss you, I'm not kissing you, I'm kissing Casanova?"

When he greeted me, one guy called my by the names of the characters I'd played.

"I'm not Katherine Jackson or Betty Shabazz or Tina, I'm Angela!" I'd say.

There was one guy who seemed to be impressed with the celebrity factor, that he was dating "Angela Bassett." He liked being seen with me in public, to go to every event, the swirl of that "fabulous life." Well, all of those events may be exciting to someone who isn't exposed to them on a daily basis, but when you do them all the time, they sometimes get a little tiresome—the hair, the makeup, the look, the dress, the smiling for the camera. I'm very social, but I can be quiet, reflective and shy, too. I just love to sit and have meaningful conversations with people, where we can just let down our guard and share—away from the noise, away from the swirl of activity. I like to feel I've walked away from a conversation having learned something about someone else or that I got some insight into an aspect of life I hadn't thought about before. But he'd badger me to go to these events until I said, "Okay, okay!"

Once he invited me to accompany him to the wedding of a woman I didn't know. I declined because I didn't want my celebrity to upstage the bride on her special day—especially a bride who didn't even know me. He insisted. I refused. Another day he read out loud a review of my work I'd told him I didn't want to hear (I thought it would be disparaging). The review was fine, but his behavior was like a slap in the face. It let me know that he didn't care about my comfort or needs. I was through with him but he kept calling.

"I was going to ask you to marry me."

You were going to get a no! I thought to myself. I was glad he lived out of town.

Another guy seemed to have gotten a kick out of pursuing

me—and, oh, the pursuit was nice; who doesn't want to be pursued? He was blowing up my phone. We were talking a couple of times a day, staying up late talking. But after I was captured—after we had sex—he suddenly lost interest, the game was over. His interest began to wane. The scale tipped and I was calling him more often than he was calling me. When I stopped calling then, guess what? He started calling again. I knew to move on. But I realized that if I hadn't slept with him, I wouldn't have cared or felt insecure by his lack of attention.

One guy I went out with had children from a prior relationship. At first that was fine. I understood that as you get older, people's lives are more complex. But I learned that when you deal with men who've already had children, you don't just get the children; you also get the mother of their children. Then you may get children being used as pawns. Or wages being garnisheed. My sister Linda shared how she had reconnected with her high-school sweetheart who by then had two children. She "loved him to life" so they dated for a while, but she knew herself well enough to know that she wanted her own husband and her own children. She didn't want to start a family with someone who had children living in another household. She didn't want him getting a call that his kids were sick and having to go but still having children with her. She didn't want a man who was torn between two homes. After listening to her I realized I couldn't deal with that, either. Deep in my heart I had never wanted to have a "half" anything in my family. I grew up in a family where it was like, "I have three sisters—no, I have four sisters. Well, I grew up with one sister, but I have two older sisters—we have different mothers. And I do have another sister, Lisa, whom I met at my father's funeral, but I don't know where she is now, in the entire world." Now, I love all my sisters, and families that are made up as mine is are just fine. And if you love someone and that's the situation, fine. I just didn't want it for my own family—the family I was going to create. I wanted to be the most important person in someone's life; I wanted my husband to be there emotionally; I wanted all the family's re-sources—emotional, financial, time, whatever—to stay on one plate. I began to think more and more about why it made sense for me to have one husband and sex only within marriage.

During this time, though I dated a couple of guys pretty con-sistently over the course of several months, I couldn't really call any of them a boyfriend. They were not labeling it that, didn't want me to, either, and were not indicating by word or deed that that was the case. On more than one occasion, I found myself sitting in the movie theater wondering why our arms were so near each other yet he wasn't holding my hand. Won-dering, "What's going on?" or "Why is he pulling back?" or "Why can't I just grab his hand?" or "I think there is something strange here." I'd go through all these gymnastics and machi-nations in my head. In the meantime I'd miss the movie.

As I experienced disappointment after disappointment, I realized just how much I wanted to be in a serious relationship. I began to wonder why I wasn't. I liked men an awful lot. I found them fascinating! I wanted to get married. I *believed* I would get married. I wanted a to have a family. And on the surface it seemed that I was dating good guys—I would think the world of them. Yet somehow it felt like I kept dating the same person over and over: exciting, passionate and nice enough to start out with, but unavailable emotionally, and, sometimes, I would learn, taken. I wanted out of this limbo lifestyle that made me feel insecure. No matter how I tried to fix the relationship, work it, squeeze into the space, it seemed like the Lord kept putting up roadblocks, saying this person needed to leave my life. "Out! Out! Out!" My love life was going nowhere. I wanted to stop hitting this brick wall.

So when I was about thirty-seven I decided it was time that I engaged in some serious introspection. I was old enough to know that the only constant in a relationship is you. If you keep dating the same types of people, you will end up experiencing the same results. You attract people who are at your level. If you want to attract a better class of person, you have to be a better class of person. I realized I needed to stay at home and work on me.

As I reflected, I considered all my previous experiences with men. My mother had told me that "I was the prize," and I knew I had some of her strength, morality and resiliency. Yet I felt that I was at somewhat of a disadvantage since I hadn't had the benefit of a daddy's love or the best male role models at home. Yes, I had Papa and some of the wonderful men in my community. But I hadn't had a good father figure to model for me what was right and how a man should treat me. I felt like there were a lot of relationships I thought I might have passed on if I'd had that. I thought I would have been stronger in my no's. I realized the love and validation I had been looking for from men—a lot of them couldn't give it. There had been a time when I was younger that I had been trying not to be inexperienced—when I wanted to gloat with my girlfriends: "How was he? What did you use—whipped cream, honey?"—that kind of stuff. The guys I had been dealing with had their own agendas and experiences, too. They were testing and trying and discovering—finding out who they were as men, finding out who they were sexually, finding out what kind of woman they wanted. Some of them may have been given lessons about needing to rack up notches on their belt, or get experience or about not settling down. But I was older and wiser now. I wanted to settle down and get married. I needed to know, on a day-to-day basis, what exactly did a "good man" look and act like? What did I need to do differently to sort through the fact that everyone's nice in the beginning, to find a man who was faithful, trustworthy and committed to me? All along I had assumed I knew, but from my results it was clear I was missing something.

I knew I had never been the kind of person who had to see a certain type of guy—a doctor, a businessman, an Indian chief. However, I had to admit that there had been times when I felt impressed by men with certain occupations, with careers that I believed were more important than mine. "Oh, my gosh, a lawyer! He's getting people off death row." Or "A doctor! He's saving people's lives." The little girl from the projects in me had to learn not to evaluate people or think they were better than me because of their occupation—or, for that matter, that I was better than them. Of course, I knew I certainly had a predilection for actors. I think actors are very interesting people, we have a lot in common, and if they're good at what they do, they're very attractive. But no matter a man's profession, I had to like him. I had to be attracted to and able to talk to him. It didn't matter what material possessions he had or even if he was poor. The truth be told, when it came to money I went for the underdog. Since I had grown up poor, I wasn't impressed with your designer this or pedigree that. I didn't think much of people who looked down on you because of the circumstances of your birth, which you have no control over. Perhaps that was so clear to me because I started out with so little and came to live in a world where many people have so much. Of course, we're human so sometimes we think, "Hey, he has more money, he must have more of everything else." But there are other things—the intangibles, the things on the inside—that matter more. What mattered to me was that a man was interesting and of high quality. Some men may have had more money or a fancy title, perhaps. But did they have more compassion? Did they have more love in their heart? Did they have more class, more grace, more appreciation, a moral compass, more talent? Did they share my values?

I wanted to be involved with someone who was nice, kind, gentle—all of those things. I wanted to be seen and appreciated for who I was: the good, the bad, the strengths, the weaknesses.

I wanted to be accepted whether it was a good day or bad day, regular me, hair-messed-up me, smart me, dumb me, good-mood me, bad-mood me, courageous me, not-so-courageous me, fabulous me, plain-ol'-colored me. I wanted to just be able to be me, regular me. But I didn't want to give away too much of myself. I didn't want to be in a disposable relationship that wasn't building toward anything. I didn't want to be in a bad relationship. I didn't want to be in a purely physical relationship, especially given the risks of AIDS and STDs. I also remembered reading girls' names on the bathroom wall in high school: "So and so is a 'ho.'" I didn't want to have a poor reputation in that way, especially in my community of actors.

But instead of taking my time and identifying guys who wanted to get married, I realized I had settled for hanging. As I looked back on my choices, I could see that I became enamored and fell in love too quickly. I'd become intimate too soon. I wasn't giving myself time to get to know the person, their values, their idiosyncrasies. I didn't take the time to see if they really lived up to my standards. I'd think, "You're odd. You're an oddball—but I *like* oddballs!" Then I'd sleep with him and project his strange behavior back on me—I'd think I was the one with the problem. No, he was just strange! I didn't need to have any more relationships like that—relationships that didn't benefit and lift me. Not only were they a waste of my time, they were chipping away at my self-esteem, at the way I saw myself. Truthfully, they were wasting something much deeper than time—something in my spirit.

I was able to figure out some things I was doing wrong, but I didn't always know exactly what I needed to change. I did know how to stop doing what I was doing, though. And I knew how to pray. I talked to God a lot.

"Lord, I can't figure this out. I'm not meeting the right men. It's not working out the way I want it to. I need your help."

My first answer came in the revelation that I should make a

sincere effort to be celibate. A couple of times in the past, I had tried to convince myself to sign a celibacy pact as part of a program at church. I had never followed through. Yet I had grown up in the church, with the Word and with a strict mama. Granted, she wasn't perfect, but I did know that the Bible says no fornicating, that the marriage bed is sacred, that sex is not a right but a gift to married people. I had learned through my religious education, at church, in Bible study, that sex was good and sacred, to be enjoyed within the confines of marriage. That ideal had been set in front of me. Yet I had spent many, many years of not paying attention, of experimenting, of growing into my sexuality, of working it out and figuring it out. Deep inside I did still believe in the values of my church and my childhood. I noticed that sometimes I'd feel a little guilty about having sex. I didn't realize that when you have intercourse you are joining spirits, joining souls, with the other person. Physically when the man enters a virgin he breaks her hymen and she bleeds. The blood seals the deal; it represents life, a promise; it is a covenant. In Christianity, the blood of Christ guarantees our salvation. When you break that promise the tie between two souls is ripped apart. That's why it's so painful. But if you don't engage in the covenant of sex, it's easier to walk away because you haven't joined spirits through the sexual covenant. When you break that promise it goes to your soul. Once I began to understand this, I abstained from sex for several years. I saw it as a deeper and more disciplined form of loving myself.

And rather than focusing on what I didn't have, I began to acknowledge that I had a great family, fabulous friends, a lovely home, a marvelous career that I love, money in the bank and I'd traveled around the world. I had a lot to be thankful and grateful for. So why was I complaining? Maybe a husband was the one thing that I just wouldn't be able to have. Maybe I just needed to dial it down relationshipwise and be thankful for what I had and adopt some children or something. I knew children were a big responsibility but maybe I'd just have to do it alone. I'd certainly purchased my condo while I was single. You can't wait for a man to start living your life. I began to consider the possibility that for the rest of my days maybe I'd be single—single and a sensation, an older woman with boyfriends. But I didn't want to do that in a sexual way, so I'd have to figure out and negotiate a new way to be.

One evening I stopped trying to figure out everything myself and decided to practice spiritual surrender, where you say, "Let Thy will be done." I told God, "I guess if I'm gonna meet somebody, he's just gonna have to knock on my door, Lord. I'm turning this over to you."

Instead of going to parties and events, I spent a lot of time at home with friends. We hung out at each other's houses, we ate together, we watched TV and movies, laughed and enjoyed good times. Wren and I spent so much time together that some people were certain we were an item. We weren't. I was just close to him and his family, including his wife, Ann. His mom, Rosalind, had taken me under her wing. That felt very nurturing and safe. I admit that sometimes being without a relationship felt lonely at times, but going out could feel lonely, too.

During this time I wasn't having sex or actively pursuing relationships, I didn't hear my biological clock ticking. I had heard other women talk about it, but it wasn't something that I thought about—not in the least. In my mind there was an order to things: get my education, establish myself, meet someone, get married, have children. I figured I was still young and biologically healthy, that there was still plenty of time. I didn't know that sometimes we women talk and pass along erroneous information about how long the childbearing years are and what is possible. So instead of thinking about marriage and babies, I concentrated on procuring and doing good work.

* * *

Toward the end of that "year of not working," I got offered three movies in a row: *Strange Days,* directed by Kathryn Bigelow, with Ralph Fiennes; then *Vampire in Brooklyn,* with Eddie Murphy; and *Waiting to Exhale,* the movie rendition of Terry McMillan's bestselling novel of the same name. I ended up filming them back to back to back, with about a week off between each of them. By then, Doug Chapin, the producer of *What's Love,* had become my manager, which was wonderful since I had already seen up close how well he worked in intense situations.

"Terry's interested in you playing Savannah," he told me when he sent the *Exhale* script over to me to read. In addition to writing the book, Terry was writing the script along with Ron Bass. It was Terry's first stab at a screenplay, but she's very vocal and vibrant. She thought I would be perfect for Savannah.

I was already a fan of Terry McMillan. I had read *Mama,* her first book, *Disappearing Acts,* her second, and then *Waiting to Exhale* on the subway. As I read *Exhale,* I could hear the different women's voices as they tried to navigate through the miasma of their relationships. That's what my girlfriends and I had been doing—talking, crying and encouraging each other.

"Oh, he's treating you like that? You deserve better than that."

"Leave him. You can come stay here." That was before I learned the lesson to just shut up and listen. "Uh-huh. *Whaat?* Really? You don't say." No more of that "Leave him alone, that ain't right," and then you turn around and she's gone back to try to make the relationship work one more time.

I knew *Exhale* had four female roles—coveted roles. Here was a balanced women's ensemble. In fact, it might have been the first time in history when four substantial women's roles were available in one movie. *Roots,* the 1977 television miniseries, may have been the previous opportunity before that. I was excited about the opportunity, but when I heard that Terry envisioned me as Savannah, I said, "Oh, no. I've read the book. I'd rather play Bernadine."

I liked the way Bernadine fought back when she was devastated by her husband's infidelity and the ending of their relationship. She fought back in such a gutsy, outrageous, extravagant, ridiculous way. Why would you sell a sports car for a dollar? I wondered. Of course, she knew it would mess him up. But to my mind doing that was just so outrageous! Burning the car and all his belongings—the scene that seems to stand out in everyone else's mind—didn't stand out to me when I read the book or the script. But to sell everything for a dollar—that's what stuck out to me; maybe because that was something I would never do. But, boy, did it seem like fun! I had never heard of or seen anything like it on-screen—a woman that bold and brash and different. Growing up, of course, I'd heard tell of aunties who, mad at their boyfriends or husbands, slashed, cut or ripped up all their clothes. I'd think, Gosh! He won't have any clothes to wear. And now he's butt naked, going somewhere embarrassed. But I, Angela, would never have had the nerve, would never have thought to do anything like that in my personal life. I'm just too nice, too fair. I could *imagine* doing it, just like I could imagine hitting someone, though I would never do that, either. So to have an outlet for those imaginings—oh, it was delicious and freeing! To tear up a closet. To burn a car. To have to say the lines and play the part but also have the opportunity to improvise. That's what made it so exciting! I think Whitney Houston and I came on board at about the same time, which, I assume, is why I got the role I wanted.

One evening in May 1994, before I headed to Arizona, where *Exhale* was filmed, I hung out at Catalina's, an L.A. jazz club, with some friends from drama school. After the set, we stood out front for a while, laughing, talking and reminiscing.

Courtney Vance was in the group. Out of the blue he asked me, "Hey, you wanna go out?"

"Oh, okay. Yeah."

I was hoping his invitation was strictly on the friendship tip. People were always asking you if you wanted to hang out. The idea of hanging easy was cool. "It's good to see you. I haven't seen you in a while. What have you been doing?" When you hang out with that kind of energy, the feeling can be familiar and warm, gentle and easy. Nothing feels pressured. You just want to spend additional time with good people in this place, Los Angeles, where everything is so spread out and everyone's always in their car. Since Courtney and I had gone to the same school, were part of the August Wilson family, knew all the same people and ran into each other occasionally, the idea of spending time was fine. But I definitely wasn't interested in having a "date." It wasn't just that I had this history of relationships that went down blind alleys, nowhere, ran into brick walls, but Courtney had dated Ahren, who I considered a friend. In my mind that made him OFF LIMITS! And I had dated Charles, who'd played with Courtney in the movie version of *Piano Lesson*. Our circles were too close. The idea of dating felt very uncomfortable. He couldn't possibly mean a date-date, could he? Oh, Lord, I thought. I hope he doesn't like me. We went out two days later. I don't remember where or what we did. The only thing I remember is trying to make sure it wasn't a date-date. Other than that, I don't remember a thing. I think I blocked it out.

The next day I was off—*whoosh!*—to film this wonderful movie. I was off to portray Bernadine!

As soon as I arrived in Phoenix, I encountered apartment drama. The apartment I had rented for $3,500 a month smelled like dog. I already thought I was paying too much, but there hadn't been much available when I looked. The other girls—Lela Rochon and Loretta Devine—had found an apartment complex I liked better. I was still dealing and living in the smelly apartment when I received an unexpected floral delivery, a bouquet of beautiful wildflowers—"Thank you for the date" flowers. From Courtney. The last person I wanted to get flowers from. I figured that if I didn't respond, maybe he would get the message and go away. But a few days later the phone rang.

"Hey, Angela, it's Courtney."

"Hey, Courtney. How are you?"

"I'm fine. I just wanted to say hello and make sure you got the flowers."

"Yes, I got them. They were nice." Then I changed the subject as quickly as possible and ran down my apartment drama. That seemed to work without being rude. I did like him—just as a friend. The call ended quickly and he didn't call me back. Months later when I had returned to Los Angeles, I was certain I'd made the right decision. I kept running into Ahren. One time I was parked on the street and she walked right in front of my car. Out of all the people in this big city. Another time I ran into her in the supermarket. I couldn't imagine saying, "Hey, Ahren, great to see you! Courtney and I are dating." I took all these sightings as a sign—an omen, really—that he and I weren't supposed to date. After being together so long, I couldn't imagine them not getting back together. So I said, "Hey, Ahren, I'm having a birthday party. Why don't you tell Courtney to bring you." And he did.

Filming *Exhale* was a lot of fun. First off, I fell in love with the director, Forest Whitaker, who's also an actor. You know him from playing roles like Charlie Parker in *Bird,* Ghost Dog in *Ghost Dog: The Way of the Samurai* and Marcus Clay in *Deacons for Defense.* Forest was gentle with all of us. We could just sit back and talk about the character or the relationship and how we saw it or wanted to play it. He was open to anything you wanted to try. I thought he was wonderful. I also got to work with some really great co-stars—Whitney, Loretta and Lela. And some really good guys came on board—people like Wesley Snipes, who I was happy to hear joined the cast, since we had arrived in New York at around the same time; as well as guys like Michael Beach, Gregory Hines and Wendell Pierce. Forest was trying to bring the best actors on board.

The environment on the set was so warm and loving—it was perfect! So comfortable that Forest let us eat snacks and watch the dailies together. We had a great time laughing at our mistakes, our little flubs or whatever. We were just *silly!* And he was very sensitive. I guess it *was* a little rude of us to laugh at our coworkers. You're going to make mistakes; that's why you do scenes a couple of times. But I guess once was enough of our laughing at each other; he banned us all from the screening room and wouldn't let us see the dailies anymore.

One of my most memorable experiences was the scene where Bernadine tore up the closet. I threw myself into the scene—just a little past the point of technique, unfortunately; I remember feeling a little out of control, banging into something, cutting my hand on a coat hanger, drawing blood. But I just kept going. I was into it, feeling the endorphins, the hormones, imagining, feeling enraged. When I torched the car, I felt like the most dramatic, empowered and hurt woman in the world. I also loved Bernadine's relationship with Wesley Snipes's character. Wesley's character was in love with his wife, but she was at home dying of cancer. He slept in the same bed with Bernadine—they were intimate—but they did not have sex. I liked the way our characters didn't cross any lines.

I also liked Wesley as a person and a friend. When I observed, "He's single and doing well. I'm single and doing well. How come people like us can't seem to get together and enjoy each other's company?" I couldn't find a brother—well, at least an actor brother. It seemed like all of them liked girls who weren't actors. I wondered, If I were a successful man, wouldn't I want a successful wife? That would make them a power couple, right? I thought that was a good thing.

Wesley play-flirted a little bit. "We should get together."

"All right, but I don't go for no shit!" I laughed. I'm still waiting for him to call.

But Wesley aside, in real life I wondered if successful men just weren't interested in successful women, if they found successful women intimidating or what? I didn't consider myself intimidating. Yet my career *was* growing nicely. *Waiting to Exhale* was a box-office success. In 1995 after it was released, it grossed over $65 million at the box office, which was a lot more money than some people ever envisioned a movie starring four black women would earn. My name recognition increased to another level. After doing *Strange Days, Vampire* and *Exhale* back to back and having each come within two weeks of the other, even I felt a little overexposed. But my bank account was growing quite nicely. My accountant told me I could afford to buy the house I'd always dreamed of owning.

House hunting was the slightest bit anticlimactic; I had always thought I'd buy my first home with my husband. Taxwise I couldn't wait. "The husband ain't here," I told myself. "You're going to have to do it alone to keep Uncle Sam out of your wallet. I'm going to have to buy another house with a husband." It wasn't the worst problem to have. I thought about it and concluded that maybe a successful woman *can* intimidate—but only an intimidateable man! I knew I deserved better.

Chapter 12

What God Brings

When I arrived in Los Angeles, I immediately liked it. It was holistic, and there was a lot of sunshine. Many of my buddies were already there. I moved into a gorgeous old apartment building in Los Feliz, one of the older, settled areas up near the famous Hollywood Hills sign. I connected with my agent, settled into my rhythm of walking Bottom and began to figure out what the touchstones in my life would be. I loved the weather as well as the people; even the customer-service reps who set up the phone and TV service seemed nicer. The rhythm in New York was faster and that was reflected in people's speech patterns. People in New York spat words at you: "Yeah. Whatever. Hold on. You talkin' to me?" In L.A. they said things like, "How may I help you? You're welcome. Thank you." At first I was taken aback. "What do you mean, how can you help me?" I thought. What's wrong with you? Why are you being so nice? After living in New York for so long, I had gotten accustomed to being mistreated.

That's not to say that people in L.A. are nicer than people in New York. In fact, I have had more instances in which people have helped me when I was in need in New York than in L.A. Suffice to say, the two cities are very different.

For a year after my move, I continued therapy with Dr. K. once a week over the phone at 5:00 a.m. PST to anchor me. The lure of pornography was fading and I was getting healthier, but I knew I wasn't ready for another relationship—after what I'd done to myself and Ahren. I was clear; I didn't want to hurt another woman. I couldn't do that again. Still, I missed their companionship. Dr. K. and I started to talk about how I could have women as friends. To keep things clean, I would have to practice being honest and letting women know where I was emotionally, and what I wanted and didn't want. I wasn't going to get romantically involved just because a woman liked me. But if I could be open and honest, I wouldn't have to back away if they wanted the relationship to deepen, and leave them hurt.

I started interacting socially again. Unlike in New York where you see people at auditions, you see people at the theater, you see them in the subway—you see and run into people every day—in Los Angeles you have to make a point of socializing. Especially if you're single, it's hard to meet folks. Everything is so spread out. Everyone lives in their little house or apartment and travels around in their car. You have to drive thirty miles here and thirty miles there, then at the end of the day you have to drive thirty miles home—in L.A. traffic, which is a nightmare. People aren't down for all of that. It's not like they're in a subway or cab. So people gather in people's homes. You meet folks at house parties. I reconnected with friends. I got into the L.A./N.Y. acting scene out there.

Actors, I learned, would also see each other at the premieres of movies. Premieres become a way and a reason to get together. The movie is supposed to start at seven-thirty but, especially with a group of black actors, might not get going until eight-fifteen, because everyone is trying to catch up with each other.

"Hey, what's up?"

"How have you been?"

"What's going on?"

"What are you working on?"

We'd share leads and opportunities, celebrate each other's successes, catch up on our love lives, talk about who was getting married or divorced, who'd had a baby, was sick, who had died. New actors are passing out cards and picture résumés. Everyone's pressing the flesh—that's what they do. That's what you gotta do to break into the L.A. scene. Lots of times they have to dim the lights a couple of times to get people to go sit down. After the movie is over you look up and people are gone. They have to drive the thirty miles home. Unlike in New York, where people would stay out late, L.A. closes down at ten or ten-thirty. Nobody hangs around. So at house parties and movie openings I would see the same people over and over—Angela Bassett, Blair Underwood, Don Cheadle, Michael Boatman and a bunch of other folks. We stayed up on each other's lives. In some ways they became like my extended family.

Through this casual social network, I slowly started interacting with women. Over several years I met a few sweet, sweet women. For the first time in my life I could talk about my feelings with them. I could have an emotional conversation. "How do you feel?" "Well, I'm feeling this and that." I was emotionally available. Yet I could also go to a movie or go to a concert and think she was nice and leave it at that. We didn't have to be intimate, although maybe we knew it could go that way. I learned that I could be honest and it was okay. When one woman liked me more than I liked her, I was up front: "I don't feel the same way about you that you feel about me."

"I know, Courtney. It's okay," she told me.

I used my good judgment. "No, it's not okay. We can't do this, because you're just going to end up hurt and mad at me. So let's just stop."

We had a nice long talk about it and parted as friends. Of course, she told her girlfriend, who then called me up, asking, "How could you do this to her?"

"What did I do?"

"You've hurt her, she's destroyed!"

"I had a conversation with her. She and I talked. How did you get in it?"

"She's my girlfriend, and—"

"Thank you very much for sharing your opinion. I'm going to hang up now."

I learned during this time that no matter how hard you try, there is always going to be hurt in relationships. All I could do was try and be as honest as I could.

I was finally becoming the kind, gentle, yet balanced soul that matched the person I imagined myself to be. For the first time in my life I was experiencing some sort of peace. Life was beautiful; work was great; I had female companionship. Everything was going along swimmingly. I even started feeling optimistic about being in a relationship again one day. But I didn't feel like I had to rush. I was comfortable taking things as they came. In the meantime, I had learned how to be patient. I'd tell myself, "I'll be tickled to see who God brings me."

In the meantime, I also had to learn how to communicate clearly with Bottom. Bottom was getting old—he was eleven years old now—seventy-seven in "dog years." His hips were starting to give him trouble. He reached a point where he couldn't get up off the gorgeous hardwood floors in my apartment, so I had to move to a small house with a yard and carpeting. Of course, I could not afford a house by myself in Los Angeles, so I needed to get a roommate. I found one in Tony Tolbert. Tony and I threw a housewarming party. I invited all my friends, and Tony, who is a lawyer, invited his. Because we were expecting a good number of people and the house was carpeted, we planned to ask folks to take off their shoes. We were in no way prepared for the hundred and twenty-five people who showed up. It was a great party and a lot of fun, but the thing I remember most is that there were a hundred and twenty-five people at our house and we had no place to put their shoes!

I had been in Los Angeles for a year when, in January 1994, there was a major earthquake. Everything shook and a lot of people's houses were wrecked. Tony and I were standing in doorways when the phone rang and I picked it up.

"The last time there was an earthquake, you and Bottom and I were together in bed and I reached out on one side and you were there, and I reached out on the other and Bottom was there. I did that again when this earthquake happened. You weren't there. It let me know it was time to call you. I'm just calling to check on you. Are you okay?" My feet floated off the ground. It was Ahren!

Two years had passed since Ahren had told me that she would "never speak to me again in life." I'd resigned myself to the fact that I'd never hear from her. Now that I was listening to her voice, I didn't know what to say.

"Yeah, I'm good. You good?"

"Yeah."

"Oh, good, I'm glad."

"Okay. I just wanted to make sure you were all right."

"Okay."

"Talk to you later."

That was it. I walked out into the street and told Tony. "Can you believe it?"

I don't know whose idea it was or who made the first call— I think maybe I called her—but a few months later we agreed to meet for tea at a little spot on Melrose Avenue and test the waters. I didn't know if I would have romantic feelings toward her, but I definitely didn't want any romantic feelings I might have to enter into things. I let her set the pace. We had a nice, gentle, respectful, catching up kind of time. We talked about all kinds of things, and she got to see the new me in action.

"*You're* having an emotional conversation, Courtney?"

I didn't shirk from the difficult questions. Just to sit and talk was all I wanted. But though I was cool on the outside, on the inside I was thinking, Lord, what are you doing here? What are you telling me?

A couple of weeks later, we got together for tea again. It was nice. Again, I let her set the tempo. I figured we should only go as fast as she said or the Lord allowed. I was just happy to have a second chance to talk to her. It was beyond what I ever thought would ever happen again. By the time Ahren and I reconnected, Bottom's hips were pretty much gone. He was a big dog and now he could barely walk. The doctors had done just about all they could do. When I traveled for work, I'd had to put together a whole network of friends and dog walkers and give them detailed instructions for how to take care of him. Ahren and I talked about that and reminisced about our good times with him. But there is only so much you can catch up on in two hours and I wanted to be able to talk more while remaining in a "safe" environment.

"What if we took a drive?" I suggested about a month later. "We could pick a gorgeous day and just drive up the coast and come back."

"Okay. That would be nice."

We gently drove up the Pacific Coast Highway. It was a beautiful day and we were having a great time, so we didn't worry about the clock and kept going.

"It's going to be dark when we get back," I told her. "What do you want to do?"

"What do you want to do?"

"Well, I know there's this funky little hotel up here. Maybe we can get separate rooms and just continue to talk. No stress, no tension."

"Okay, that would be nice."

After all of the tough, ditch-digging work and soul-searching

I'd done, I was thrilled—this was more than I could take. I would think, Lord, I don't know what you're doing but I'm grateful to be having a second chance. I'm having a great time. We spent the night in separate rooms in this very funky, famous pink hotel that reminded us of the Flintstones. We had the *best* time!

We drove back to L.A. the next day. Everything was great and we went on with our lives. We weren't in constant contact with one another. Every couple of months we would get together and do something casual. In the meantime, I just kept working, walking Bottom and paying attention to my dreams.

In addition to Bottom's hip problems, he was suffering from a host of other illnesses. He basically required 24-7 care. I just didn't know what I was going to do. I couldn't expect my dog-sitters to do everything I was doing for him. I knew I had to start thinking about putting him down. But how do you lay down a dog who's been your child, your rhythm, your life? I remember talking to him: "Bottom, what are we going to do?" One afternoon I asked him where he wanted to lie—on the front lawn so he could lie in the sun and watch what was going on, or in the backyard where the grass was soft. He wanted to go out front, so we went and sat out front for a while, then I went back inside and kept peeking out at him. Toward the evening, he wanted to sit on the grass in the back. So we walked back there together then I went back in the house. I must have fallen asleep or forgotten that he was out there. All of a sudden I remembered, "Ohmygoodness, the sprinklers—Bottom can't get up!" I ran into the backyard and was relieved to see him lying there chillin'; the sprinkers hadn't come on yet. But I looked at him again. Something was wrong. Brown stuff was coming out of his mouth.

"Bottom? Bottom!" He didn't respond. I was frantic. I picked him up—ninety pounds of dead weight—and carried him to the car. I drove him to the animal emergency room and rang the bell. They came out and looked at him.

"Is he going to be okay?"

"Sir, he's gone. He's gone."

"Oh…"

"We'll keep him on ice until you decide what you'd like us to do with the body."

I sat there in shock. I didn't know where to go. I didn't know what to do. So I called Ahren and broke down.

"Bottom's dead! I don't know what I'm going to do…"

She and I talked. I realized he'd stayed around just long enough for Ahren and I to reconnect. And then he left. The circle was closed. Now he could move on. To comfort myself I volunteered to start walking Wren's mom's dog.

One night a week or so later, I decided to get over my grieving and go hang out with some friends. I went out to the jazz club Catalina's with some of my friends and Angela was there. We had a great time listening to the music, catching up and having fun. Afterward, as we stood outside shooting the breeze, it suddenly dawned on me: Angela's not seeing anybody and I'm not seeing anybody. Maybe we should go out. So I asked, and she said yes.

I don't remember where we went or what we did—all I remember is the date being painful. It was a "quiet disaster." What I'd envisioned was something casual—Court and Ang just hanging out. Instead, we both felt awkward. She's shy, I'm shy and we didn't know what to say. I couldn't get it together. I kept thinking, She's Angela—she's my friend! What are we doing here? I wasn't able to be cool, glib—nothing. I don't even want to know what she was thinking of me. All I remember is pulling up to her house in my little station wagon and thinking, Okay, please leave so I can just go. I didn't want the end of our date to make her wonder, Is he going to kiss me? Do we hug? What do we do? I thought, "Okay, Angela. Thanks so much, blah, blah, blah. Please let it end!"

Afterward, to be polite, I sent some happy-birthday/sorry-for-the-lousy-date flowers to her on the set of *Waiting to Exhale,* which she had flown off to film in Phoenix. When I hadn't heard back from her after a few days I called to make sure they'd arrived.

"Hey, Angela! Did you get the flowers?"

"Yeah, I got them. Thank you so much." Then she launched into some drama about her living arrangements down there. I was so glad she changed the subject. I felt like I had a way out of an awkward conversation.

"It sounds like you got a lot going on, girl," I told her. "Okay, I'm gonna let you go."

I was just trying to be a friend and move on. I didn't run into her again for a while.

In the summer of 1995 one of my buddies asked me if I had heard about the auditions for a major role in the movie *The Preacher's Wife* that would star Denzel Washington and Whitney Houston. I hadn't heard anything about it from my agents, but I as soon as I brought it up to them I was able to get an audition and went through a whole series of callbacks. Penny Marshall, the director, wanted to find the right person to play Whitney's on-camera husband, Reverend Henry Biggs. Between Whitney and Denzel, she had two big stars to work with. She wanted someone who was "steady," who wouldn't give her any "drama." (I guess all that work on myself had paid off; I was being considered "steady"!) Eventually, I was called to her house in the Hollywood Hills. I knocked and rang the driveway buzzer, knowing it was a moment that could change my life.

"Courtney! How ya doin'? Come on in!"

Penny opened the door and greeted me in her distinct Penny Marshall "New Yawk" accent. We talked, and she showed me around her house. I could see that Penny and I got along and that we wouldn't have any problems working together. I'd won my first major, major movie role!

That fall of 1995, before we started shooting, I finally decided to walk down that church aisle to the altar and give my life to the Lord. I had been going to the Abyssinian Baptist Church in Harlem whenever I was in New York, and the church's minister, Reverend Dr. Calvin O. Butts, was serving as our technical adviser for the film. The winds of change had been blowing in my life for a while. Before we began shooting, I realized that I didn't want to play the role of a preacher and stand in a pulpit if I wasn't baptized. I wanted to make a statement to myself and to the other people in the film that I was very serious about giving my life to the Lord. When I went down in the water, I had the most amazing experience. A shift happened. I didn't know the Bible, I didn't have any spiritual tools; yet I was being rinsed clean—I could feel it!

We shot *Preacher's Wife* for five months in and around New York during that winter. Everything went wonderfully. The movie was about a man realizing that his family is the most important thing in his life and that was necessary for him to reorder his life to make sure they remained first. That was exactly the kind of work I was doing in my own life. The whole movie was a metaphor for what was happening to me.

One fun behind-the-scenes story involves the movie's ice-skating scene. The scene could have been shot in Manhattan, but Penny wanted to travel to Maine, where she could guarantee that it would be cold. So we all went up to Maine and raided L.L.Bean and all the other winter stores so we'd have the latest woollies and cold-weather gear. I was very excited because I had grown up playing hockey in Detroit every Friday and Saturday night. I would finally get the chance to show off my skating skills in a movie.

It was 20 degrees when we arrived in Maine. The crew had gotten there a good month earlier and put a foot and a half of water on the lake just in case the temperature went up. It was frozen solid and deep. But on the day of the shoot the temperature soared to 50 degrees and kept climbing. Denzel and Whitney were able to complete their scene, but by the time my part of the shoot came, the lake was mush. I was crushed! Denzel and Whitney couldn't skate, yet they got the opportunity to skate on film; I knew how to skate, but my scene had to be cut. Thank God they saw fit to put that extra water on the lake, otherwise the whole day would have been ruined. Other than that little glitch, it was an important and wonderful shoot for me.

When I returned to Los Angeles, Ahren and I had a couple more teas—a couple more get-togethers—but a couple of hours together didn't seem to be enough.

"Why don't we drive up to Big Bear," I suggested. So we decided to spend a weekend at the mountain resort, located about an hour and a half north of L.A. We decided to rent one of the big log cabins they have but stay in separate bedrooms. We didn't know what was happening between us—we were getting to know each other again slowly. And it was good; it was easy and there was no pressure. We had a great time. By the end of the weekend, we were staying in the same suite but sleeping in separate beds.

"Courtney, how do you feel about me? Do you feel attracted to me?" Ahren asked me. It was just a question. She had this way of getting right to the point but in a gentle way. I didn't want to play games with her; we had both grown beyond that.

"I don't really know how to say this, Ahren, but right now I really don't," I told her honestly. "I'm not feeling any sexual tension or attraction. That doesn't mean it won't be there, but right now I'm just basking in the fact that we're here. That's more than enough right now." After what we had been through, being in each other's presence was a miracle in itself. It was a *miracle!*

"Okay. Honest question, honest answer," she said.

I didn't ask her how she felt; I didn't really want to know. I liked that we were getting to know each other again slowly. Talking about whatever feelings she may have had for me would be moving too fast. Over the past few years, I had been forced to do what she'd told me to do, which was to let her heal. I'd focused on working on myself. Now, the Lord had brought our relationship back around. For what purpose, neither of us knew. But it sure felt good.

The next day we had a blast, gigglin', laughin' and cleanin' up after ourselves before we left—it was one of the best times we'd ever had.

"Remember the last time we left somewhere?" she asked.

"Wow, tears…" I recalled.

But this time we were just laughin' and squealin'. When we closed the door to the cabin we raced to the car and took off back down the hill.

For the first time in our relationship I had been present with her. That left me feeling fulfilled. When we parted, we said, "Okay, I'll talk to you soon." There was no "What does this mean?" or "What are we doing?" We were just gently getting to know each other, slowly putting our toes in the water. We went back about our lives. I won parts in a couple of cable movies. I picked up golf. I was consoling myself about losing Bottom by walking Mama Bear's—that's what we called Wren's mother—dogs.

A few months later, early in the summer of 1996, I called Ahren up and asked her to go to a play with me. *Having Our Say,* the story of the hundred-year-old Delany sisters, was in town at the Taper Theater.

"I'd love to come. But I'm hectic right now," she told me. "Can I call you at the last minute and let you know?"

"Absolutely. No problem."

At the last minute she called me up to tell me she couldn't make it.

There are times in our lives that turn out to be pivotal

moments, when we make choices or walk through doorways through which we can never return. Unbeknownst to either one of us, Ahren's decision not to join me at the play that evening would turn out to be one of them. To this day I don't know what was going on in her life; I only know that she couldn't come. I asked my buddy Henry Woronicz, my friend from the Boston Shakespeare Company, to go. He had been staying with my housemate and me for the past several months while he checked out the L.A. acting scene. When we arrived at the theater, I saw Angela milling around the front of the theater with Mama Bear.

I didn't know Angela knew Mama Bear, I thought. I didn't even know Mama Bear was coming. She didn't say anything about it this morning.

Since Angela had blown up after starring in *What's Love Got to Do With It?* and *Waiting to Exhale,* the photographers were all around her. I didn't feel like getting caught up in all that so I figured I'd talk to them later. During the play's two intermissions I got up and walked around looking for Angela and Mama Bear, but I didn't see them. After the play ended, I kept my eyes open for them again, though I was more concerned about getting backstage. The Taper Theater is round and I didn't know where the stage door was located. I was wondering where it was and hoping Hank wasn't getting mad at me for taking so long, since it had been a three-hour play. I knew we were both exhausted, and I had to get up in a few hours to walk Mama Bear's dogs.

I was standing in front of the theater as people were streaming out, and suddenly Angela popped up in front of my face.

"Lookin' for me?"

"Actually, yeah!"

Gordon Davidson, the artistic director of the theater, popped up right next to her. He asked, "You guys going to the opening-night party?"

I said, "No."

Angela said, "Yeah!" as if to answer for all of us.

"I guess we're going," I said to myself. I wasn't convinced we'd stay long, but given the artistic director's invitation, I couldn't say no. Backstage, we got to see our friends and tell them how much we liked the show.

"You going to the party?" they asked us.

I said, "No."

Angie looked at me and told them, "Yeah, we goin'."

I looked at Hank. He looked at me and shrugged. So I reluctantly said, "All right, let's go."

When we got to the party, I started doing what I do. I got chairs for Angela and Mama Bear, got them coffee, set up things for them, then stepped off to the side with Hank and away from all the commotion.

"She's nice," Hank observed.

"Who?"

"Angela," he said. "She's nice, Court. You should date her."

"Hank, Hank. Please don't do that to me. There's history here. Please don't put that in my mind…"

"Courtney, she's nice," Hank repeated. "I think you should date her."

Now, where this was coming from? I wasn't thinkin' about Angela. I wasn't lookin' at her like that. She was just Angela—as sweet as can be—but I wasn't lookin' at her like that.

"What about her?" Hank insisted.

"No, no, no, Hank. I went on a date with her. She's shy, I'm shy. It was ugly. I embarrassed myself."

"But, Courtney, she's nice, you're nice. You guys should date—that's all I'm saying. I mean, come on," he continued. "What's the problem?"

"Okay, Hank, okay. I hear you. I don't know that I'm going to do anything about it, but I hear you."

So we did our thing. I talked to our friends. Then at about 2:00 a.m. I excused myself.

"Okay, Mama Bear, we're gonna check out. I'll see you in the morning. I'll call you five minutes before I get there."

Angie said, "For what?"

"I'll be there to walk her dogs."

"You're gonna walk her dogs in the morning—it's two o'clock now!" She stared at me in amazement.

"Yeah…"

"Will you marry me?" she asked and laughed.

"Ah, yeah!"

"You're not going to change your mind, are you?"

"Uh, no."

Hank and I got waylaid, so we didn't leave right away. When we finally did start heading out, it was at the same time as Angela and Mama Bear.

"Courtney, we've got to walk them to their car," Hank reminded me.

"Oh, right."

He nudged me the whole time we walked behind them.

I whispered, "Will you stop it already?"

His matchmaking continued when we got back to the house.

"Court, you've got to call her to make sure she got in."

"Oh, Lord!"

"Call her, Court."

"Okay, Hank, I'll call."

I called. She answered.

"Did you get in okay, Ang?"

"Yeah, I got in."

"Okay, I just wanted to make sure."

"Thank you."

"Okay, I'll talk to you a little later."

"Okay…"

In the morning I dragged myself up to walk Mama Bear's dogs. When I got back, Henry kept pushing.

"Courtney, you know you need to call her."

He was unrelenting. "You've got to call her for a date. She's so sweet, Court."

"Hank, I had a rough time the last time we went on a date. I just don't think it's gonna work. She's busy, she's got all these people around her, I don't want to bother her. I'm just doing my thing."

"Court, just give her a call."

To this day I don't know what Henry saw that caused him to hound me so hard. Eventually I relented. I had planned to go to the driving range that afternoon anyway. I wasn't trying to do a real date, so I figured I'd put them together. Golf. Date. Golf date. I called her.

"Angela, whatcha doin'?"

"Nothin'."

"Let's go hit some golf balls."

"I ain't never hit no golf ball."

"No? So let's go do it."

"Okay..."

"I'll pick you up."

At the driving range, since we had something to distract us, things between us were a lot freer than they'd been on our dinner date. "Okay, here's your pail," I told her as I set her balls alongside her. I demonstrated. "Now put the ball on the tee."

"Like this?"

"Yeah. Now hold the club like this."

"Okay..."

"Now swing it gently."

And she'd swing and the ball would dribble off to the side somewhere or go off on some crazy angle and we'd laugh.

"No, like this." I'd demonstrate again.

"Like this?" She'd swing and the ball would dribble off again. And we'd laugh. She couldn't get the ball to go anywhere.

"No, Angela, let me show you." So I stood behind her and put my arms around her, positioned her hands on the club and showed her the swing motion. I wasn't tryin' to do nothin' fresh, but all of a sudden the whole idea of being up behind her all close was like, "Whoa boy!"

Now that we weren't having to look at each other and think, This is really weird. I hope she don't like me, we ended up having a blast—an incredible time acting silly and laughing. When we finished at the driving range we got something to eat. Then we talked for so long we closed the restaurant down. We compared notes about Yale. Reminisced about the good times in August Wilson. Talked about what it was like to be black actors. Shared about how it was going—our successes and failures. The challenges we were having with our managers and agents. Everything flowed gentle and easy.

The next day I invited Angela to get something to eat. We talked about our families, our careers, relationships. By the end of the night we were laughin' too loud, babblin' and finishin' each other's sentences. Everyone was looking at us like we were crazy. We closed that restaurant down, too. The next night we went out and did the same thing. I noticed her beautiful hands. The gleam in her eyes. I let my mind go there: She had the softest-looking lips…. The night after that we went to Manny's, my favorite health-food restaurant, and closed it down. Then we stood outside talkin' and standin' in the street.

"Whatchu want to do?" she asked me about my life. "How many kids you want to have? When you gonna retire?"

Angela was as loud and just as country as you wanna be.

"Shh…Angie, keep it down. People are sleeping."

"Oh, okay." She lowered her voice for about two seconds before the volume crept back up again. "Yeah, but anyway…"

I was laughing inside, saying, "Oh, Lord, she's country! *Ooh,* she's *country!*" She kept saying, "I'm fittin' to do this," and "I'm fittin' to do that," pronouncing fixing like "fittin'." Now, Angela can lay her Yale on you—she can talk proper when she wants to. But she had gotten all comfortable and the Yale came down and she let the St. Pete's come out. It was so endearing. I thought, "Lord have mercy, what have we here? I had no *idea!*"

I was feeling very attracted to her though we hadn't touched or kissed. Nothing romantic had been said. But we had been doing so much sharing. Our conversations were so intimate. She had such a kind heart. Suddenly it dawned on me—THIS IS WHO I WANT TO MARRY!

I tossed and turned in my bed all night. Sensing that Angela was "the one" gave me so much joy. But the thought of letting her know frightened me. I wondered if I was the only one catching feelings, or if she knew, too.

Angie's my friend, I'd think. It may not even be what I think it is. It may just be that we have fun and like to talk. I was too shy to come right out and ask her if she felt the same way.

I couldn't even begin to think about Ahren. We hadn't talked about or promised anything relationshipwise and we weren't even seeing each other often, but it was clear we had been exploring the possibility of getting back together. The stakes were very high. The thought of hurting her again made my heart feel heavy. I had to know how Angela felt about me. After obsessing about how to do it, I decided to send her some flowers with a note. It took me three days to write it. Trying to fit everything I wanted to say into a space the size of a Post-it note stressed me out. I must have torn up a hundred and fifty of them.

I knew what I said had to characterize my feelings and would get her to give me an answer. What I finally came up with went something like this: "We're both shy. We're both like family. I like you. Do you like me? Check one…" Then I drew two boxes: "Yes" and "No." I took the note to Rita's Flora on the corner of LaBrea and Sixth, where I ordered a bouquet of flowers.

"This note has to go with them," I told the cashier.

"Okay."

"No, you don't understand. This note *has* to be with my flowers."

"Okay, sir."

"No, you don't understand. This note HAS to be with those flowers. These flowers cannot go to Angela without this note."

"Okay, sir." She smiled. "I get what you're saying." Then I went home and sat down and waited for the phone to ring....

I have never sweated so much before or since as I did waiting for Angela to call me. When the phone finally rang, my heart was pounding out of my chest like you see in cartoons.

"Hello?"

"Hey, Court!" I noticed that her voice was all high and scratchy.

"Oh, Angela. How are you doin'?" I tried to play it off but my voice was about six octaves too high.

"Hey…"

"What's up? Whatcha doin'?" Sweat was pouring off of me—the phone was about to slip out of my hands.

"I got your flowers…"

"Oh, the flowers. Oh, yeah. Do you like them?"

"Yeah…"

"Did you get the note?"

"Yeah, I did. I got the note—and, oh, boy, was that a 'note'!"

"Is that a good thing or a bad thing?"

"That's a good thing…"

"Thank you, Jesus!" After all those dark years, after all the work I had done on myself, after having faith that God would bring me someone special, I knew I was about to park my heart.

I also knew that I had to dial back with Ahren and tell her what was going on. I didn't have Dr. Kornfeld to help me on this one. I would be on my own. Over the past several years I had developed the ability to be honest and have difficult conversations. I knew that talking to Ahren would try those skills; it felt like it was the biggest test the "new and improved" Courtney could possibly face. I had to step up, be a man and navigate whatever emotions came up by myself.

Ahren and I met in a park near my house and took what turned out to be a three-hour walk through my neighborhood. I told her everything that had happened, beginning with the night of the play. Honestly, she was stunned. One part of her was excited for Angela and me; she knew us both and felt very strongly about us. She was also thankful that I was being so open and honest. Although Ahren would never allow her feelings to cloud my joy, I suspected that another part of her was extremely disappointed. Fortunately, because I had been so forthright with her, although she was disappointed, she didn't feel betrayed. By now I knew Ahren well enough to leave her alone and allow her the space to heal. I hoped that in her own time she would reach out to me and want to be in touch again.

We didn't talk for a long time. Six years passed but then Ahren called me to tell me her mother had died. She wanted me to come to the funeral. Angela agreed that I should definitely go. Ahren's mom had been like my mom for over eleven years—her family had been my family. And since her father had already passed away, this marked an important transition in her life. As I watched Ahren at the service, I marveled at what a wonderful and amazing woman she'd become. Yes, God had a different plan for me in terms of who I was to marry; yet I value and cherish the fact that over time we've been able to navigate our way back to friendship. Ahren and I have reconnected and remain friends to this day.

A couple of days later I asked Angela if she would help me pick out a gift for my mom's retirement party. We would both be leaving L.A. at the same time. She was going to Italy for a fashion show, and I was going home to Detroit. When we walked into the jewelry store everybody gathered around us—not physically, but with their eyes; a collection of eyes followed Angela. As I looked at bracelets, I'd ask her opinion. We narrowed down the selection together. I was going to choose from those. While I was considering my options, Angela moseyed around the store. I noticed that people kept looking at her, then looking at me and smiling. After a while I noticed she was examining some piece of jewelry and talking to a salesperson, so I wandered over to see what she was looking at.

"What do you think about this, Court?" she asked. She held out her hand. She was wearing a diamond ring on it with three different stones in it.

"That's nice!" I answered and didn't think anything of it. But the man behind the counter said, "I think something's happening here. I think something just went down!"

"Whoa!" I told him. "It's nothing like that." Then I dragged Angela out of the ring section. "Help me finish with these bracelets." But I knew she had just dropped a monster hint. I bought my mama's bracelet and got on out of there.

That night I stopped by her house to say goodbye to her before she left in the morning. We talked for a little while and I gave her a tape of a sermon I thought she'd appreciate. I hadn't planned to kiss her good-night; I had learned to be a gentleman and let the woman dictate the pace. I would have been fine with a hug now that I knew that she liked me. But as we stood next to her front porch on a secret path behind the hedges that run around the house, I don't know if she went to kiss me or I went to kiss her; the next thing I knew we were kissing. And let me just say that Angela Bassett's lips feel just as soft as they look! I'll leave it at that. We kissed for a good long time then we kissed a little more. And then kissed a little more. It went on for quite a while. As a matter of fact, I was surprised by how long it went on. That kiss was amazing! I was giddy. I think I floated home. I just remember calling my mom and telling her, "When I get home I have something important to tell you!"

Chapter 13

Gently, Sweetly, Concretely

One day I was minding my business at home when the messenger from Rita's Flora arrived at the front door. There are times in your life when you get flowers and you know exactly who they're from. But once you reach a certain level as an actor you're always getting flowers. You never know who they're from until you read the card. Someone might have sent them for some little good deed you did or an appearance you made somewhere or anything. My manager at the time would send me flowers for the least little thing. He was a sweet flower sender. The messenger handed me a big bouquet of wildflowers—purple and green and yellow. Little-bitty buds—almost like weeds. Really cute.

"I wonder who these are from?"

There was a big card attached to them—not the little 2x2-inch card that all the flower shops have where the clerk writes in this nondescript handwriting whatever the customer dictates. But a bigger card—a 3x4- or 4x5-inch stationery note card. I opened up the envelope and there were two note cards in it with a name across the top: Courtney B. Vance. The cards were hand printed. His handwriting, obviously, because it was somewhat illegible—letters leaning to the left, to the right, straight up, close together, letter on top of a letter—that kind of stuff. Still, I could see that he had taken his time with it. I read what he had written.

I like you. Do you like me? Check one—yes, or no.

"Ahh…"

It was really sweet. He was just layin' it out there. "I really like you and would like to spend time with you but I'm not in a rush. We don't need to rush this thing. In your time…" I remember feeling all excited and getting butterflies, then getting really quiet. I knew this was monumental. This was a moment—a really big moment. I remember lying down on the couch. I thought about it.

Well, we had been having a good time together. Maybe we could move from a friendship to "well, let's try it this time." I thought about the first time we went out, when it was, "Oh, Lord, I hope he don't like me in that way, in a romantic way. Let's be friends. Let's just continue it how it is—as friends. There's nothing wrong with it. It's not broken so let's not fix it—fix it and break it."

Now here were these flowers and this letter where he was clearly professing his desire to be with me—to be my boyfriend, to develop another kind of relationship. It was sweet; it was chivalrous. I had just experienced a number of relationships that were not right—back to back to back in rapid succession. Not the right person, not the right circumstances. Just wrong! I felt a little beat up emotionally. A part of me was thinking, Do I really want to go back in that ring again? Do I really want to roll the dice? Do I want to try my hand again? Is it just going to end up like all the others? Or could it possibly be different?

But by now I'd known Courtney for many, many years. I knew he and Ahren had broken up and had stayed broken up. I had admired his committment to her for the many years they'd been together. When people go together for that long and they break up, you just know they're going to get back together. But it seemed like they hadn't been together in a long time. I knew he had dated other women; I'd heard mention of it through the grapevine. I also knew he was secure in himself. Here was someone who could care about the essence of me. Who could care for who I am now *and* who I can be.

I had to take to bed and lie down and compose myself. I knew I had to make a decision. They say love is an action—a choice. I had to make one quickly. Being raised right, I knew I had to respond and let him know I'd received the card and flowers and say thank-you. Then I'd have to make some kind of response to his overture, either that I was interested or I wasn't. I probably needed to figure that out and do that in my next conversation. I didn't know that I wanted to put him off, though he was being really kind and patient. (He's been rushing me ever since!)

I thought about how at another time he probably would have been that guy where I would have said, "He's just so nice—too nice." You always want that passionate guy, the bad boy. But that type of man is not all he's cracked up to be. I had an appreciation of the "nice guy" at this point. I was interested and hungry and ready for that. I thought I deserved that, at least, as a given. I deserved someone who is kind and gracious and supportive and encouraging. That should be a certain thing—the first thing—not the last thing or a thing you're hoping for. That's what I deserved; that's what we all deserve.

I reflected on my girlfriends talking about different men and telling me, "He's so nice, he washed my car!"

"That ain't *nice*," I would tell them. "That shouldn't be a big deal! Men are supposed to wash cars."

Or "He opened the door for me." Please! That ain't nothin' special! People are supposed to be nice and not take you for granted—call when they say they're gonna call, show up when they said they will.

So after thinking about it, I called him.

"Hey…"

"What's up?"

"I got your flowers. They're beautiful!"

For years I could remember the rest of the conversation. Funny, I can't anymore. I just know the relationship started there. Gently, sweetly, concretely.

At the end of that incredible whirlwind week, Courtney had to go home to Detroit to attend his mom's retirement party, and I had to leave for Milan, where I had been invited, all expenses paid, by designer Giorgio Armani to attend one of his fashion shows. The night before I left, Courtney came by my house under the guise of dropping off a tape. I think it was a tape on vocal technique, vocal warm-up or something like that. It might as well have been blank, as far as I was concerned. It was his excuse to come say goodbye. Before he left we were standing on my front steps. The big moon was out—a big ol' fat moon and a clear sky. Then he kissed me. I felt like I was a teenager. It was truly reminiscent of my first puppy-love kisses. I got pinpricks and chills up the back of my thighs and across my butt, up my neck, across my scalp—everywhere! There were these electrical impulses just coursing through me. So we just stood out there and kissed for a moment. Now, everyone can't kiss good. Kissing is an art! To some it seems to come easier than others. Courtney was a good kisser. He had good "pillow" lips.

Milan is one of the most wonderful cities in the world. Home of Teatro alla Scala, the world-famous opera house; and Duomo, an amazing cathedral that seats forty thousand people and one of the most famous buildings in Europe. Milan is well known as the location of the some of the most renowned fashion houses in the world—Armani, Dolce & Gabbana, Prada, Gianni Versace—as well as some incredible shopping. I was visiting the city for the first time. Mr. Armani was wonderful and generous. He doesn't speak English and I don't speak Italian. Our interactions were short.

"*Ciao, bella. Bellissima!*"

"*Grazie! Grazie! Spaghetti!*"

After his fashion show I had dinner with Eric Clapton back at Armani's *palazzo*, while sitting with Sophia Loren. That was pretty cool!

Under any other conditions I would have been enthralled by Mr. Armani and his amazing fashions, the city's arts and culture, the beautiful fashions and fabrics and accessories, by being in another country. Yet on this trip I hardly paid attention to any of it. I couldn't concentrate; I missed Courtney. The three days I was gone seemed like forever. I don't think I ever went to sleep; I didn't even rest well. I don't know if it was the time-zone difference, the newness of love, talking on the phone with him at all hours or the combination of all three. What I did do was talk my girlfriend Jean Mori's ear off for the entire plane ride—over and back. I processed and reprocessed, thought about and rethought everything about this amazing man who had just shown up in my life, though in some ways he had been right there all along. I must have dissected every tonality, phrase and look he had given me. Thankfully, Jean was very patient with me. How true a real girlfriend can be! I was already dreaming that I would be married to him and we would have children together. My heart bubbled over with passion, desire, excitement—it just brimmed over.

When it was time to leave Milan, Courtney offered to pick us up from the airport.

"Tell Mr. Armani to cancel the car, I'll come get you."

"You sure?" I thought that was so considerate.

"I'll be there."

When we landed at LAX, I could hardly wait to see him, but Jean got stopped in Customs for trying to sneak back some Italian sausage. While I was waiting for her, I thought I would die.

"Come on, girl. Come on! Come on!"

When we finally got through he was waiting for us with a big smile on his face and two dozen roses—a box of yellow roses for Jean and a box of red roses for me. It was very sweet. It was very kind. Jean was so impressed.

"If you fuck this up…" she whispered to me.

"*Jean!* You never use curse words!"

"You just make sure you don't mess up!"

Chapter 14

Parking My Heart

When Angela got back to Los Angeles, I picked up a bouquet of flowers for her and one for her girlfriend Jean and gave them to them when I picked them up at the airport. Now that Angela and I knew that we liked each other, our relationship was officially on. I was head over heels, and tickled to see who God had finally brought me!

Angie and I started to spend a lot of time together. We spent as much time as possible in each other's company. If I wasn't auditioning or running errands, I was hanging out at her house. At first we would sit and look at each other and say things like, "It's you? I'm amazed! I can't believe it's *you!*"

"I've been looking all this time and it's *you!*"

I was always trying to think about unusual things to do—a different movie to go to, a new place to eat. We would go to little tiny restaurants or little hole-in-the-wall places. We would also go to church together. Before long, Angela saw that I have a spirit of service. I'm always asking, "What can I do? How can I help?" When she got sick, I came right over with my bags of health-food stuff—I was the herb doctor coming over. I headed straight into her kitchen, grated some ginger, boiled it down, then added honey and lemon. It was like an elixir—that bad boy was strong! I served it to her then I left. She said, "Wow! That's not the norm anymore." My willingness to serve resonated with Angela. It was what she responded to. I was someone who could assist her, emotionally secure her, help her take care of herself—which is a basic feminine response. Angela made more money than me at the time—she made a lot more money—she didn't need me for that. But it wasn't about money, it was about "He's a good man, he's a kind man." She is a gentle woman and she needed a gentle man.

Even though I had been baptized and had given my life to Christ, back then I didn't know anything about the Bible. I didn't know what it said or its rules of conduct. Throughout my life I had lived by the values my parents instilled in me: love of family, hard work and academic excellence. But there were biblical laws that, as Angela and I moved toward marriage, I would desperately need exposure to.

As we talked about what we wanted for our relationship, Angela said, "Courtney, we should do this right. We shouldn't have sex until we're married."

I didn't have to think about it; her suggestion just confirmed what was in my heart already—she was the real deal. "You're right," I told her. "Let's make this special. Let's do what is right." So before we married, we kissed and hugged and cuddled and caressed but we did not have sex. Sometimes it was hard—but she had said we were going to do it, and I was committed. Along the way she got weak a couple of times.

"Court, maybe we could…"

"No, Angela, we are *not* going to have sex. We're going to do this right."

"Okay…"

Abstaining became a big thing to me. God had finally gotten me ready for the woman he wanted me to marry. And I was determined to make our relationship special.

In the coming months, we talked about rings. Initially we

went around to all these jewelers and all they wanted to talk about was "the rock, the *rock*, the ROCK!" It was all about the size of the ring. "Do you want a four-carat ring or a seven-carat?" No one—except us seemed to care if the ring looked good. Neither of us is ostentatious; our style is understated elegance. And it wasn't about what the ring symbolized—our undying commitment and spiritual union to each other. Finally we met a jeweler, Martin Katz, who suggested, "Don't worry about that carat thing. It's the aesthetic. Get something nice." In time Ang and I whittled a long list down to two or three options. I learned that she has a very unique way of making decisions. She's gotta feel it out, then walk away, then talk it through with about ten or twelve different people and come to the exact choice that she was going to make in the beginning. That's her!

"What do you think, Court?" she'd ask me.

"I like this one," I'd say.

"Hmm…I don't know. What do you think, Martin?"

The jeweler would share his thoughts.

She'd consider them, then say, "Oh, I can't make up my mind."

In the meantime, I'd be saying, "Oh, Lord, girl! You know the one you like!"

"I know, but what if I like that one tomorrow?"

"Okay, you're right, you're right! Okay, Martin. We'll be back."

She's that way to this day. I have a different decision-making process. I may talk to one or two people, but then I know, "I like this one" or "I like that one." None of this back-and-forth. She and I end up at the same place but go through a different process. So once she whittled the options down, I chose the antique ring she liked.

In December 1996, *The Preacher's Wife* opened in Manhattan. I felt like everything had finally come together. This was the largest movie I'd ever done; I'd gone through this incredible journey to gain peace and become the man I saw in my mind; my mother and sister were here to celebrate with me following our devastating loss; and I'd found the woman I wanted to marry! Tonight, unbeknownst to her, I was going to get down on my knee and propose. That premiere was also everyone's introduction to Angela and me as a couple. By then, a lot of people had heard we were together, but this was the night we "came out" to the press. The media was excited—wow, a new black couple! "When are you going to do a project together?" everyone wanted to know.

Chapter 15

The Real Deal

I didn't need anyone's admonitions to know I had finally found my husband. Courtney reminded me of my great-grandfather Slater Stokes; they had the same qualities.

Oh, he's just so nice, I thought. Someone who thinks of me and cares for me when I'm down. In my experience, women were usually the caretakers. I wasn't used to nurturing men. I had never experienced a guy taking care of me. That impressed me. We spent a lot of time together, sometimes at home and other times out doing something special—anything to see each other. We'd go to the movies, get dessert, take a road trip—drive somewhere far out then turn around and drive right back. We went to my little church, First Southern Baptist, in North Hollywood, together. (Courtney went to a large church, but I liked my real small, little family church, so he came to church with me.) Each time I would hear *knock, knock, knock* at my back door and see his little face through the window and I'd feel my face light up like a Christmas tree. I was always so happy to see him.

With every passing day I observed him display little thoughtful and caring behaviors that I might not have paid attention to before. Or behaviors where the old Angela might have thought, Oh, he's such a nice guy. Boring… Now it was like, Oh, stupid! Forget the guys with all that drama, this is the kind of person you're looking for. After that series of bad dates, small things loomed large, were underscored. I could tell he was genuinely concerned about the well-being of others—not just of people he knew and was close to, but anybody. He was really nice to everyone. Courtney actually makes the world a better place because he really does care for people. I had already discovered that he walked and groomed Mama Bear's dogs, which took a lot of stress off her. When we would meet for dates at night, he'd call to make sure I got home safely. He would send a bouquet of flowers for no particular reason at all. He loves to plan gifts and surprises. Some days he'd call me up with a great and creative idea or he'd book some wonderful getaway. That was really a plus; in my experience the woman had to plan those kinds of things. So he'd plan them, and I might embellish them in some little ways. But lots of times he'd already thought of the little boat ride or side trip I'd been thinking about. We'd go to a different restaurant for breakfast, lunch and dinner, and then we'd visit some sight, then go on a shopping spree. He'd run us around until we were worn out and tired. I learned that was all a reflection of his curiosity about different places, his inquisitiveness—the "Henry the Explorer" in him, because he had grown up around a lot of books.

So I fell in love with Courtney's inner beauty first, but shortly thereafter I swooned over his rich, deep brown, soulful eyes. Looking into his eyes I felt like I could feel his spirit and his soul, and that was amazing to me. To this day when I get upset with him, he just looks at me like he really, really wants to work things out. It's impossible to stay ornery. I observed that he took care of himself, healthwise. He was always sharing something with me about some vitamin or herb. And he always looked nice and well groomed, which was a relief. As a woman in Hollywood, dressing myself is stressful enough without having to dress my man. He knows what he looks good in and wears it. Sometimes I found myself staring at his hands. My mother always would joke about a man having a nice smile, but hands so to' up and dirty that you'd be afraid to let him touch you. Courtney has really beautiful hands—nice, strong and well cared for. He has affectionate hands; his hands were always touching me, holding me, caressing me, embracing me.

For the first time in my life, a man actually felt safe. I knew I was just brimming and bubbling over, but I didn't ever worry that I was falling in love and might hit bottom and bust my head open. I didn't feel like I was falling at all. For the first time in my life, love didn't feel uncertain, it didn't feel stressful, it didn't feel rushed. It slowly began to dawn on me that true love felt calm, peaceful, so certain. I knew it was right. I could tell it would last. As Dr. Phil says, I'd found a "soft place to fall."

As our time together revealed these and other wonderful qualities, I knew he wasn't putting on airs or anything to impress me—you know how Chris Rock says when you first start dating you send your "representatives" to meet his "representatives"? Well, I could tell that the qualities I was seeing was just who he really is. Sometimes when he didn't know it, I would sneak looks at him. He looked really human in the best ways; I could see his sensitivity and vulnerability. I realized that he, indeed, is fearfully and wonderfully made—made in the image and likeness of God.

In around October 1996—at about the one-month mark in our relationship—I wrote Courtney a letter expressing how grateful I was for him and how much I appreciated his love and care. Courtney is sensitive. I could tell he didn't want to hurt anyone's feelings, he didn't want to misstep and he didn't want his heart to be broken. I wanted to give him a little encouragement, to let him know how much I cared for him. In my letter I told him that I could see him as the father of my children. I didn't have a daddy he could ask for my hand in marriage, but I wanted him to know that if he wanted to marry me, I was going to say yes, that it would be fine. I thought he needed to know that.

Shortly after I wrote him the letter, he began to give me little hints that he had gotten the message. Though we never really discussed it, over the next month or so we looked at engagement rings a couple of times, which was very sweet and intimate. The shopping itself was a little overwhelming. I had never had a picture in my head of what I wanted my diamond to look like, and I thought, "Argh! Too many choices." I knew I wanted something radiant; that was about all I knew about diamond shapes. But Courtney's the type of man to go to the diamond information center or something and talk to someone so he can learn all the fine points. Fortunately he has good taste and he's so good at this kind of thing. So I figured that as we looked I'd narrow down the choices and then he could pinpoint the right one.

Before long I could tell he was planning something and would be presenting me with a ring. When he's preparing to do something really special he gets really quiet, very officious, sort of stands up straight. Then he does this really jokester kind of thing where it's like he's pulling a girl's pigtail, where he's got a big proclamation, but can't wipe the smile off his face. It's like he's holding on to a secret and he doesn't want to burst, or here comes his part in the school play and it must be perfect. It's really quite endearing. Well, I could tell that a special weekend would be coming up, though I didn't know when.

In December 1996, Courtney experienced one of the biggest nights of his career—the premiere of *The Preacher's Wife,* the biggest movie of his career. It was also a big night for us as a couple. I met Courtney's mom for the first time. I wanted to make a good impression.

"Mom, this is Angela."

"Hi, Mrs. Vance. It's a pleasure to meet you. You have a wonderful son."

Today I know Mrs. Vance is very warm, loving and friendly. That night she was pleasant, but kept a little distant; she was definitely studying me. I was a little bit nervous. Still, I was glad to meet the woman who had raised this wonderful man I was seeing. We also formally "came out" as a couple to the media for the first time, which had its own stresses. And a couple of Courtney's old flames attended the opening, which threw me for a moment. With so much going on, I felt a wee bit insecure; it was a lot to deal with at once. Courtney reassured me. Then after we watched the movie and engaged in the evening's festivities, we went back to the hotel. We were just talking about nothing, when he handed me a little box and dropped to his knee.

"Angela, will you marry me?"

I opened the box and pulled out a beautiful ring in an antique setting. It was simple, yet really beautiful. I slipped it on. It fit. Of course I said, "Yes!"

The next morning I called to tell Mama my good news. I was stunned to find out that she had an attitude, her feelings were hurt. Apparently, several days earlier and totally unbeknownst to me, the news had gotten out that Courtney and I would be getting engaged. Somebody somewhere knew something and leaked it to black radio. My mother's coworkers had told her we were engaged before we actually were. From her perspective it must have been hurtful and humiliating to believe I hadn't told her—my own mother—about my engagement, yet the media—and her coworkers—knew about it.

"But I wasn't engaged, Mommy. He didn't propose until last night."

"You knew it was coming."

"I didn't, Mama—not really, not *when*."

Unexpectedly, what should have been an exciting time—the happiest day of life!—was fraught with hurt feelings. I had been prepared for her to respond to my news with excitement, with bright red or maybe a brilliant purple. Instead, I was met with beige. Just beige. There was no particular color, no particular excitement in her voice. The occasion was no longer awash with hues of joy. She hadn't even met Courtney, and she'd decided she didn't like him.

He and I talked and decided to fly down to Florida to assuage her hurt feelings. When we arrived, I called her up on her job.

"Mom, Courtney and I are here in Tampa. We want to see you so we can talk to you."

"Oh, you don't have to come to see me."

Oh, I was just so hurt. And I felt badly that her feelings were so bruised. She refused to see us.

"Courtney, Courtney, let's just get back on the plane. Let's go. Let's go…"

"No, no." He was really calm. He kind of understood the situation. He knew that if he had flown off the handle it could have precipitated a broken relationship or slowed down the healing process. "We're just going to have to go through it. We're going to go through it together. It's going to be okay."

"You think?"

I was glad to have him calm, strong and steady. I'm not always the best at handling confrontations. I had been ready to run away. But he said it with such confidence I believed everything was going to work out fine. I went to my mother's house alone. Her car wasn't in the driveway but I knocked on the door. She didn't answer right away but eventually she came to the door.

"Mama…" I hugged her and showed her my ring. We sat there and talked about how, on what should have been the happiest day of my life, I had been bested, usurped…by the radio! I was a casualty of the ratings war. I learned to never underestimate the power of black radio. I mean, that is how we got our news for a long period of time, wasn't it? Don't sell them short!

That night we all went to dinner. Courtney, being the charmer, won my mother over. They've been best friends since. He talks to her every other day—more often than I do.

Chapter 16

Tying the Knot

Now I had a wedding to plan. Oh, that was fun! As a little girl, I'd daydreamed about getting married. I had never planned it out in my mind exactly like some women do—you know, some women know exactly what dress they're going to wear, what flowers they want, what wedding invitation. I was thinking about things like that for the first time, which made the experience especially enjoyable. Every wedding invitation I received in the mail I replied to saying I would attend. I even went to weddings I wasn't invited to. I was, indeed, a wedding crasher! At each wedding I'd glean ideas that helped me know what our ceremony would be like.

One time Courtney and I went to some little resort he'd found up in the Napa Valley. When we arrived, there was a small wedding going on, maybe twenty or thirty people. There were the hills, the mountains, the bride, the groom; it was really picturesque.

"Ooh, look, Courtney! Let's peek."

We stood in the hotel on a balcony above them, peering into their ceremony. I loved that it was small, beautiful and intimate. I loved that it was outdoors.

We originally scheduled our wedding for June 1997, but

later pushed it back to October to accommodate my work schedule. My sister D'nette and Courtney's sister both lived out of town, so they couldn't help me in the same way they would have if they lived in L.A. That was okay. I read all kinds of wedding books, and the idea of planning my own wedding didn't stress me out. I enjoyed coming up with ideas; it was as if I was being my own director/producer. Why don't we release some butterflies? "Ooh, that sounds like a cute idea."

I wanted our ceremony and the process to clearly express who we were and our belief systems—our love of God, our families and friends, our love of our community and culture. I wanted the people who loved us to participate. I read in one book that a marriage ceremony might include writing a letter to each other's mothers. We did that. I wrote Mrs. Vance a short note expressing my gratitude for how well she had raised her son and telling her how much I appreciated the wonderful man he'd become. I promised to take care of him from this point on. "Ain't much finishing of him left to do," I wrote. But I promised to do my best to help him become an even better man.

Every wedding I went to I'd take the best and make note of the worst. I went to another ceremony and their cake was divine. I didn't want a whole lot of desserts; I wanted ours to be one good cake, not dry or tasteless. I chose one that was lemon, raspberry and coconut. I heard a song sung that addressed receiving praise and glory but the glory really belonging to God. I thought that was appropriate for us because of the profession we're in. God empowers us to do whatever it is that we do. That's the reason we're getting the glory. I wanted that song for us. At one ceremony the pastor was wearing a microphone but the bride and groom weren't. You could hear the pastor's words but you couldn't hear the couple's wedding vows. I made a note to be mindful of that. At another wedding I realized how much a difference it makes when the soloist could really sing. At still another they played Pachelbel, the classical music often played shortly before the bride enters the sanctuary. I realized that it didn't touch my heart. I'm not European. I don't want European music, I thought. I wanted jazz music instead—jazz standards. Jazz touches me—Ella Fitzgerald and other music from our African-American idiom. For flowers I chose simple lily of the valley, with its little white bells.

Given our celebrity, I wanted the wedding to take place somewhere comfortable and safe. We live behind gates, so that would give us added security. We walked the neighborhood looking at homes where we might like the ceremony to take place if their owners were willing to rent them for a day. I was at home napping and the doorbell rang. Lou Rawls lives in my neighborhood. He walked over, offered his home and asked if he could sing at our wedding. Of course I said yes! That was a *tremendous* blessing.

I crafted the vows for the preacher to recite, but I didn't want us to have our own vows. "Oh, you are my lover and my friend." "Lovers, best friends, soul mates, blah, blah, blah…" I didn't want that. It seemed corny. A close friend, Donna Denize, is a writer whose work I enjoy and admire. She wanted to write and read us a poem.

One of Courtney's friends, stylist Phillip Bloch, helped me identify a gown. I already had a relationship with Escada, and they had offered to make it. I wanted something simple. They drew up a sketch. I liked it. They made my gown. It wasn't a big production.

Almost everything proceeded smoothly; however, the plan I came up with for the first dance almost caused our first argument. We took classes because I wanted our dance to be choreographed. You could bring the actual music you wanted to dance to and this guy would come up with steps. I wanted to dance to "At Last" by Lou Rawls and Diane Reeves. When I danced with the instructor, who was a choreographer as well as a professional dancer, he put one hand in the small of my back and gently held my other hand. He led me: go this way, go that way, step back, step up. I was just following; I felt very secure. Well, dancing with Courtney was a little bit different. Since he was the gentleman, he was supposed to lead, but he didn't have it locked down. So I started leading.

"Baby! Let me lead," he told me.

"Then lead. Come on! You gotta hold on tight."

"I am."

"You aren't doing it right. Do it like this."

"I can't because you keep trying to lead."

"Well, you're not doing it right, so someone's got to lead."

"Babe!"

"Don't call me baby when you're upset with me."

One day after practice we got in a little fight on the drive home. Next thing I knew, he had pulled the car over to the side of the road, got out, came around my side of the car, opened the door and knelt down as traffic whizzed by us.

"Baby, what is the problem?" Those big ol' eyes were looking up at me.

"I don't know…"

"He just don't know how to teach us, does he?"

"No, he doesn't."

"Well, forget that. I think we can dance just fine on our own."

"Yeah, we're actors."

"You're an actor, I'm an actor…"

"And you know how to dance and I know how to dance."

"We'll just act it out on our own."

COURTNEY: In the days following our engagement, as we began planning our wedding and life together, Angela and I shared our hopes and dreams about love, marriage and family. One of the things that I set on the table of our marriage from the outset was that divorce was not an option. It was a given that issues and problems would arise in our marriage, as they do in every marriage. There is no such thing as a perfect marriage. I took seriously the symbol of the wedding ring. We would soon be stepping into "the ring" and whatever issues might come up between us, we would take God and the spirit of forgiveness into that ring and work out our differences. I wanted us to step inside the circle and close the circle—we would not step out. Angela agreed. We promised each other we were going to marry one time and one time only. Since we weren't going to get divorced, there was no need for any prenuptial agreement.

During this time I met a physical trainer who trained Olympic athletes, Dr. Frank Little, while shooting *Twelve Angry Men*. From the outset I believed that Doc, as I came to call him, was heaven sent to guide me during this period. I would be preparing for a role in *Space Cowboys,* which had some difficult physical requirements. Before long I learned he was also a Christian marriage counselor. I knew Angela and I would be entering that very emotional, volatile first two years of marriage when two individuals are attempting to become one. How that oneness happens is a mystery. And as I came to see, men need to be counseled along that journey. I soon understood that Doc's real purpose in my life at this time was to help me learn the Bible and become the husband God and Angela needed me to be. Angela already had in mind what kind of man she would respond to. She had told me about her grandfather, the Reverend Slater Stokes, and her uncle Grover. She took me to meet her sisters' husbands. They were all godly men with a "servant spirit." Angela's sister Lynn and brother-in-law, Al, sat us down when I went to visit for the first time. Lynn advised us to keep the focus of our marriage on our relationship as husband and wife. This would be especially important when the children come, she said. "My children would not be here if it wasn't for my husband." I hadn't thought about it that way before. The advice they shared with us had a very powerful impact.

My parents had instilled a lot of wonderful values in me, but they hadn't provided the biblical role model of unconditional love and cooperation in a way for me to know that this example that she was describing and showing me is what a true husband does and is. Over the next two or three years Doc and I trained every Monday through Friday. As we worked, he introduced me to biblical principles and taught me how I needed to walk as a Christian man. One of the most important lessons he taught me was "family order." He taught me that God should come first in both of our lives. For the husband, the wife should be his first thought after God. That was an eye-opening revelation for me. It changed my entire life because it opened the door to accessing the remaining part of that man I had seen in my mind and was trying to be in real life! The key idea that I hadn't learned yet was the spiritual concept of service.

Not surprisingly, it didn't take long before I faced my first challenge in this area. I tagged along with Angela a lot as she organized and structured the wedding. She had a very clear and specific idea in mind and wanted me to go with her as she pulled the event together. At first I found tasting all those beautiful but bland and dry wedding cakes, and tagging along and sitting in on all those meetings with florists and wedding planners, boring and frustrating.

"What do you want me to *do*, Angela?"

"Courtney, I just need you here to help me. Tell me if you like things. I just want you to be here."

I didn't know what that meant; I wanted a specific assignment: go to the store, drop off these invitations, call the musicians—something! Doc helped me understand that my actual assignment was to be at her side as she had asked me. I had no idea that being the "husband" wasn't always about doing things; sometimes it just required being there and allowing her to be the "wife." So I followed along, watched, listened, offered my input and learned what she wanted. That turned out to be important. Two weeks before our ceremony, Angela had to leave town to shoot some scenes for *Stella,* and left me in charge.

"Courtney, please make sure they do what I've asked them to do."

"Baby, just tell me what to do."

ANGELA: We both agreed to get premarital counseling. I thought it would be good to do because I'd heard the statistics that one in two marriages fall apart. I didn't want that to happen to me. I'd rather just not get married. I didn't want to entangle only to have to unentangle. What did Shakespeare say? *This knot is too much for me to untie...* Well, I didn't want to tie a knot and then have to untie it. So I thought it would be good if we could talk about some of the issues.

I had caught glimpses of what a good marriage looked like when I visited my auntie Golden and uncle Grover. I also had my two older sisters, whose husbands, to me, were standard bearers. They were men who could take care of business militarywise, but also walk in the door and be very loving. "Honey, what can I do for you?" They were important role models for me. During our engagement I took Courtney on a family tour so he could meet everyone. I wanted him to see what kind of marriage I had in mind. The mutual respect, the mutual taking care of each other, the not taking each other for granted.

As actors when you prepare for a role you have to do your research. I was preparing for the role of a married woman. We were preparing to be husband and wife. I wanted him to meet my amazing sisters and brothers-in-law. I wanted us to see how they interact, to bear witness to how they treat each other, to gain whatever insight we could. I especially remember watching Lynn and Al. Al gets up at 4:30 in the morning, exercises, then goes to work. He is bone tired when he gets home at five or six o'clock. Late in the afternoon Lynn would be at home cooking for him. As she prepared the family meal, she'd speak with such pride and such gaiety about her husband, his work, his actions, the things he'd say. She'd laugh, "I'm preparing dinner for Mr.

Askew," just giving him respect in a playful kind of way. Dinner would be ready before he came through the door. What stood out for Courtney was that when Al came home, he greeted her and the family first then said, "Sweetheart, what can I do for you?" Even though he had been up since before dawn, out all day and working hard for hours, he walked in with an attitude to serve her. You might have thought he'd go upstairs, take a bath, read the paper, go into a cave to decompress and not come out for hours. But he didn't. She'd greet him, of course, then tell him to sit down. When he asked what he could do to help, it made her feel good to tell him, "Absolutely nothing. You sit here. You put your feet up. What would you like to drink?" It was her way of saying, "Thank you for being so thoughtful, but I've got it covered." That's what I wanted for us.

Aside from these good examples, I didn't really know what that kind of marriage looked like from firsthand experience. I hadn't grown up in a home seeing a mother and father work together. As an actor—a person whose life and job it is to daydream and make believe—I felt it was important for me to have realistic expectations of what marriage should be; rather than my fantasies of being married to one of the Jackson 5. I didn't want my expectations to be grander or higher than the reality of what was going to happen. We wanted to make sure our expectations were in synch with each other. I didn't want to be disappointed because I was married and Courtney couldn't read my mind or because he wasn't exactly like me. I didn't want us to take each other for granted. I wanted us to appreciate each other and be grateful and say thank-you no matter how long we were married.

"Thank you for doing this."

"Thank you for doing that."

"Thank you for picking me up."

"Thank you for washing my car."

I want to feel appreciated for the things that I do and want to show him that I appreciate him, too. I knew we'd have to mindful. I'd heard psychologists talk about being careful with children with how you use you "no." How you shouldn't "no, no, no" them all the time—"don't, don't, don't." The admonition loses its power. You want to applaud children, reinforce them positively. I wanted to do that with my husband, as well. Thank him, be grateful, give him positive reinforcement and encouragement. I knew we needed help to get there, so we got it.

Chapter 17

Getting in the Groove

While I was planning my wedding, I was offered the lead role of Stella Payne in *How Stella Got Her Groove Back*, another Terry McMillan bestseller. I had already worked with Terry, the producer and the studio before, so that was good. The studio selected another male director, Kevin Rodney Sullivan, for this women's movie. (It's *so* hard for women directors, especially sisters.) But I fell in love with him, too. He treated me well and has a wonderful sense of humor.

Shortly after we met, I asked Kevin what he had in mind for the love scenes depicted in the script. I was pretty fine with doing them, but still needed to know what my director was thinking about how they would be performed. There was going to be some degree of "clothedness" and nakedness in the love scenes, and I wanted Courtney to be fine with it. The last thing I wanted was problems with my fiancé, my husband-to-be. I'm modest in that regard, but I really didn't want *him* trippin'.

"What do you see in your mind?" I asked Kevin. I left the conversation comfortable that the loves scenes would be more sensual than sexual. Sensual worked for me. I knew how to do it: a wrist, a look, the back of the neck, that kind of thing.

Before we started filming the movie, Kevin asked me to participate in a screen test with the three guys who were auditioning for the part of Winston Shakespeare. A tall brother from England was the oldest of the bunch. Physically, he was beautiful. He was a wonderful, very experienced actor with an impeccable Jamaican accent. But he was very slim about the chest—okay, let's just call it skinny. If you like your man skinny, he was right up your alley. There were also two American men of about the same stature; medium build, but more muscular. One was very, very fair skinned. He looked so young, like a baby—a little too young, to me. And then there was Taye Diggs, this beautiful chocolate drop. Taye was a young actor; his accent wasn't as perfect as the brother from England. But he was the cutie, heartbreaker, sweetheart type. *Stella* was supposed to be a woman's fantasy. Taye had more of the complete package—acting, looks, personality, physique. All of it!

We also wanted to identify hairstyles that would work for Stella. We needed looks that were sexy and free for her vacation in Jamaica and ones professional enough for the corporate environment where she worked. My personal hairstylist had asked if he could do my hair for the movie. Since I was allowed to request someone, I said, "Why not? You take care of it, that's what you do," and didn't think about it again. *Mistake!* I should have said, "Let's get together every weekend and figure it out together." It turned out he didn't braid hair. So in the month we would have had to get it together, he asked someone to sew some big, thick braids onto some fishnet stockings configured into a cap. The contraption was so heavy that when I put it on, my head snapped back. It almost gave me whiplash! Even the white woman in the room who had no clue about black women's hair was saying, "That don't look good. That don't look good at all!" Then there was this wig, which was supposed to be the corporate hair. But Kevin thought it looked like a helmet, not sexy enough. I was a little disappointed in myself because I hadn't stayed on it like I should have.

Anytime I'm filming a movie, there's always some dilemma. For this one, it became the hair. There was a surprising amount to think about: my own hair? braids? no braids? big braids? small braids? micro-braids? vacation hair? corporate hair? We were filming the movie out of sequence, so one day I might need braids and another day I meet need corporate hair. Plus, Stella was traveling back and forth between Jamaica and the United States. With the job she had, she couldn't just show up at work in some big, unprofessional-looking braids. Couldn't you just see her managers' reaction? All this had been set up in the novel; now it was left to us to figure it out logistically. We settled on a braid wig for when we were filming in the United States, and real braids in Jamaica, where three women braided my head into micro-braids over the course of twelve hours. The black woman's hair is always an issue.

The same day that we were trying to get all this hair stuff together, Kevin handed me the videotape of a French movie favorite of his he hoped would give me an idea of how he envisioned the more sensual scenes. I went back to my trailer, popped the tape in and started watching. The scene began with a man in an apartment lying on the sleeper sofa. Then he jumped out from under the covers and started walking around butt naked with his penis flopping all around. At first I was just shocked. "Oh, my gosh! There is *no way!* This is what he says *sensuality* is?" Later I asked the makeup artist who was applying my body makeup at the time for the Jamaican commercial, "Does that look sensual? It looks pornographic to me." I remembered visiting Paris and being blown away by the uninhibited sexual nature of their commercials. So just imagine.

Later on I said, "Ah, Kevin, before we start shooting these love scenes, I need you to draw me some pictures, give me little cartoons, stick figures, whatever. Because these people are full frontal in this ol' movie you gave me to watch."

He laughed. Yeah, he laughed. "Okay, fine. Okay, okay,

okay." Then he agreed to have it storyboarded, where images of the scene are drawn in sequence so you can see them and get a sense of what the director wants it to look like.

The second time I met Taye was on the day we rehearsed the logistics of the love scenes. "Hey, Taye, nice to meet you. Let's get into bed." While we rehearsed the positions, Kevin walked around the room with a video camera trying to figure out how he was going to film us. We did the bedroom sequences, the love scene in the shower and the sequences getting in and out of the shower. Needless to say, it was a little awkward.

During that rehearsal, I first saw the storyboard depicting the love scene in the bedroom after they get out of the shower. In succession the frames showed them lying on the bed kissing, then the man's head going down her body, then out of the bottom of the frame, then it popped back in again and he's smiling. Well, you knew what that was!

Oh, no! Oh, no! I don't like that, I thought. It was just so blatant. And I remembered this TV movie I had once watched—Laurel Avenue—where the male character was making love to his wife, he went out of the bottom of the frame, you imagined what was going on. In the very next scene the doorbell rang. Another woman at another house answers the door. The same man is now at her door. He kisses her and walks into the house. "EWWW! DO YOU KNOW WHERE HIS MOUTH HAS BEEN?" They needed another scene or needed to see him brush his teeth. Something! That's what this story-board reminded me of.

Since I have never filmed a love scene this graphic before and I was feeling uncomfortable, I figured it would be smart to ask Courtney about it. I lay the images on the kitchen counter.

"Courtney, I want you to look at this storyboard. I'm concerned about it."

Courtney looked then said, "I don't want to talk about it."

"Oh, come on, Courtney.... Give me your take on it. I need to know, what does it look like?"

"I don't want to talk about it."

"Are you serious?"

"Yes, I am."

"You're gonna be like that?"

"Angela, I told you that I don't want to talk about it."

I was shocked. Courtney acted like I had drawn the storyboard myself. In his defense, he was probably dealing with the scene from a "this is my woman" standpoint. I guess men don't want to imagine their women with other men, either for real or simulation. On the set some hormones and stuff can get rollin'. Many a romance has blossomed on a movie set. Here I had a costar who was really cute and young and virile. It's a real bed. And you really don't have your clothes on. I mean, you might have a few pieces on, strategically placed—a woman may have on a patch and a man may have on this sock contraption, especially if they're trying to show the sides of our bodies. By and large you're naked. I recalled having gotten pretty excited on the couch with my boyfriend at age fifteen and we had jeans and clothes on. But Courtney was going to see the scene eventually, during a preview, surrounded by a whole bunch of other folks. I thought if he and I could be comfortable about it, then we could go into the experience without hesitancy.

"Courtney, I'm an actor, you're an actor. We have love scenes with other people from time to time. I've got a director who's showing me French movies. I need to figure out how much we're showin'. I need somebody to bounce this off of. Look at the board. It looks like he's going down on me. How do you feel about it as an audience member? Am I being hypersensitive? Am I too close to it? Am I too prudish? What do you think?"

"Angela, this is hard."

"Please, Courtney? What's wrong? Come on... I need you to help me with this. I'm not trying to aggravate you or hurt your feelings. I don't like this. This is my job. I'm just asking you to look at it for my sake and help me so I can go back to Kevin sure and strong and say, 'No, I can't do this.'"

"Okay. I'm sorry. I just…"

"It's terrible, ain't it? Isn't it too much?"

"Yeah, it's too much."

Once we got over a few sticky moments, we were able to talk about it and work it out together. We decided that my natural reserve and caution could be part of the dynamic of the scene. After Courtney and I worked it out together, I went back to Kevin with my ideas about the scene and that's how it ended up being shot. During the shower scene, Taye wore the sock thing with fish wire holding it up. But it was cutting into his body and created a crease in his side that showed on camera. That wasn't working so they told him he couldn't use the sock.

"Do you mind if I don't have anything on?" he asked me.

"Oh, that'll be just fine. That's fine," I answered a little too quickly—I'm sure my nervousness showed. I tried to play the scene without looking down. Well, truthfully, one part of me kinda wanted to look; the other part didn't want to get caught. So I didn't look, I didn't see a thing. I don't believe I felt anything, either.

I *didn't*.

Chapter 18

At Last

ANGELA: On Sunday, October 17, 1997, I woke up without a care, without a worry. It was two months after my thirty-ninth birthday. Less than a year earlier I'd thought I'd never get married. Yet here it was, my wedding day. When I drew back the curtains, the sky was a beautiful turquoise blue—all hope and possibility. Usually the L.A. sky is pale, nondescript, and I miss the fluffy white clouds that float across the bright blue sky down South, back East, in Hawaii. The day before it had rained hard. Rain always washes the smog from the sky. You know the following day will be brilliant blue-blue with the white fluffy clouds I love from back home. These skies make me feel so happy. I get a sense of what California must have been like back in the 1930s—before smog. All sunshine and orange groves—very "Go West, young man."

I was excited that morning, but not "Oh-my-God" excited. You sometimes hear stories about wedding-day jitters. I was calm; I didn't have them. I guess you're not nervous when you're sure it's right, when there aren't any of the red flags people talk about. I hadn't seen one red flag. I hadn't had to duck one bone tumbling out of a closet. I knew red flags well; I'd certainly ignored them before. Instead, I felt calm and peaceful—the assurance you feel when you're doing the right thing and are really sure of it. I took a leisurely bath, made breakfast, read the paper. I didn't talk to Courtney; I would see him soon enough. It was just chill, chill, chill. Just me. Later, my bridesmaids—my sister D'nette, his sister Cecilie and my girlfriend Pamela Tyson—came over. We walked over to Lou's house, where the wedding would be performed, took the rollers out of our hair and got dressed. Later, my niece Alexandra (Lynn and Al's daughter), who was the flower girl, and Mama Emma, the ring bearer, joined us. I wore an ivory-colored V-neck Escada dress with a lace inset and little buttons going down the back and a little train. I thought I looked beautiful and elegant. While we dressed, the photographers took pictures of the wedding party. I wanted our photographs to be candid shots. I didn't want all that posing, nor did I like the idea of taking the bride and groom and crew far away for an hour and a half while everyone's starving and waiting and nibbling hors d'oeuvres. A couple of posed pictures or a smile here or there was fine. But I didn't want all that "come over here because the light is better." I just wanted the photographer to just catch it—grab it—and let us enjoy the moment, each other and our guests.

The wedding was scheduled for two o'clock, enough time for people who often work late into the night to wake up and get moving. We had invited about two hundred people. I wanted to keep it simple; I didn't want it to be over the top; I wanted understated elegance. That's how I like to describe myself, and that's how I want to keep it. We had tried to keep the wedding somewhat quiet, but somehow it was reported in one of the rags. You never know who will tell on you, sell you down the river for a prize, I guess. We had to fend off a couple of wedding crashers.

B. J. Crosby, our soloist, can really sing. She put her foot into "To God Be the Glory" by James Cleveland. The way she sings it, it really swells up and grabs you hard. She has such drama in it!

COURTNEY: Our wedding took place on the most beautiful October day. We had planned it to take place outside—without tents—and everyone had been worried about what kind of weather we'd have. There was a big storm the day before, but on our wedding day it was all blue skies—balmy and clear. I had stayed up late the night before—stuffing envelopes, doing this and doing that to get the space together. I wanted her to be able to sleep like a baby so she could be the beautiful bride everyone expected her to be. That morning I got up at 6:00 a.m. and got a haircut. I wore a black eight-button tux by an African-American L.A. designer named Dion Scott. My three groomsmen stood with me—Wren, my cousin David Daniels and Theron Cook—and all my guys were there, including Henry, who had pushed me to date her. Our two mothers and Angela's grandmother were sitting in the first row along each side of the aisle. I remember looking up and seeing Angela in her wedding dress. It was the most moving sight I'd ever witnessed—she was so beautiful! As I watched her walk down the aisle all gorgeous and giddy and silly, I welled up with emotion. To see how happy she was and how perfect everything was turning out and to know that I had played a role in helping her have the wedding she'd wanted really filled my heart. Yes, I was moved because it was our wedding, but it was made perfect through service. I realized what a gift it had been to her that I had overcome my frustration and practiced serving her as her soon-to-be husband. I felt proud that the first thing we had done together turned out exactly the way Angela had planned!

After Angela arrived at the altar, B. J. Crosby sang "To God Be the Glory." I listened to her words about thanking God for the gifts he'd given us. I thought about where I'd been just a few short years ago and where I was now. I was a "puddle" after that.

ANGELA: Two young men walked my grandmother down the aisle to steady her. She held the pillow with both rings on it. Had my father been living, I would have asked him to escort me. He hadn't been there to raise me, but he *had* contributed half my chromosomes. Since Daddy wasn't around I asked his brother, my uncle Jerry, who has been loving and kind toward me throughout my life. In modern times we're getting so feminist—feminists that some of us are. I didn't trip on that at all. I wanted my walk down the aisle to symbolize moving from the covering of my father's house to the covering of my husband's for protection and as the head of my household.

"Who stands with this man in marriage?"

Mrs. Vance stood.

"Who stands with this woman in marriage?"

My mother stood.

"Who stands with this couple in marriage?"

Our guests stood. Our whole world stood with us.

I stayed calm all during the wedding our vows. Courtney got choked up. I often wonder why so many grooms cry at weddings. Maybe they're feeling that now they've got to be responsible. Before, they could do willy-nilly what they wanted, when they wanted, how they wanted. But now that they are going to be married and bring children into this world, maybe they sense in that moment the gravity of life. Everyone is going to depend on them for everything—for food, for clothes, for shelter and for boundaries.

After we took our vows, Courtney slipped a beautiful wedding band onto my finger. It is intricately carved, like a leaf and grapevine. Filigree or something like that. Similar to the ring his mother wore while he was growing up. There's a plaque on the inside of the band that reads "ABVGODCBV" to symbolize that it's just the two of us—but we keep God in the middle.

I had purchased a ring for him that looked like the band his father wore.

Courtney acted a fool during our wedding kiss. He kept kissing me and kissing me. He wouldn't let me go.

COURTNEY: Angela's always been dramatic and you can bet she was when it came time to recite our vows. She was cute and funny and people just fell out! "This girl's crazy!" When the minister told me, "You may kiss the bride!" I said to myself, "Lord, I've been waiting to do this for a long time!" So I wrapped my arms around her and kissed her. And kissed her. And kissed her. In fact, Angela let go of me and held her arms out wide as if she was saying, "It ain't me!"—we had a little comedy routine going on. But I kept kissing her and kept kissing her. It was a beautiful moment....

After we all finished laughing, the minister said, "I now present you Courtney and Angela Vance." We turned to face our guests and walk out. As I walked past my mother, I reached out and touched her hand. I saw her face break. Seven years earlier my father had killed himself. After all we had been through together, her baby was finally getting married. I broke, too. We'd made it—we were all okay!

After the wedding everyone walked up the street to another neighbor's house for the reception. It was gorgeous—the flower arrangements, the chairs with gold things—I don't know what they were—on the back of them. I mean, it was just beautiful! When we had our first dance, we gave *them* a dancing lesson. We had taken a dancing class together but we had thrown that out the window after trying to figure out who was going to lead and who was going to follow. Instead, while Lou Rawls and Nancy Wilson sang "The Best is Yet to Come"—*Out of the tree of life I picked me a plum*... We just went out there and had the greatest time. Our dance was sexy and fun and funny. The party was the bomb!

In all, ours was the most beautiful wedding—understated and elegant. I had begun to learn that through service I would be able to make my wife happy so we could have the peace I envisioned us having in our home. Little did I know we'd have to go through a long process to get there. But that day was a celebration we enjoyed with our friends and family. That night was a celebration of our coming together in the way that we had decided we were going to come together. We had said that we were going to respect each other and respect God and we had done that. It was an amazing time to say, "Come here! We really did this. Thank you…."

Chapter 19

Back to Work

Even though we were on our one-day honeymoon, I was still working. I had to get my hair rebraided because I had to go back to work the following day. Ten hours of my one-day honeymoon were spent putting micro-braids in my hair. We spent one more wonderful night together. The next day we headed off in different directions. I went to Jamaica to finish filming *Stella,* and Courtney flew down to Mississippi to film *Cookie's Fortune.*

As we shot *Stella,* this women's fantasy, in that beautiful environment, I thought about how easy it must be to love when you're in idyllic settings. It's fun to be spontaneous and exciting. Yet a whole lot of life is lived in the mundane. It's about decision-making and making sure the water's running and the grass is cut. You have to return to life at some point. I realized it would be important for Courtney and I to schedule out time together—to do things that were new, things that were exciting, to enjoy little experiences together. *Stella* wouldn't be the last time I'd consider sex and nudity on screen. Perhaps because throughout history so many black women have been abused sexually, perhaps because of my religious values and perhaps because I was fondled as a child, I'm not comfortable being portrayed as a sex object. I've passed on wonderful projects over nudity. Most notably, *Monster's Ball.*

After we finished filming we went on our real honeymoon in Nevis, a small Caribbean island. Once we returned home, Courtney moved into my house. He had already been spending a lot of time over here, coming and going every day. Since he had been renting his house, we figured this house was a good place for us to start. We began to accommodate and make space for each other. I knew that for him to feel like he belonged here I had to make room for him. There was definitely an outstanding mortgage, so we could certainly contribute to that expense. I'd never want him thinking I could say, "It's *my* house!"

As we settled in, Courtney made it clear to me that I was now the most important priority in his life—ahead of work, ahead of his mother, ahead of his family, ahead of everyone else. Nobody had done anything to cause him to broach the subject. His mom or his sister hadn't made me feel bad or demanded an inordinate amount of his time—they wouldn't do that. Yet he kept repeating to me, "You are the most important person in my life. The wife's gotta come first. Everyone else is going to have to get in line." He wanted our situation to be in line with what the Bible says: *Therefore a man shall leave his father and his mother and hold fast to his wife, and they shall become one flesh.* (Genesis 2:24). His assurances made me feel very secure. A lot of problems come up when a grown man still put his mama first in his life—whatever Mama wants, Mama gets—as opposed to placing his wife first. Instead, a man should become the head of his own family, as husband. At the same time, Courtney also turned into the son my mother never had. He just loves her, and they talk, they get on really, really well, which is fantastic. As often as he talks to his mom, he talks to my mom. He keeps up with my family; he doesn't differentiate between my family and his. He keeps up with everyone.

Of course, we were eager to have children, but with our pastor's guidance, we decided to hold off for two years and establish ourselves as a married entity first. How do we work? How do we problem solve? How do we do things together? I knew how I had done things for thirty-nine years without input from another person—I might seek counsel but I still made my own decisions. But how would we do this together? We thought it was important to enjoy each other and work on our marriage for a while without the added pressures, demands and responsibilities of raising children. In some families children become the center of the family. We wanted our relationship to form the center, the nucleus, and have the children join us. I was healthy. We thought we had time.

Courtney took very seriously the responsibility of being the head of the household—of being the man, securing the household, that kind of thing; he took it to heart. In addition to putting his touch on our marriage, he began to put his touch on our household. Right away, he wanted to fix up the house. When I bought it, the walls had been painted a neutral white so it would be easy to sell. I hadn't done much since moving in. Spending a lot of money made me nervous because I never quite knew when or where my next job would come. That made it hard to plan for major expenditures. Courtney wanted our house to feel more like a home. He also wanted to organize and consolidate our finances and business affairs.

As we embarked upon this process of coming together, we began to discover that no matter how much you love someone, marriage is a lot different than going together. When you're single, *you're* the head of your household. Even though you're dating, ultimately you do your thing and I do my thing. You have your house and I have my house. You take care of your business and I take care of my business. We get together around some things, but my decisions are my decisions; your decisions are yours. Whatever you want to do with your life, your home, your things, your career, your money, your travel, your plans—they're your decisions. Of course, we had planned some things and done things together before. But to really accommodate and listen to each other in all those areas, that was different. Now that we were married we realized this is *our* house, that's *our* tree, that's *our* grass, this is *our* phone, this is *our* stuff, these are *our* bills! Two really must become one. Yet we kept behaving like two individuals, with two personalities and two ways—different ways—of doing things.

I still made my own decisions about the work I was going to do. If we wanted to talk about it, we could. But I thought it was best for us to continue to make our own decisions about the projects we wanted. I knew what I wanted to work on, I had been pretty good at choosing them so far, and I knew what satisfied my soul. I figured I might ask his input or ask him to read a script for further confirmation. But instinctually I know if a project is something that I want to do or not. I thought that for stuff that affected me, I should still make my own decisions. And as a woman—a fully grown woman, at that—I certainly had my opinions about things. Sometimes I had strong opinions and I could be set in my ways. I liked things done in a certain way, in a certain order and a certain time frame.

Now here came Courtney trying to change and rearrange things. Thinking we should paint the house, buy new furniture, create a family calendar, adhere to a household budget, put together a financial plan, work together to decide what projects we'd take, that kind of thing. The whole time we dated we had hardly had an argument. Not one cross word, not one "watch your tone." It was just happy to see you, all polka dots and moonbeams. But as soon as we got married, it was more, "Uh, that tone!" Courtney is sensitive, he's very sensitive. All of a sudden we'd be driving home from church talking about something, and maybe I'd make a joke or a sarcastic comment, and he'd ask, "What did you mean by that?"

"Do you think I'd hurt your feelings intentionally?" I might have taken a little jab or whatever but I meant it in fun; I'd never hurt his feelings on purpose.

One set of arguments we had revolved around decorating the house. It's funny now when I think back on it, but it was very tense at the time. I had hired a painter to paint a couple of rooms. Along the way, he found all sorts of other little projects to do. He was an inside painter but he might see something on the outside of the house he thought we should repair. I'd say, "Well, that does need fixing," and he'd fix it. Yet he tried to fix the shower door but ended up making it worse. Now the shower door wouldn't close. I had to hire someone else to fix it. That meant I'd paid to have the shower door fixed twice, but he didn't want to incur any of the additional cost. (That's when I learned the "stay in your lane" lesson. You're the painter, you don't need to be "fixing" the shower door.) And with every little thing he found to fix, the job lasted a little longer. And each thing he fixed, I paid him a little more money. Eventually with all his fixing of other things, he ran out of time to paint because he had another job that was already scheduled. In the meantime, there were places that weren't finished, places he had missed—part of a ceiling, inside a door frame, that kind of thing. He said he had to leave and start the new job and would come back.

At first I agreed. However, now we were on the honor system. Now, I'm good on the honor system, and I guess he figured he was honorable, too. But when he wanted to be paid the balance of the money I owed him, I told him, "I'll give you five hundred dollars now, and when you complete the rest of the job, I'll give you the other five." He got very indignant. He thought I should pay him and trust that he would, on his word, come back. When I wanted to hold back part of his payment, I guess to him I was insinuating something negative about his integrity. He told me he had basically done the whole job, so he expected and wanted the whole amount. At some point in the back-and-forth I said something not so nice about holding back part of his payment. He just got so upset that I said something like, "All right, all right, all right, here's the whole thing!" We left it that he'd come back and finish.

So after some time passed, Courtney called him to come back. The painter said something about me. It may not have been all that outlandish, but to Courtney's ears the man had insulted me.

"He insulted you and I don't want him back in here," he told me.

"I don't care if he insulted me or not," I told him. "He didn't finish doing what he was supposed to. I have paid him. He didn't do his part. I want him back in here."

"Well, I'm not going to allow someone in my house who has insulted my wife."

"I paid him complete and now I want the job complete. You're suggesting we should pay someone else to come and complete this job because you think he insulted me? Huh! He's gonna get his behind over here and paint this—or send one of his guys!"

We had one big ol' fight over that one. We were running up and down the stairs, this one overtaking that one, one of us out-shouting the other. I think I ended up in the bathroom with the door shut and locked. Courtney sat on the floor on the other side of the door. And waited. And waited. In the meantime, I sat on the toilet with my hands over my mouth, trying to keep the sharp words inside. Courtney kept waiting. Eventually I had to come out.

"Please, please," I finally asked him. "Courtney, can I just have this one? This man has gotten on my last nerve! I'm gonna lose my mind if he doesn't come back here and do what I've paid him to do."

"But you're my wife, he insulted you."

"Listen, Courtney, I'm asking you. I know you feel strongly about this, but will you acquiesce and let me have this? Can I please just have this one the way I want and need it? For me?"

"Okay," he relented. "For you."

Which was a good thing because we were at an impasse—over some paint. Some nothing.

We had another set of arguments when he wanted to start talking about children before the two years was up. I definitely wanted a family but now that I was presented with the reality of it, all my fears welled up. We both traveled when we worked. So how was that going to work? And I couldn't stop working—I was making more money than him, and it wasn't like either of us got a paycheck every two weeks. And I was a forty-year-old black actress. I'd seen what had happened to many of my female classmates and peers, regardless of their race. Roles are few and far between for middle-aged and older women. I felt like I needed to make hay while the sun was still shining. Plus, I love being an actor. I wasn't ready to stop working yet.

Sometimes we'd be talking about something and one thought would jump into my head and I'd start to say it, but then another thought would jump in and say, "Keep that to yourself—don't say that." He'd wonder why I didn't want to talk—he'd keep trying to get me to talk. But I needed to think about what I was going to say. Sometimes I'd realize that what I was going to say could be taken wrongly. Or maybe it wasn't nice. Perhaps it was the first thing that came into my head. Or perhaps it was something I'd heard someone else say at some point—there were a lot of feisty women in my family. But it wasn't always lovely. And it wasn't always constructive.

On more than one occasion I have to admit, I've been known to just say those kinds of things to D'nette. Sometimes when I see an area I think needs improving, I can be on her like white on rice. "Oh, I've got a new thing for you to try." When we were younger I used to constantly bring up the short end even though I was just trying to help her improve. Of course, that's not always how she saw it. I'd be telling her something I thought she should do, then all of a sudden I'd hear that choke in her voice that let me know I'd hurt her feelings. I'd feel badly that I hurt her. I'd try to make nice and change to another subject. Then I'd tell myself, "I'm not going to do that again. I'm not going to be concerned with the short end anymore. Just live your life and do your thing, and let her do hers." But then I'd find myself tempted to bring it up again. With my girlfriends I'm much more conscious of being gentle. I may say, "Why do you think of that?" instead of "Let me tell you what I think about that." But with my sister sometimes it's, "Listen, I know you're smarter than that and you need to do this, that or whatever." I can get on my sister's nerves—and I know sometimes I do—but she can't get rid of me, she can't divorce me. I knew my husband could if he wanted to. I began to think about my behavior differently.

As actors we learn that there is the text and then there's the subtext. There are the actual words that are spoken and then there's the meaning behind the words. There's your tone, and how much of it. Sometimes you might try to say something but the person only hears twenty percent of what you say because eighty percent of what you're communicating is conveyed by your tone. If your tone of voice isn't positive and supportive, sometimes the ear hears harsh or harsher words than are actually spoken. On the other side of the equation, we can often bear critique if the tone has love in it.

So during that time I'd start to say, "Oh, Courtney, why don't you do so and so because you never…" But that was wrong when I did it with my sister, it was wrong when I did it the last time to him and it is wrong now. Sometimes I'd catch myself; sometimes I wouldn't. But I'd think, Oh, girl, you know you gotta watch what you say and how you serve it. Sometimes my mother's voice would echo in my head: It's not just what you say, it's how you say it. I know *I* don't want to get hit over the head with the truth all the time. So I began to learn to start asking myself, "Do I really need to say that? Is it going to edify or enlighten? Is it something we both do? Is that something I need to say right now? Is this the right time? Is it the right tone?" Many times I'd decide to keep my own counsel—or change my tone of voice. Other times I might decide that it *was* something I wanted to say, but now wasn't the right time to say it.

As much as I tried, there were many times when I'd mess up. One time we were in Santa Fe having a wonderful, fabulous weekend. Riding back to the airport, something happened— a misunderstanding, a wrong tone from me or something. Next thing I knew, he was pulling over to the side of the freeway, getting out of the car, coming around, opening the door and kneeling in front of me.

"What just happened, babe?"

"It's okay. It's okay. It's nothing."

"No, it's not nothing, your voice changed."

"It's okay, Courtney. It's okay!"

Then, as traffic was whizzing by us on the highway, I looked into his deep brown eyes and realized that he really was committed to working things out. That talking it out, working it out was what was important to him—to the point of possibly missing our flight.

"Please, let's just try to talk about it. What the heck happened, babe? What did I do?"

But I'm not the kind of person who just gets over things. When I'm pissed or upset, I run away from the situation. I gotta work through it, process it, think about it. "Oh, it could have been this way." "Oh, I should have said that." "I should have countered this way." I think about where I was wrong; I have to work out what happened, how I was complicit in our blowup. Then I'd have to figure out, how does it work now? What do we do next? What must I do next? So it might take me a long time to come out of my little funk—not a month or anything like that or I'd have no friends left; usually just a few hours, maybe half a day or maybe a day at most.

Courtney, on the other hand likes to stay and deal with the situation.

Sometimes I would say, "I don't want to talk about it, I don't want to talk about it, I don't want to talk about it," trying to get away from the situation, and with him pulling me back in. At first he always wanted to talk right then, but I wasn't always ready to talk yet; I'd still be thinking about it. He had done therapy; I'd just done girlfriends. I needed to think about things first. I had learned that I didn't want to say the first thing out of my mouth. Now I wanted to say what I had to say in a way that was kind, and where he was not just listening but he really heard me, heard what I was saying. It can be so different trying to figure out how to talk to a man so he really, really hears you. I was still learning how to do that.

When I'd get all worked up, Courtney would take me by the shoulders and look me in the eye—look at me with his big, brown soulful eyes and say, "No. We didn't get married too soon. All couples go through this. It's not perfect all the time. We are going to go through this and we are going to get through this."

And he was sure about it and his confidence made me sure. I needed a man in whom I could see strength and resolve. His assurances made me strong in those weak moments. I learned that I'm not fickle at all; I needed the right man for me. Just looking into his eyes, I couldn't stay in my attitude, my fury, my righteous indignation. I found out that when we're upset with each other, our five-bedroom house suddenly becomes mighty small. I might be upstairs and he'd be downstairs or I'd be in one room and he'd be in another, but it would feel like there was a dark cloud all throughout the house. It would feel really oppressive and sap me of energy. And I couldn't not talk to him or go out into the world and, say, stay out late on purpose, thinking, Oh, yeah. He can just wait 'til I get home. I guess he misses me now. I didn't want to walk around with the weight of being upset on me. Every time I'd see him in front of me earnestly trying to work it out, it would just melt my heart.

About a year into our relationship—about a year after all this arguing, combining and consolidating—Courtney frantically awakened me one night while we were sleeping.

"Babe, babe!"

"Hey, yeah. What's wrong?"

"I think I'm dying!"

"Huh?"

"Call Dr. Young. Call my doctor."

Courtney had just been to the doctor. He takes good care of himself, always working out and taking vitamins. I knew he was very healthy. I realized he was feeling upset, but I didn't have any reason to believe something serious was wrong. It seemed more like he might have been having an anxiety attack. An anxiety attack is real, especially to the person who's having it. You do feel like you're dying.

"It's four-thirty in the morning now. Do you think you can wait until like eight, to a more decent time?"

"I can't."

"Okay, baby. I'll call him right now. It's going to be okay."

Dr. Young answered the phone as if he was awake, just waiting for the call. When you have an appointment with him in his office, he's the kind of doctor who doesn't just see you for five or ten minutes; he'll talk to you about your year and how it's been going. You think you're just having a conversation, but he's steadily gathering data. At the end of the conversation he'll tell you, "Okay, I want you to go do this test and this test" because of something you said, something you mentioned in passing and haven't thought about anymore. When Courtney saw him, Dr. Young probably realized that he had been trying to do everything. He knew Courtney wasn't dying. He talked to Courtney in a very calm and soothing voice.

"Don't you make any decisions. You have a wife there and you allow her to make the decisions and care for you."

And in that weak moment I had the opportunity to be strong for him the way he's always strong for me.

Chapter 20

How Two Become One

When we returned home it was the first time we'd lived together for more than a few days at a time. Before our wedding we had decided that I'd move into Angela's house. I had been renting, she owned her home and it was big enough for us. A few people had warned me "a man shouldn't move into a house a woman already owned." But we thought it made sense, and it has been one of the best decisions we have made as husband and wife.

I remember when I first brought my clothes over, she had cleared space for me to put them in her closet. I appreciated her thoughtfulness but turned down her offer. I already knew how that was going to play out over time. I needed some room to hang up my tux, my suits, shirts and shoes, but most of my wardrobe consists of T-shirts, sweats and blue jeans. Even when we go to formal functions, I wash, comb my hair, brush my teeth, put on some lotion, dust off my tux and am ready to go. For Angela, it's an all-day process. She has a stylist help pick out clothes and jewelry, a person to do her hair, she gets her fingernails and toes done, has someone "beat" her face, then she pulls it all together. With all that drama and its related accessories, I knew that eventually she would slowly but surely reclaim the part of her closet she had allowed me to occupy and I would eventually be left with a drawer! No thank you! It was a nice gesture that I was *supposed* to turn down. See, husbands have to know these things! She also "gave" me three or four drawers and my own cabinet in the bathroom. That worked. Of course, now I'm down to one drawer and half a cabinet in the bathroom, but at least I'm still in the room!

After I moved my clothes in, I wondered, "Now what?" We started figuring out some household logistics.

"You leave the dishes dirty like that? Okay."

"You don't like to cook or clean? Oh…"

"You do like to put flowers around the house? Okay."

"Well, I like to grocery shop. I take care of that."

"Are we going to create a budget? No? Well how are we going to manage our finances?"

During the first six months after our wedding, neither of us was home very much. Even though we were married and acting often requires being away, our love of our craft is so great neither of us wanted to give anything up. I had my list of projects I was planning to work on and she had hers. On top of that, we had separate management teams. She had her agent; I had mine. She had her manager; I had mine. She had her business manager; I had mine. She had her publicist; I had mine. For years we had followed our teams' recommendations and trusted them. But it quickly became clear to us that having so many people on two different teams directing our moves was causing chaos in our household. We needed a vision about how we would run our family. We were married, but the way we lived and approached important decisions about the amount of time we spent apart, our finances and priorities, we still acted single.

I felt that it was my responsibility as man of the house not to be the breadwinner, but to create an atmosphere of safety, stability and love within our family. I wanted to bring order to our household and thought I should lead the process. I knew that if Angela and I were going to thrive professionally for the long term, and successfully provide for and raise the children we envisioned, rather than all these people pulling us in different directions, we'd need to surround ourselves with people who had a vested interest in our family and our values. When I had been on the set of *Space Cowboys,* I got to see how Clint Eastwood worked. Clint arrived on set at six in the morning and left at six in the evening. Each day we rehearsed the heck out of our scenes but only shot them twice. Then he hopped on his helicopter and headed back to his home in Carmel so he could be with his family. That was the model I wanted to follow. I wanted to put family first.

During our premarital counseling our pastor had suggested that Angela and I spend two years getting to know each other and solidifying our marriage before having children. We thought that was a good idea; but we hadn't considered the implications of marrying later in life and her biological clock. I brought up the subject of children early on in an attempt to talk about creating a plan for them.

"How are we ever going to have children if both of us are always working and traveling?" I asked. "How are we going to raise them if neither of us is ever home?"

"Courtney, that's too much for me to think about right now," she answered. "We said we weren't going to have children for two years. I'm an actress, I love what I do. I don't want to think about children yet."

"But, Angela, we have to start planning now…"

"Courtney, that's too overwhelming. I'm doing this right now. I can't think about that."

"But, Angela," I pushed.

The next thing I knew, Angela was yelling at me and was closing herself up in the bathroom.

Oh, my goodness! What just happened? I wondered. "Angela. Angela…" I sat on the floor outside the door. What

had I done that was so horrible? For a few moments I pushed
for an answer, but the Lord told me to sit still, be quiet and not
to raise my voice. An hour later she came out.

"Baby, what did I do to get you so upset?" I quietly asked her.

"Oh, Courtney, it's not you, it's me. I shouldn't have—"

"But, honey, did I do something?"

"You didn't do anything, Courtney. It was me."

"What happened?"

"Courtney," she began slowly, "I want to have babies and start
our family, but there's so much on us right now. We said that for
two years all we were going to do was get to know each other. I
want us to do that. Thinking about babies right now is overwhelming to me. I want to have a family but I also love what I do.
If I stop working, am I going to lose my career? Will I have to
leave my craft? How will I make money? It's too much right now."

I understood what Angela meant; I was concerned about
some of the same things. Acting careers are very tenuous. No
matter how good you are or how much money you make, there's
no job security. Your livelihood can disappear overnight if you
make the wrong career move, someone decides you're not "hot"
anymore or you fall out of the public eye. Our careers were going
well, but Angela and I weren't kids anymore. There are not a lot
of roles for middle-aged people, especially women. There are
fewer roles for black, middle-aged actors and actresses. I wanted
us to figure out how to navigate through all these issues together,
but I didn't know how to get us on the same page.

"You've got to go to school—you have to study your wife," Dr.
Little would coach me. "You have to learn what she likes, dislikes
and how she likes things to be and go. That means you've gotta
be home sometimes and you've gotta pay attention. Then you
have to apply what you learn. It takes time, Courtney.

"You have to get a Ph.D. in Angela. Once you study her and
learn how to meet her needs, she's a good woman, order will
come to your household."

There was a part of me that understood that Dr. Little was right. I respected him and it was clear from his own life that he knew what he was talking about. He had a wonderful wife and five children and he'd recounted stories of how they'd survived challenging times. But we needed to make changes quickly, I thought. And there were times when I resented having to do additional work on myself. I had done so much work with Dr. K., I mistakenly believed I was done improving. I thought—*poof!*—our relationship was just supposed to happen. Although I had gotten saved, had been going to church and we had entered a spiritual union, I didn't realize I wasn't yet spiritually mature—or that spiritual maturity was important. And I didn't understand what marriage was about or how much *work* and *sacrifice* it is. There were times when I didn't *feel* like learning more about my wife. Did "putting Angela first," as Doc suggested, mean putting her needs before mine? Wasn't a marriage supposed to be 50/50?

Every marriage goes through rough patches. Ours happened early on, as we dealt with these kinds of issues. We struggled for several years, during a time when many marriages are still in the honeymoon stage. For my part I didn't know how to keep going emotionally during times when our union felt like 75/25 or 100/0. I didn't know how to get us working like a team. I didn't know how to keep going while I was waiting for my wife to understand that I had her best interests in mind, and trust me. I didn't yet understand that being the "leader" of my home wasn't the same as telling her what to do. Instead, I pushed her, manipulated her and tried to win and be right. When that didn't work, I'd sulk and pout. Rightly so, Angela resisted me a lot. Sometimes it was because she needed to grow in certain areas, but it was often because of how I approached her.

"I'm the only one trying to figure this out," I'd say to Doc then complain about something Angela had or hadn't done.

"Courtney, it's your job to 'cover' your family—to be the

'priest of your home.' That comes from practicing loving-kindness and making sacrifices. Sometimes it's not 50/50. Sometimes it's 100/0," he'd tell me. "Christ gave us the example of unconditional love, and you've made a commitment—a covenant—before God. Your role is not to 'fix' Angela. You need to put your nose in that Bible and work on understanding what a 'good man' really means. In the meantime, be patient with her, show her the example of the servant leader, and let God do the changing."

"Well, how long is that going to take?"

"It's none of your concern. You talk the talk, Courtney, but can you walk the walk?"

Walking the walk required a tremendous amount of effort. Sometimes I succeeded; other times I failed miserably or would resort to old tricks to feel more in control. Whenever I would complain, Doc would call me on my behavior.

"Men have been lying and trying to manipulate Angela for her entire life. You have to show her you're different. Just love her, Courtney. Lead by example and be patient enough to let God turn her. God will order your household by ordering you first. As he works on you, she'll see God in you and a different dialogue will begin. But he can't move on her until he orders you—you're the key. If you don't allow him to work on you and through you, nothing in your family will work."

"But, Doc…"

"No more buts, Courtney; just do it. This is on God's timetable, not yours."

"What am I supposed to do in the meantime?"

"In the meantime God will take care of you," Dr. Little reminded me. "God has your back, Courtney."

As I struggled to master various spiritual lessons, our relationship, which I had thought was so strong, floundered.

"Maybe we got married too soon," she said a couple of times within the first year we were married.

Oh, no! In my mind divorce could not be an option. I took off my wedding band and held it between my fingers in front of Angela's face.

"Do you see this ring?"

"Yeah…"

"This circle represents the continuity of our marriage. We are going to stay within it. There is no divorce—we *are not* getting divorced! We are going to figure this out—and we're going to figure it out together! Everything we need to do is going to happen within this circle."

"Okay…"

I knew that I didn't want to get divorced, but I didn't know how to be married. I often rebelled against the lessons Dr. Little was teaching and the ideals I was learning in the Bible. I longed for the freestyle kind of lifestyle I had experienced before I was married. I resisted so much that God began to box me into a corner to get my attention. During the first couple of years of our marriage, my career opportunities slowed down. For the first time in my adult life there were times when I wasn't working. That weighed heavily on me. I had been making less money than Angela, but that didn't bother me; I was working and making a solid financial contribution to our home. Now I wasn't working for months at a time. That had never happened to me. I felt very insecure—as an actor and a man.

Angela was facing similar challenges, but things were going much better for her. For the most part, she stayed busy. It had never occurred to me that my career would suddenly slow down. And in a profession where you know how you're doing partly by the way people respond to you, I had never considered what it would be like not to get the same amount of recognition I was accustomed to receiving. With my career stalling, my ego got fragile. From time to time when cameras would be popping around Angela, I would feel a little slighted. I wondered, What about me? We're a couple. It should be about both of us.

So many things were going wrong—from business teams undermining the order and organization I was trying to establish, to the shock of having all these disagreements with the woman I loved, to my disappointment that I hadn't yet earned my wife's respect, to now not having enough work. I reached a point where I felt like a broken man. One day I just fell to my knees.

"Lord, I can't do this anymore," I prayed. "We need order in our household—is that asking too much? What do I have to do?"

As I knelt by the side of my bed, I finally began to surrender my will to God's will. I knew I had been resisting the messenger of the Word he had sent to me. Doc had been trying to get me to read the Bible more, to practice what I preached and to be the "priest" of our home.

"Jesus came to serve not to be served. As the leader, you're setting the tone of love in the household. Follow Jesus' example and be a servant leader. If you start serving and supporting Angela, she'll see that you are the man you say you are and give you the respect you're looking for. Don't *tell* Angela what to do, *show* her. Do your work for two years and I promise you, God will reorder your home. He will bring you the desires of your heart."

I knew Doc was right. I needed to stop pushing back and to just do what God had been telling me through him.

"Not my will, God, but thy will be done," I prayed.

Once I surrendered, God began working with me. Now that he had my attention, he could take over. Everything started to change.

I decided to take up Doc's challenge to begin to look at life's circumstances as opportunities to practice the lessons I was learning as I studied the Bible. I realized that he was challenging me to apply Dr. K.'s advice to be patient—to let the "mud settle in the water"—but from a biblical perspective. I was beginning to understand why I needed to be patient; not just with Angela, but with everyone—rather than trying to force everything to happen myself, I needed to sit back and allow God to do his work! As I considered my life in this light, I realized that the times when I wasn't working presented a perfect opportunity. I stopped worrying as much about my employment situation and what Angela was or was not doing and went into study mode. I just focused on the Bible. When I woke up in the morning, I'd pray and read scripture before I did anything else. The more I learned, the more I realized that Doc's advice that marriage was a wonderful opportunity to practice walking like Christ was right.

While I "put my nose in the Bible," I also began to "study" Angela. I remembered Dr. K.'s observation that Bottom and I were so intertwined I knew how he was feeling even though we were unable to speak. How come I'd known when my dog wanted attention or needed to be left alone, but I didn't know that about my wife? Something was definitely wrong with that picture! I needed to take that lesson into my marriage.

As I paid more attention to Angela, I realized Doc was right—she is *very* complex. Men and women are different anyway, but women are *extremely* complicated. I had to learn to pay attention. Once I did, I realized she was easier to understand. Timing is everything with Angela. Her emotions and ability to focus are great gifts and they help her be a phenomenal actor. When she gets excited she focuses on something and really throws herself into it. But when she's focused like that, it's not necessarily a good time to talk to her about other things. Lots of times she doesn't feel like being bothered. That has nothing to do with me; it's just part of her nature. So why get sensitive about it? Now that I was paying attention, I began to be more subtle and flexible.

"Honey, I want to talk to you about managing our finances. Is this a good time?"

"No, not right now."

"Okay, no problem." I wouldn't take it personally; I wouldn't try to push. I knew it wasn't about me. I began to move at a pace that was comfortable to her and prayed through the rest of it.

The more I paid attention, the more I also realized that Angela wasn't always ignoring me when she didn't follow up on things I asked her to. I figured out that she gets overwhelmed when she's presented with too much information. When that happens she's likely to put things off. Before I realized this, her delays and indecision had been making me feel crazy. When it came to our family finances and business decisions, instead of overwhelming her with information, I started researching our options and presenting them to her in a positive and encouraging way. I'd show her what I'd learned, explain what our options were and what decision I thought was best and why. Then I'd answer all her questions, and we'd pray for God to help us make a good decision. Sometimes she liked my ideas, sometimes she didn't. Sometimes she'd answer things when I wanted, sometimes she didn't. I had to accept that. At least she would go through her process and eventually get back to me. I didn't feel dismissed or ignored.

As I began to acknowledge that she wasn't as unreasonable as I'd believed, I also admitted that by trying to be right and to win our fights I had been contributing to the situation. I decided that in the future I'd be willing to apologize first, to say I'm sorry for something I didn't even know what I was apologizing for, and even to get a little "mud" on my face so there would be peace in our home. It wasn't always easy; it was a process. At first the "natural man" in me would say, "I didn't do it. I'm not apologizing. *She's* gonna apologize to *me*." But I was learning that God can't heal a situation where there is no forgiveness. If two people are at an impasse, someone's gotta take the first step. And that is the major part of leadership. The spiritual man in me decided I was willing to go first.

"I'm sorry, Angela. I'm not quite sure what I did, but I didn't mean to make you upset."

"Courtney, you didn't do anything…"

While I studied Angela, I also practiced performing the task Doc had challenged me with: making the effort to walk like Jesus by loving and serving my wife. I started asking her new questions:

"Is there anything you need, baby?"

"How can I help?"

"What do you want me to do next?"

Rather than "keeping count" of who had done what for whom, I began looking for ways to please and serve Angela. I started focusing specifically on making sure she was happy. I took responsibility for being the "priest" of our household and bringing love into our home. I knew that Angie liked flowers but wouldn't buy them for herself. So on Tuesdays and Thursdays I started getting up at six in the morning and going to the wholesale flower mart. Believe me, I didn't want to get up at six but I did it anyhow. I'd buy flowers for the whole house and arrange them in vases so she could put them wherever she wanted. By the time she'd get up, the flowers would be lined up on the kitchen counter and I'd be off to the gym. I wouldn't even bring it up. I'd fill the refrigerator with groceries and not look for "extra credit." I'd cook for her when she wasn't expecting it. I started planning little surprises for her birthday and our anniversary. For her fortieth birthday I told her I was going to treat her to a weekend on the town in New York. I wined and dined her and took her to functions and plays. But the trip was a diversion; back home, I was throwing her a party. When we landed back in L.A. she wistfully said, "I guess that's it, huh?"

"Well, there's one more thing back at the house," I told her. "There's something for you sitting on the front steps."

She picked up the package and I opened the door for her. As soon as she stepped in, all her friends yelled, *"Surprise!"* She was in shock. All the people she had just seen in New York, plus her mother, D'nette, all her L.A. girlfriends, Mama Bear, almost everyone was there.

Another time for a birthday gift, I had the backyard land-scaped and lighted for her. On the night of her birthday, I held an "unveiling." Then fifteen of our friends jumped out and we had a surprise dinner party on the patio.

I planned little trips and couples outings with people we liked. I tried to make sure there was a smile on her face.

As I began to serve Angela by submitting my ego to God, the way she dealt with me changed. I was amazed by the results! A thaw started to happen. We stopped fussing and fighting almost altogether—today we rarely get in an argument. She responded to my needs and she gave me the respect I needed. She raced to do things for me before I could do them for her.

We soon reached a point where we both started to want to do things to please the other person.

"Well, I was going to do that for you."

"Oh, I was going to do it for you."

"Ohh…"

When that starts to happen, the marriage kicks to another level. I began to feel more like the man I aspired to be in our relationship. I didn't feel insecure. When we'd go out in public and the photographers would call her name, I'd encourage her to step forward and I'd move out of the way. While the flashbulbs were popping and people were calling her name, I'd chill and talk to the publicist. In a few minutes she'd call, "Honey, come over here. They want to take some pictures of the two of us together."

Doc informed me that I was experiencing one of God's

many dichotomies: "When you humble yourself before God, he exalts you. Humility," he said, "is the greatest virtue in the kingdom of God." I was seeing how wonderfully it worked. And in a society that focuses so much upon women submitting, it was amazing for me to learn "the power of a submitted man"!

Chapter 21

Fearfully and Wonderfully Made

Over the first two years of our marriage, Courtney and I got our differences ironed out. For the most part it's been smooth sailing since then. I was forty-one when we began trying to have children. We started the old-fashioned way. About six months passed and nothing was happening, so we added in temperature taking—charting when I ovulated by measuring my temperature. I had this chart by the bed and when my temperature rose over 98.6 I knew I was ovulating.

"Come here, Courtney!"

Well, that was fine by him. Early on. But I'll tell you what—love on demand can become a drag.

So we did the temperature thing for a few months, but it wasn't working. The doctor would ask me, "Are you under stress?"

"I don't feel like I'm stressed."

Maybe I don't know what stress is if it's not anxiety or butterflies in my stomach. I didn't have any butterflies, anxiety, worries or fears. I was just trying to figure it out. Then there were months when we didn't keep up with it because one or both of us was working on a project and we weren't physically in the same place. We weren't so conscientious that on the day I was going to be ovulating one of us would jump on a plane.

We didn't take it to that degree—*that* would have added stress to our life. It was just we're here, my temperature is up, let's try it this time around.

When that didn't work, the doctors conducted tests to make sure my fallopian tubes weren't blocked. Some of the tests were kind of painful—shooting dye into me, for example. But that was just part of the process of making this happen. I was willing to go through it. Then they tested Courtney to check his sperm count and sperm motility. When both of those were fine we moved on to artificial insemination. Artificial insemination seemed pretty easy—when you're ovulating they get the sperm up as close to the egg as they can. But it didn't work for us. So the gynecologist suggested that we step it up a notch and try in vitro fertilization. In vitro is a commitment; it's an everyday thing and it's expensive. Fortunately we've been blessed to be able to do it without being concerned about the cost. When you do in vitro they're constantly testing your blood and you're back and forth to the doctor. I had to take shots twice a day in my stomach—in the morning and evening—to stimulate the ovaries to release a lot of eggs every month instead of just one. They look at the eggs using ultrasound—there's one, there's one, there's one. Then they aspirate them out of you, put the sperm in them and see which will grow in a Petri dish. An embryologist watches the cells subdivide—first in two cell, four cells, then eight. They then take the healthiest-looking ones, tilt you up and put them back in so that they'll implant in your uterus.

At some point I learned that the eggs wouldn't implant; my uterine lining was too thin. But one month, the nurses told me my hormone numbers had started going up. "We don't want to give you any false expectations, but maybe you will get lucky," they told me. Well, I don't believe in luck; I had been praying on this for years and believed my prayers had been answered—and on what better day than on my birthday. And at some point Courtney had had a dream that we would be having twins. I was so excited! It was too early to take a pregnancy test but at my birthday gathering at our home that evening I shared the good news with our friends. Many of them already knew what was going on, but I filled everyone in on what we had been going through and gave them the good news that we were finally pregnant. It was a wonderful evening. We ate good food, cake, hugged and kissed, and there were kids all around. It was a glorious, glorious night!

A few days later Courtney and I traveled to Martha's Vineyard for vacation. Now, I'm pretty in tune with my body. Women, you know how right before your period, your breasts get tender or you crave sweets or whatever, then your cycle starts and your breasts are fine or you can walk on by the sweets? Well, nothing like that was happening. After a couple of weeks I was feeling quite like myself—in fact, right regular. I didn't feel like I was pregnant; it didn't feel like anything special was goin' on. I couldn't wait 'til we got home so I could get to the doctor. And, sure enough, once we got there I learned that nothin' was goin' on. The embryo had dissipated. I guess they call it the "miracle of childbirth" for a reason. And maybe that's also why people tell you to wait three months before you tell anybody.

Needless to say, I felt sad and disappointed. But I didn't feel devastated—it wasn't like I wanted to take to my bed and not come out from under my covers or anything like that. It didn't work out, so I knew it wasn't meant to be. I thought that maybe God had a bigger blessing in store for us that I couldn't see with my limited human vision. I know I can't see what's going on behind my head and that my peripheral vision is limited. I also know that God holds the whole world in his hands. He's omnipotent, omniscient, omnipresent. I know I can't be everyplace and know everything. But he can. So I leaned into my faith.

One Sunday at church a guest preacher said, "All women who want to have children, come up to the altar." I walked forward. This preacher prophesied over me, "I see you with two babies." People have different spiritual gifts. Some have the gift of prophesy. So knowing that this man had been so clear and so sure, his vision strengthened me.

As we continued through the process, Courtney and I talked to other people we personally knew or heard tell had gone through similar experiences or recommended their doctor. Brooke Shields shared with me that she had gone through in vitro a number of times. I hoped I wouldn't have to go through it as often as she had. Along the way I actually got pregnant twice without the in vitro. I miscarried both times.

Sometime in the middle of all this, Courtney was offered a recurring role on the television show *Law and Order: Criminal Intent*. It would require that he spend a great deal of time in New York. Now, Courtney and I are homebodies. We love to spend time together, we have fun together. He loves to putter around the house, doing this, doing that. We went back and forth about whether he should take the role.

"Tell 'em no!" I told him at first. But later I thought, How could I say that? He enjoys what he does; I enjoy what I do. I wouldn't want him to tell me, "No, you can't go someplace to do a project that means a lot to you." I wouldn't want that for anything in the world. I realized I really had to eat my words. It wasn't like he was going to the other side of the world. Other people we knew had done the bicoastal thing and done it well. He had other cast members who were married and bicoastal. Some of them make it work even though they have children. We didn't have to factor children's best interests into it.

"Do you really want to do it, baby? Will it satisfy your soul?" I asked him. "If you want to do that, then go. We'll make it work. It will be fine. It will be wonderful. It will be perfect!"

I realized that Courtney's new job would give me the perfect excuse to go to New York more often. The television-filming schedule is similar to the school year. They start in September and go until Christmas. They break and return in January, then finish in late June. We decided I could visit him six or seven times in the fall—about every two weeks. Then I'd be done with it because New York winters are too cold. He could come home for the holidays. I'd go out a couple of times in the spring. Then he'd be off in the summer and live in Los Angeles. I knew that sometimes it might disrupt our attempts to get pregnant, but we might as well do it while it was just he and I.

When Courtney isn't here, I enjoy my own company and spend a lot of time with friends. When Courtney is around, it's me and Courtney. We have a good time and we hang out and I don't see a good deal of my friends. It actually works well.

Eventually, after three doctors, seven in vitros, two miscarriages, taking drugs, drugs, drugs—drugs to thicken my uterine lining, drugs to make me ovulate, drugs to make me not ovulate—getting acupuncture, drinking those nasty, muddy teas to strengthen my chi because it's been shown that it might be helpful and some people claim it worked for them, after driving to this doctor, to that doctor, after crisscrossing town to find the right specialist on top of keeping up with work and my life, I started getting a little weary, a little discouraged.

"My gosh, aren't I doing enough?"

A part of me wanted to give up, but the bigger part of me knew I had to maintain my faith, that it still could happen. I'd pray, I'd cry. "Oh, my God, it's not going to happen." If I only knew how many more times I had to go through the process, I knew I could make it. "Oh, four more times? Okay, I can do that," or "Is it never going to happen? Okay, just let me know." I knew I could live with it.

Courtney had always said, "If you want to quit, that's fine with me," but I knew he really wanted children. I'd seen him with children; he was wonderful with them and seemed to enjoy them so much. I wanted to give him his own. And now that my biological clock was ticking, when I'd see a little baby I'd think, "Ohh, so cute!" I started noticing babies everywhere. They were all so precious. But I'd hear Courtney differently now when he'd say, "You can quit." In my life I'd learned you're supposed to keep going, keep going, keep going. And when he'd tell me I could quit, in my own mind it became a bit of reverse psychology; it became a challenge.

"You can quit."

"No, I won't quit."

"You're tired, Angela. I understand. If you don't want to go through the blood draws, being stuck with needles, running all over town, reading books about people who have gone through this, talking to people, it's okay. It's really okay."

Eventually I began to consider other options. We began talking about the possibility of adoption. I started talking to different people about it—my mom, Courtney's sister and her husband, who had adopted a boy; my oldest sister, Jane, who had adopted two children; Courtney's cousin and his wife, who had adopted a little boy. We were comfortable with adoption; it's part of our family tree, our family makeup. It's no big deal. We began exploring the different adoption Web sites.

And that was the plan until I ran into my friend Kathy.

"Angela! Guess what?"

"What?"

"In five months we are going to have triplets!"

"*Whaaat?*" I looked at her; she didn't look pregnant. "What are you talking about?"

She explained that she can't have children, yet her partner always wanted to have a daughter. So they hired a surrogate. They hadn't planned on having triplets but that's what happened. "Their coming is a blessing and we're going to work it out," she told me.

Oh, my God! I thought. I didn't know that I felt comfortable with the notion, but could this possibly be the way?

Well, I came home and relayed the story to Courtney to kind of feel him out.

"I was with Kathy today and she told me they're having triplets, and how it's happening is through surrogacy." I explained what little I knew. "What do you think about that?"

"That sounds great, hon. Let's check it out." Courtney was very open to it from the beginning. But that's him, Mr. Quick Draw McGraw. Give him a directive and he's going to make it happen.

Me? I need to feel it out. I'm just sort of gonna suss it out, feel it out, talk it out, see if the timing feels right. "What do you think? Oh, okay…" Maybe in the days and the weeks to come, I'm just gonna kind of think about it. It may not seem like I am but somewhere in there, I am. It's just like how I pack for a trip. You may not see me pack the week before, but I'm thinking about the things I have to take. So the night before, when I finally pack, I've already thought it out.

Courtney was so certain, I got kind of scared—because I know him. I knew that if we went into this thing, if we got on this train, we would have to see it though to its final destination, to the end point. The idea was different from anything I'd ever considered in my life, but I had to admit it was kind of intriguing. It would still be our DNA, so we could be the natural parents, which is what we had been trying to do. But it seemed like it could be fraught with problems, expensive, and it seemed unnatural. Did I really want to do this?

I didn't bring the subject up again, but a couple of days later Courtney nudged me. "What about that idea you mentioned? Maybe we could talk to the woman who helped Kathy."

"Oh, okay, I'll call. I'll set up an appointment."

We couldn't be against this idea because it could possibly make our dream come true. I find that when you don't understand something it's easier to be against it. But we needed to know more, so we talked to the head of Kathy's surrogacy program. The offices of the program were located really close to our home. (Hmm… How convenient. Who knew? Was this a sign?) We talked to the woman for about three or four hours. We got info, were just learning, just hearing. What is it about? What is it? How does it work? We learned that there are quite a few surrogacy programs around Los Angeles. California is one of the states where the laws are favorable to the intended parents. In California, the intended parents are legally the baby's parents, so you don't have to legally adopt the child from the woman who carried him or her for you. We learned that there are a lot of ways to approach surrogacy in terms of the baby's DNA. One way involved doctors administering medication that would shut down the surrogate's ability to ovulate. She would also abstain from sex with her husband. Then our embryo could be placed in her uterus and she would carry the baby to term.

After the appointment was over we were definitely open to the idea. I mentioned it to my mom. She was against it. I really couldn't even talk to her about it. Fortunately, her lovely son-in-law explained the whole deal to her and she heard him. It was wonderful. I don't know what his mom said, but she must have been all right with it. Anyhow, I wasn't ready to do anything with any of the information. So I just let it go and sat on it for a couple of months.

Well, after a while Courtney being Courtney, he started chompin' at the bit. He had already come to find out that with me timing is everything. He's come to know that I'm feeling it out, feeling it out, slowly mulling it over. Eventually he brought the subject back up.

"Babe, what's happening?"

"Um, I don't know…."

It was still a very fresh idea to me. I felt I had more to learn.

And I was wondering if this was the right organization to work with. It was the first place but was it the right place?

"Let's talk to somebody else, let's talk to another place," I suggested. I figured the more times you talk about it maybe different things will come up, different considerations; something another person didn't bring up that could make a difference. And it's a very expensive proposition. Having your own baby costs a certain amount. But when you're hiring a surrogate, there are all kinds of things to consider. If she has twins, it's more; if she has a C-section, it's more; she needs insurance; you both need lawyers to keep things nice and clean; you want a maid to come clean her house; she needs a wardrobe for maternity; she has to go to the doctor; if she and/or her husband take days off from work, you want to compensate them—that kind of thing. Adoption was much, much cheaper.

In the meantime I kept praying. One of the women in my prayer group at church offered to be our surrogate. My assistant at the time offered to carry for us. They were so sweet. We never considered taking them up on it, but I was touched; my heart was warmed by their compassion, their sincerity, woman to woman.

That December 2004 we took part in the Kennedy Center Honors, the lifetime achievement awards for people in the performing arts, that takes place at the Kennedy Center in Washington. That year the awards were honoring James Earl Jones, whose performance when I was fifteen lit the spark for my career. Courtney was asked to participate in the program, as were Charles Dutton and Kelsey Grammar. Before the ceremony the three of them spent a little time together getting their parts right. I remembered that I'd read someplace that Kelsey and his wife had had a baby by surrogacy.

Later I asked Courtney, "Would you feel comfortable calling Kelsey and asking him what company they went through?"

"Sure, babe!"

Kelsey was kind enough to talk to us. He referred us to another surrogacy organization. Whereas the first was a more boutique "mom and pop," this place was more corporate—"We've been doing it from the beginning." We talked to people who ran the company, couples who had been through the experience and women who had been surrogates. We met people whose opinions ranged from "We are helping you create your family" to the woman who quoted from the Bible: *Now faith is being sure of what we hope for and certain of what we do not see* (Hebrews 11:1).

Our comfort level increased. I left feeling encouraged in my spirit, excited even. "Okay, we're going to have faith. We're going to have this baby!"

We began to believe that maybe this was the way the Lord was blessing us. We had known of one way—traditional childbirth—but God knows of many ways. Maybe the old-fashioned way wasn't the way; the Lord had something different in mind: adoption, surrogacy, maybe even somebody leaving a baby on our doorstep. I started telling more people what we were thinking, to see how they would react. I talked to my college roommate and told her what was going on.

"Mary was Jesus' surrogate mother."

"Oh, my gosh! I had never thought of that." I'm not trying to compare myself to Mary or our children to Jesus. But the idea that Mary had carried a child that was not her own made me feel more comfortable.

Eventually we decided to go for it.

At the company we selected to manage the process for us, you don't just select your surrogate, they have to choose you, too. (Another girlfriend of mine had a different experience. She was given the files of ten different surrogates to look through. She chose the woman.) Courtney and I had to put together a book that told our story, which the company would present to the potential surrogates. It became our little production. Courtney began to write out our story. I thought the first draft was a little heavy duty, a little too "I love the Lord!" I thought it might put somebody off; you don't know who your surrogate is going to be. So I worked on it and shaped it a little bit. I wanted them to know that God is important in our lives, but I thought they should see more of who we are as people. I had fun selecting the right book, going through our pictures and trying to make them match the text, almost like a silent movie. Then I made five copies—four for whoever would get them and one for us to keep, that's a part of our history. We'll share it with our children. Then we anxiously waited. We didn't get any information about what was going on—until we learned a couple had chosen us.

Now, meeting your surrogate family is a very, very interesting and surreal experience. It's very, very intimate. It's hyper-intimate. You don't even know them, yet you need them so much. They're going to carry your baby and then give it to you and go back to their lives, yet they even don't know you. Ours was a first-time surrogate, married and already a mother. (To protect their privacy, I'll call the couple Stephanie and Kevin.) I don't know how Stephanie was feeling, but I was very nervous. What do you talk about with someone who you don't know but who might make your most precious dream come true? What do you say to someone you don't know whose baby you're willing to carry then part with because you're that giving, that loving, because you know that you've been blessed?

Stephanie was very quiet and sincere. Kevin was very kind. They were very, very, very kind and sweet.

"Have you ever done this before?" I asked them.

"It's our first time," Stephanie answered.

"What makes you want to do it?"

"We love our children. I love being a mother. We've been

blessed to have children and to be able to be parents. We'd like to share our blessing."

"Wow…. You're amazing people. That's incredible."

"What would you expect from us afterward?" Courtney asked. Relationships with surrogates can look many ways. Some families stay in touch with each other, others send occasional photos, others never see each other again.

"Oh, we don't expect anything. It would be nice to see pictures of your family from time to time—how it turns out, how the children grow."

"Well, you wouldn't have to worry about that," I laughed. "We've got Mr. Shutterbug here. You'll definitely see some pictures."

It was incredible to me that in Stephanie's spirit all she wanted was to help someone. It takes an incredibly, incredibly special person to do something like that. It's beyond my imagination. Thankfully, Stephanie and Kevin selected us.

Now while all this was going on, Courtney had been having a dialogue with John Guare, author of *Six Degrees of Separation* and one of the most accomplished playwrights in the country, about performing in a play, *His Girl Friday,* a movie from 1940, at the Guthrie Theater in Minneapolis, one of the foremost regional theaters in the country. At some point it came up that I would be perfect as the character Hildy. Courtney mentioned the possibility to me, but he knows it takes me a while to read something unless you tell me it's starting next week. So we all got together for lunch—Courtney, me, John and Joe Dowling, who I'd never met before but who had been running the Guthrie for the past seven or eight years. They were delightful and fun and I decided I wanted to do the play. Courtney and I were going to spend the summer in Minneapolis!

Of course, Courtney and I had never worked together before and were very excited to do so for the first time. We discussed what it meant to be working together as a married couple and came to some agreements. We wanted to provide the best possible model of Christian love and respect and cooperation. We were determined not to give them any marital drama whatsoever. And I resolved that I was not going to try to direct my husband.

Once we arrived at the Guthrie, we saw that Joe had assembled a phenomenal cast. Minneapolis is a theater town—they appreciate the theater, they love theater. If you're an actor you can make a living in Minneapolis. In fact, I learned that one of my drama-school classmates, Izzy Monk, is just beloved there. I'm sure the other actors had probably seen us in films and on TV and may have been thinking, "lazy actors!" It's a whole lot harder to do theater than television or film. Onstage, you've gotta get it right the first time; there is no "take two." But even though Courtney and I hadn't been onstage in years, we were going to work as hard as they did and be up to the task and surprise them. We could have shown up as celebrities and rented a house, gotten a maid and acted all grand. Instead, we took it back to our regional theater days. We just wanted to get back to our roots and just work. "This is the housing for actors right across the street for the theater? Okay, that's where we want to stay." But since we were two different actors, we did ask for two separate apartments.

So it was a good time. But it was stressful—good stressful—especially for Courtney. He was the star of the play, the engine of the piece. He needed to have a high level of energy and intensity and focus. My role wasn't as important as his, though I had to gun it, too. The play is a lot about rhythm and pace. The dialogue is quick, quick, quick. You finish each other's sentences. I mean, to the point you are just out of breath! Once Courtney and I started working together we discovered that we were a little different. Courtney is the studious type. Of course, he had a lot to memorize—the play was two hundred pages and they were shaping and cutting and taking away lines and adding new lines. He claims I have a photographic memory, but I think it just comes a little easier to me. I could sit up and watch *Entertainment Tonight* and get my lines. I'd go to bed at ten and leave him working. But when I'd get up, there he'd be—still studying. Poor thing. I felt so sorry for him! I'd want to run lines with him but that wasn't the way he studied. He had such a hard time for the first several weeks.

The apartment across the hall from me seemed like his little prison cell. I wasn't sure we were going to have enough time to get it together before we were in front of an audience. Still, I knew he'd done three-character plays where you don't have twenty-five other people to take the heat, take up some of the words, and plays where he'd had to do South African accents and things. So I knew he was up to it. He just wasn't ready to run lines yet, though I *would* have liked to be able to do our lines together—for him to just be able to run them with me so I could hear another voice and know my response. We also thought about our workday differently. I'd have liked to rehearse in the evening so I would have had a little preparation before I went in with the other actors the next day. I wanted to get to tomorrow's work tonight. Courtney does the opposite. The work he does onstage that day, he wants to revisit in the evening. Tomorrow's work he wants to worry about tomorrow. He greets the day and starts from there.

Even though I promised myself I wasn't going to direct him, as soon as I got there, I was like, "Courtney, I think you should…"

"Angela, you promised not to do that!"

"Oops!" He done shut me up. My feelings were a little hurt. I wanted to shut my own self up. Instead, all I could say was, "Yep! I know you're right."

Three weeks or so into the process something clicked for him. He started to get it.

And I could say in a more supportive tone, "You know what,

Courtney? You did that with this and that was great. But I was thinking this other thing. What do you think? Am I crazy?" I could help my husband be his best, and he could hear me, and it could turn out okay.

Opening night before we went onstage, I remember I was in my dressing room putting on my false eyelashes. Courtney came into the room. He was so dedicated, he had been at the theater for two or three hours getting warmed up, drinking tea, doing his Linkletter freeing-the-voice vocal exercises. You're only required to be there thirty minutes early. I might get there an hour early. We said a prayer that we all have a great performance, that it's a great night in the theater for everyone. Then he'd start rocking back and forth with his towel around his neck. He's gotta pump up his energy because that's the way his character is—he bursts onto the scene making deals and twisting the truth. Then maybe twenty minutes into the play Hildy—my character—would show up. I'd have this fantastic red suit, red coat, red hat, red purse and heels. I had the 1940s thing down—the cigarette, movements I don't usually make, the hands on the hip, the banter, the *je ne sais quoi*. I remember feeling aware of my body, my voice and the audience. I would look across at Courtney. I'd see him with his hair conked—processed—that pencil-thin mustache, that 1940s suit. And for a quick flash of a second I might see him working and hear the audience laughing and think in passing, I *love* to work with Courtney! But then he'd have so much energy that he would jump on my line—cut me off too soon. Then I'd think, "Courtney, you'd better cut that out! Look at the script." It was hard work, but it was gratifying. We were just in awe every day. After all of the challenges we'd faced early on in our marriage, we had loved each other and ourselves and worked through them. We had worked through our differences in how we worked as actors. We learned how to approach our parts separately yet meld and come together. We learned how to accept each other's uniqueness. And now we were working together. We were in awe and it was brilliant! It was brilliant!

Night after night the audience loved the play. The audiences in Minneapolis are so appreciative and so savvy. It didn't matter that Courtney and I were black and playing in roles from the 1940 movie starring Cary Grant and Rosalind Russell. They paid their money. They bought the seats. The lights went down, we told them the way it was and they agreed. They bought it. They believed it. And that's what theater is all about: transporting belief. Opening night, Izzy came to the show. So did Sharon Reich, one of my freshman-year roommates. Today she is a doctor at the University of Minnesota. I got to meet her husband and daughter.

Meanwhile, back in California, our surrogate was going through the process of preparing herself to get pregnant. We knew the process was in capable hands—hers and the doctors'. One, two or three occasions Courtney and I had to ask for a break in our rehearsal schedule to participate in activities related to our surrogate. When the doctor places the embryo in the surrogate, we participated by conference call. I'd been through that process before and knew it was private and that we wouldn't be in the room anyhow. Courtney wasn't even in the room when I did it. But we could have our voices there in the room so we could talk to Stephanie and support her. We could all talk to each other. That was good. We had been told the odds—there was only a sixty percent chance that each egg would work out positively, so we had agreed to implant two embryos. But at the last minute the doctor said he was going to implant three embryos to increase our odds.

"You've been through so much," he said, "I want to put in three to give you the best chance."

We had already agreed we were going with two. She was younger than me. You're supposed to have babies in your twenties, so her uterine lining was thicker than mine. We figured we'd have the doctor put in two and see what we get. We'd either get none, one or two—unless one or both of the embryos split, in which case we could get three or four. It's rare, but it has happened. So we had all discussed this from the beginning and agreed upon two. We were all clear. None of us wanted to do more than that. Now at the last minute, the doctor was talking about three. We were caught off guard. She didn't want to try to carry three. And we didn't want to make the decision of—they call it selection—decreasing the number by aborting one. We just couldn't do that. Our beliefs wouldn't let us do that. We'd wanted children for so long, we couldn't just say, "Okay, now we're getting rid of one of them." You don't know who you'd be getting rid of.

We started to defer to his expertise.

"What are the odds of all three taking?"

"You only have a five percent chance."

"But if that happens it's like a hundred percent." I was just so emotional. I was leaning toward giving in to this professional who's been through this and knows we're not going to end up with triplets. Because as he said, "Triplets are nobody's friend." He was just for putting them in and getting one or two.

With hesitancy, I said, "Okay…" We stayed on the phone and the doctor talked to us as he performed the procedure so we could hear what was going on.

Stephanie said, "We said only two. Two only!" She was worrying that maybe she might hurt our feelings, but it was a relief.

I told her, "Yes, yes, yes! Thank you! Thank you! *Somebody* had to have the presence of mind to make a good decision." Because all we wanted was two. We didn't want more. "Thank you for being stronger and remembering what our first conversation was. Let's go ahead with that."

We stayed on the line and the doctor talked us through it. We're all talking on the phone and hearing what's going on. After the procedure Courtney asked, "Can we say a prayer?"

Yes! Being a man of faith—he's Jewish—our doctor offered a prayer in Hebrew.

Two weeks later we would find out whether Stephanie was actually pregnant. We could have gotten the information on a Friday, but Monday is the day off in the theater. We didn't have to be there but we wanted to be as much a part of the process as we could. Some people can't—they live in Japan or another foreign country or have other reasons. But we could. I wanted to be there to support Stephanie. How could I not support someone who is giving me such an amazing gift and I am believing that they will treasure themselves to take care of my baby. You've gotta show that you care. In my mind, not to would have been negligent. I also wanted to be there because for years I had tried arduously so I could have the experience. Okay, so my body wasn't physically going through it, but I wasn't gonna miss it. I didn't want to miss it.

"If we can wait until Monday, we can fly there. We want to be there for the ultrasound instead of just hearing it over the phone."

So Courtney and I flew home and went to her ultrasound appointment. We got the most amazing news—she was carrying twins. I was stunned! Several years earlier Courtney had had a dream that we'd have twins, and the minister had prophesied that I'd have two children.

Now another woman was carrying my baby—not just one but two! There are no words to explain how appreciative I felt—feel! You can't tell them enough. *Thank you* doesn't get it. And they told us, "I'm just glad I was able to help you, I did it for you. Here. Have the wonderful life that you want."

"Oh. Okaay…" It's strange; we can never give enough thanks. We don't visit each other back and forth. But we can make sure you're well attended to. How are you feeling? What do you need? We'd see each other at Stephanie's monthly doctor's appointments as we all looked at the ultrasounds together.

* * *

We weren't sure exactly how we were supposed to interact. We had agreed to be open but weren't certain how to do it or where the boundaries lay. As the holidays neared, Courtney said, "We could knock on their door for Christmas or something like that." We decided to get them a Christmas present. How could we not? They were such sweet people, although we knew there was no way to thank them. But we wanted them to know we were concerned, we cared.

Then at our December appointment Stephanie whispered in my ear, "I don't know if we're supposed to do this or not, but..." and handed me a present.

"Oh, you beat us to the punch!" Courtney told them. Over the nine months we grew closer and closer to each other.

Before the babies were born, Courtney and I went to see our business manager to get our wills together. Years earlier we had written wills as if we had children even though we didn't. Now that children were actually on the way, we needed to answer some hard questions we hadn't answered before: what's going to happen if somebody dies—that kind of stuff. We drove separately. Afterward I think he went home. But the meeting went on so long, I had to get something to eat. And I had some errands I wanted to run, some stuff I wanted to get to help pull the babies' room together. Then I decided to make a couple of stops—I was just out in the street lollygagging. I didn't have my cell phone with me.

By the time I got home it was about three-fifteen. I came in through the back door into the kitchen. It was quietish. Nobody was here. Courtney wasn't here, his mom wasn't here, our assistant, Tracy, wasn't here—only Dmitri, who doesn't speak English, who was tiling our newly remodeled bathroom. There was just nothin' goin' on—no phones ringing. Nothing. For some reason my overnight bag was sitting in the middle of the floor with a yellow Post-it note on top of it. I wondered why it was sitting there but figured I'd grab something out of the fridge and check my messages first. So I got some tapioca pudding, which Courtney was into at the time, then started listening to my messages. The second message was from our surrogate.

"Hi. I hope you're having a good day. I was just here at the hospital for an appointment and I want you to know that my water broke—"

"OOOOOOH, MY GOD!"

Any fool knows that means the baby's comin'—the babies are comin'! But what does that mean? Is everything okay? We had just had a doctor's appointment two days earlier. Everything was fine then. The hospital is across town, which might as well be another country since we were in Los Angeles on a Friday afternoon and rush hour had started at eleven. You don't want to be on the freeway leaving Los Angeles on a Friday afternoon. I tried to listen to the rest of the message, but it was hard to listen. I heard something about delivery at four, but my brain was just jumpin' around and tryin' to figure out what to do next. I was tryin' to listen. *Delivery at four! It's three-thirty now.* In traffic I was about three hours away. What should I do? What should I do?

Then it dawned on me that maybe that my luggage sittin' in the middle of the floor had somethin' to do with it. I read the note: "Go down to Mattie's house. She's going to drive with you." Mattie is our neighbor down the street. Mattie? My mind was like "WHAT? WHAT? WHAT?" I was trying to make sense of this note and figure out what to do next. I had packed my bag weeks earlier, so I knew I had all my stuff. I knew that babies would be early—they were scheduled to be delivered at thirty-eight weeks—and I wanted to be ready to go. But I didn't think they'd be five weeks early!

The phone rang. I snatched it up.

Courtney.

"Hey, how are you?" Mr. Cool, Calm and Collected.

"COURTNEY, TELL ME WHAT'S GOING ON! TELL ME WHAT'S GOING ON!"

"Okay, let me tell you exactly what's happening. Everything's okay. Everybody's fine. We have time. The delivery's at four. We're going to wait for you."

There was no way I could get to the hospital by four. All of a sudden I felt like one of the parents I'd heard stories about at our initial surrogacy consultation. People who lived in Japan or someplace and who tried their very best to guesstimate when they needed to be in the United States for the birth of their baby, but the baby came early and they were trying to get here from Japan as quickly as possible but just couldn't get here in time. When I first heard these stories, I thought, "I'm glad I'm right here in Los Angeles." Right now, as far as I was concerned, I might as well have been in Japan.

"ARGH!" My heart! My heart was breaking. I just felt so disgusted with myself. A part of me wanted to burst into tears, but another part of me knew I'd be good for nothin'. You could already sell me for half a cent; I knew if I started cryin' you could give me away for free.

"Don't even go there," I told myself. "If you cry you won't be able to turn it off and that's gonna make it worse. You gotta hold it together, hold it together in case it works out."

Why hadn't I carried my cell phone? How could this happen to me? How could I be so close yet so far? I had tried to be there to support Stephanie and experience it all—every doctor's appointment, even from Minneapolis. Me and this not carrying my cell phone! I knew I hadn't been one of those people with their cell phone tied to their hip. I would easily run out and forget it. "I'm not gonna carry that cell phone." But when you need it, it comes in so handy. And now Courtney was at the hospital and it was his mama who was there with him. *I* wanted to be with him. *I* wanted have that experience with him. I wanted it to be me and Courtney—not Courtney and his mom! Not that I have anything against his mom, but I'm his wife. Oh, it was disturbing! It was distressing! All these thoughts were going through my mind.

So Courtney had told me to go down to Mattie's, so I went down to Mattie's. I'm waitin' in the car, waitin' for her to come out of the house, but nobody's comin' out. Finally, after about five minutes, I'm wondering, "Golly, what's goin' on?" I call Courtney. He tells me Mattie's picking her son up from school and must not be back yet. But her son goes to the school across the hill and it's Friday at rush hour. Oh, Lord! I don't know where they are in her travels. Where are they? I call her husband, Michael.

"Where are they? Where are they?"

He's all calm. "It's gonna be okay. She's almost there."

"Oh, Michael, I can't believe I wasn't ready."

"Angela, nobody's ever ready. Nobody in the history of birth has ever been ready." Then he laughed. That was calming and reassuring—for about two minutes.

Okay, I've got a few minutes, I thought, so I drove back to my house. Let me make sure I have everything I need to be comfortable: some sneakers, whatever. I didn't need anything. I'm just trying to keep myself busy until she comes back. Then I drove back down the street to her house. Then I called Courtney.

"Courtney, I'm leavin'," I told him. "I can't wait. I can't wait. I'M CRAZY! I'm gonna drive myself."

"No, baby," Mr. Calm, Cool and Collected instructed me. "Wait for Mattie so you two can get in the carpool lane and get here faster. Everything is okay. We're going to wait for you. We're all just sitting here tellin' jokes." I guess it wasn't going down like on the Discovery Channel where the water breaks and the vaginal hard labor happens. "Everything's calm and nothing's gonna happen 'til you get here."

That calmed me down a bit—but could I believe it? Yeah, I kind of believed it—for a minute. Then I called Michael again.

"Where is she? I'm leaving." I think I drove around the corner when the phone rang again. Courtney.

"Wait!"

"Okay…"

I park again. Oh, I'm just sittin' there in the car and I'm twitchin' and nervous and I wanna cry. I'm so frustrated. I'm so excited. I'm so where I don't wanna be. I just wanna SCREAM! Meanwhile I remember that the baby shower is tomorrow and I have friends coming to town and stayin' at my house. I'm reachin' into my purse to get out my spare key when Mattie and her son drive up!

"Look, Jonathan," I say as soon as her son hops out of the car. "Go put this key under the door because we've got company comin' and they have to get into the house."

Then Mattie says, "What are you doing in *your* car? *I'm* driving."

So I park my car, get in her car and we head toward the freeway. Well, Mattie is a conscientious driver. She drives the speed limit and obeys the traffic laws, and I'm thinking, "You gotta get out of this lane! Get over into that lane!" Then I'm tryin' to have a conversation, tryin' to talk about it a little bit, tryin' to talk about *anything* to get my mind off it. Tryin' to make the time go by. But you can't really have a conversation when you're in the middle of a situation like that!

Finally, we get onto the freeway and into the carpool lane. But as soon as we get into the carpool lane the regular traffic starts flowin' faster. Mattie loosens up a bit. Now we're crossin' double yellow lines back into the regular lanes. When that tightens up, we jump back over into the carpool lane. We know we're not supposed to be crossin' double lines but here we go and do it anyway. We finally get to the hospital and Mattie drops me off. A one-hour ride had taken two hours, but that was better than three if I had tried to do it alone.

When I go in, everyone's waiting for me. Courtney had been there the longest. His mom and Tracy had arrived about twenty minutes before me. So I went in and said hello to Stephanie and Kevin and their families, who were there with them, and saw that everything was, indeed, fine. The doctors and nurses told me how it was going to go in about twenty minutes. We washed up and stood in the hall—Kevin, Courtney and myself. Courtney—Mr. Shutterbug—was taking a couple of pictures. Then we went in and stood up there by Stephanie's head. There were two teams of doctors—one for each baby. So there were about a dozen people in the delivery room. A drape had been set up over her abdomen and the doctors were doing the prep work. At one point they told us we could go around the drape and look. "Oh, gosh! I'm not sure if I'm ready to look yet." Then I got it together and came around and watched the whole procedure.

To see the human body opened like that! To watch them do their first incision and see all the various layers of muscle and tissue and sinew in the human body—it's just amazing! *We are fearfully* and *wonderfully made* (Psalms 139:14). And then the doctor reaches in and out comes this perfectly formed human baby—our son! He came out very calm. His body language was all curled up. I jumped and I think I said, "OOH! OOOOOH!" I just started crying and hyperventilating.

Everyone was asking, "Are you okay? You all right?"

"Yes, it's a baby!" Like it's a wonder—it's a wonder! "Wonderful, wonderful yet again," as Shakespeare said. Wondrous. They had to work to get the second one out. By the time she came out, I had calmed down. I had seen it, so I wasn't crazy. "Wow, look at that!"

Courtney and I were just standing there holding each other. He had given the nurse his camera. Since she knew what would be coming next, she was taking all the pictures. We stood there in awe, watching this incredible woman having our babies and the doctors and nurses do their thing. The nurses and technicians were weighin' them and wipin' them and cleanin' them. Then they let us hold them up close for a second. I felt like I was dreamin'—like I was in a dreamlike state and maybe I would wake up. You just don't believe you're holding them. You don't believe they're yours. It's kind of like: Really? Truly? Finally? Honestly? After all that? They're ours?

We would name our son Slater Josiah after my great-grandfather, Slater Samuel Stokes, and the most powerful king in the Bible. Our daughter is Bronwyn Golden, named after Ahren's sister who, coincidentally and unbeknownst to Courtney and me, we both had hired as our assistant at one point and loved, and my Auntie Golden, who had cared for and nurtured me when I was a little girl. Aunt Golden had been ill. But she stayed on this earth long enough to see her namesake arrive. She would pass away five days later, but stuck around long enough to make sure they got here safely.

But right now one of the doctors is lookin' at Bronwyn's nostrils flarin'. They're saying she's experiencing a little respiratory distress. They tell us not to worry about it. They're telling you it's not optimal, but it's not an emergency. As an actor I'm listening to the subtext, I'm listening intently, trying to ascertain just how serious this is. I'm trying to listen to the type of words they're using, I'm trying to listen between the words. I could almost take it in and get emotional, get distraught. But they're capable and they're giving us a lot of information—they're disclosing, they're not keeping us in the dark.

"They're twins," they say. "This happens a lot to the second one coming out because they're in there longer. It's nothing out of the ordinary. It's just going to be a couple of days."

"Oh, okay…"

"It's nothing that she won't be able to get over."

But they have to get them to the neonatal unit, so they whisk them out of our hands. All of a sudden it's like, "What do we do?" They're taking the babies away. They're amazing. I want to go with them, yet Stephanie's body is still open—and she's bleeding. To go with the babies is like abandoning her. I want to go with them but I'm torn. We're torn. I almost wished someone would just tell us what to do. It's just so intimate all the way around and such an interesting human-relational dynamic. But Courtney and I are thoughtful people so we think about it for a minute. We decide the babies are in the best possible hands. The doctors are doing their thing with them. We don't know if we can go down to the nursery with them anyhow. So we stay with Stephanie.

"Thank you!" we tell her. "We can't tell you how much we love you. We are just so grateful!"

Finally someone tells us what to do. They tell us to go with the babies because the doctors have to do some work on Stephanie. It isn't an emergency but they have to get on it.

"Thank you for helping us know what to do." We head to the nursery.

When we get there the nurses are getting the babies hooked up to all these monitors—all tubed up. They're taking blood at the heels of their feet. They're getting poked and pricked. I am about to cry—I know how much I hate needles. But Slater isn't crying at all. He's a strong baby boy.

We learn we can't hold our babies yet so we just reach into the oxygen tent and touch their lips or something. Slater looks so small. He's very yellowish; he has my undertones. Bronwyn is getting some oxygen through a little tube into her nostrils. She's a little bit bigger than him. Her color is a little bit ruddier, like Courtney's. They are both very fair—a lot lighter than we are. We check their ears, around their fingernails for signs of color. We don't find any yet. Maybe it's too early. We watch and watch and watch them. We wait and wait for them to open their eyes. After a while Slater opens one of them for just a millisecond.

"HE OPENED 'EM! OH, MY GOSH!"

Just for that second I could see one black pupil, a glimpse of the eyes I'll soon stare into lovingly. Our amazing journey was about to begin!

Chapter 22

When God Takes Over

In 2004, I was invited to film the pilot episode of a new drama called *Law and Order: Criminal Intent*. I'd never done a TV series before so I was tentative about it, and taking the job was a big deal because the series was being shot in New York. But Angela and I sat down and talked about it. We felt that, after all our struggles, our marriage was now on solid ground. The distance would be a big deal but we felt we could work with it. I had grown up seeing the model of my grandparents' long-distance relationship, and Angela wanted to give it a go. We knew it was doable as long as we both were committed. So we agreed that we would talk every night on the phone and not go more than three weeks without seeing each other. In the beginning, I traveled back and forth every two weeks between L.A. and New York. Eventually we rented an apartment. Between missing Angela, the apartment not feeling like home, traveling back and forth and trying to learn my lines, I found doing the series very difficult at first. In time she and I got into a rhythm and it just became our routine.

Although I was now working in New York and Angela and I were living in Los Angeles, emotionally we had finally gotten on the same page. We had begun to "secure the perimeter" logistically and financially, so whenever we were together we started trying to have a baby. We bought books and talked to people and watched live births on the Discovery Channel. But the natural methods didn't work. We moved to fertility treatments and then to in vitro fertilization. These fertility treatments meant Angela was constantly getting shots, going to the doctor and getting poked and prodded. The procedures were very invasive and some of them had to hurt her. She toughed them out but I felt guilty. We had reached a very wonderful time in our marriage when we wanted to do things for and sacrifice for each other. As much as she wanted children, I knew she was going through all this for me because she knew how much I wanted kids. I dreamed of being a father. One night I dreamed we had twins!

In spite of the fertility treatments, we went through menstrual cycle after menstrual cycle with no results. We went through the hopefulness, the joy, the pain, the heartbreak and the questioning when we considered whether to start all over. But throughout the whole process of trying to conceive, I am very proud that we remained focused on loving each other. We did not implode and begin blaming each other. On my end, this was chiefly due to the Bible telling me to "love my wife." I also recalled Angela's sister Lynn's advice to take care of our relationship. Lynn's encouragement also reinforced in my mind what Dr. Little kept telling me and I was reading in the Bible—that my wife is first and must remain so!

After much trying, praying and soul-searching, we let go of our dream of having our own biological children, and moved on to the next option—adoption. I was fine with the idea. I thought the idea of giving a child a loving home was a good idea. "My sister did it, we'll do it," I figured. Angela thought so, too, and we began to research the process. Adoption was the plan until the day she came home and told me that one of her friends was about to have triplets through something called "surrogacy."

"I really don't know what that is, honey," I told her. "Talk to your friend and we'll do whatever you think is best."

Angela started investigating. Her friend thought we should talk to the folks at the surrogacy place she used. So we sat down with the director for a couple of hours and thought it was very, very interesting.

"Someone else can carry our egg and our sperm?"

"These are pictures?"

"Wow!"

"People come from all over the world to California to do this?"

"Who knew?"

The meeting went well but I recognized right away that if we went on this journey it was going to be very emotional, expensive and fraught with all sorts of opportunities for disaster. I was almost obsessive about making sure we were working with an organization that knew the landscape very well and could protect us and guide us down this very tricky path. For me to feel comfortable that we would be protected, I thought we needed a company that was more corporately structured and organized than this one was—that could orchestrate the whole thing, act as intermediaries between us and the surrogate, manage all the finances and make sure that both we and our surrogate parents were legally protected. The last thing we wanted was to get in the middle of the situation and find out that it cost more than we'd planned and that they'd quoted us the bare minimum. Or end up with a surrogate who's pregnant with our babies but doesn't eat right and take care of herself. Or have some other kind of emotional disaster. I couldn't allow our family to be exposed to that. So we called some very good friends, who recommended a larger organization, where the process is much more formal and comprehensive. There, in addition to speaking with the director, we went to a day-long education process, met with people who walked us through all the financial aspects of surrogacy, and talked to the legal department and people in the counseling department. The company assured us the surrogates are screened and tested emotionally for months so they can be matched with the right people. We were impressed. When we left, we understood everything. We decided we were going to do it and began to go through the process.

Before long, we met the woman (and her husband) who was considering being our surrogate family, we fell in love with them. They were a quiet, humble couple with a loving and servant spirit. Apparently, the woman had read something about surrogacy and decided she been blessed with beautiful babies and easy pregnancies, and wanted to share her gift with someone else. At first her husband asked, "What are you talking about? No!" But she explained her reasons and he told her, "Talk to me in six months." Six months later, when she still wanted to do it, he agreed and got completely behind her. As they told us the story we were struck by the fact that after six years of marriage and two children they still made goo-goo eyes and held hands. They made me want to hold Angela's hand—and I did—that's how loving they were. Once we saw their spirit we knew they were the right people for us. You can't pay anyone enough to do something like this for you. There's no dollar value to set on it. We felt blessed that they wanted to share this gift and knew God had brought them to us. And as a man, I particularly appreciated the husband. I knew it took a lot for him to be on board—to have his wife carrying another couple's child. In fact, I was in tears over this man. Angela and I were just weeping.

That same spring of 2005, Angela and I agreed that our marriage was strong enough to try acting together for the very first time—people had been asking us about it for years. Over the previous summer I had reconnected with John Guare, the writer of *Six Degrees of Separation,* when I traveled to Valdez, Alaska, to be a part of the Last Frontier Theater Festival. John and I taught a master class together, which reminded me how much I missed working with him. About six months later, John called me up with an offer to perform the leading role in *His Girl Friday.*

My agent at the time suggested that Angela might enjoy performing in the play because it had a great leading role for a woman.

"Do you think she'd do it?" John asked when I brought the idea up.

By now I'd learned not to try to think for Angela. "Her decision-making process is very different from mine," I told John. "I'll give the play to her and we'll have to wait for her to read it."

So I gave her the play and explained the opportunity. I hoped that she would do it but I knew to let it go and allow her to make her own decision. After a month John called. "What does she think, Court?"

"She has the script and she knows you're waiting to hear from her. She'll read it, but I've learned not to keep asking her."

A few weeks later Angela had read the play but still hadn't decided what she wanted to do, so I suggested that we have lunch. That way Angela could meet John and the director, Joe Dowing, and learn more about the play. We met, and Angela fell in love with John and Joe. "Courtney, I've been wanting to do something new and exciting. I think this is it!" she told me.

When Angela decided to come on board it was a momentous occasion for me. I had been not been onstage in twelve years and had never done physical comedy. Angela had not been onstage in at least five years. But we knew the foundation of our relationship was strong enough for us to be able to work together. To top it off, shortly after we began rehearsals we began our surrogacy process. It was a *very* exciting, very full time!

* * *

In the end of May we headed to Minneapolis's famous Guthrie Theater, where the play was being staged. We fell in love with the city and were surprised to discover how beautiful and well developed a theater town it is. We stayed close to the theater in two separate apartments, across the hall from each other. When I first suggested getting two apartments, Angela thought it was a good idea: "Our guests will have a place to stay." But I didn't want guests to come anywhere near that apartment; I intended to rehearse in it. That was the smartest thing I did. Angela and I have different rehearsal processes. Angela is a genius. She has a photographic memory. She can watch television at the same time she's learning her lines and blocking. Someone can change the script, and she can look at it once and say, "Yep. I got it. Okay, Court, what's for dinner?"

My process is much slower. It takes me longer to learn lines. While Angela can lie on the couch and learn her part, I need to physically walk through my blocking as I state my lines because I remember the lines based on what I'm doing and where I am on the stage. Walking through my performance causes it to drop down into my muscle memory. I need to do this as I learn new lines each day. Doing this would require my own space. The second apartment was going to be that space. Plus, I have my own process for building up my confidence to be onstage. *His Girl Friday* is a very complex play, and my role was very demanding. There was a lot of movement, and my actions and dialogue drove the whole play. Every member of the cast was reacting to my character. If I didn't know what I was doing the whole piece would fall apart.

I was used to having six weeks to rehearse, but this was a regional theater so we would only have four. I was very excited to be doing this play with my wife, but I was also very frightened. I kept my head in my script and notes. At the theater I picked dressing room 33, downstairs and as far from the stage as possible. The theater staff said, "Are you sure you don't want to be next to Angela? She's up by the stage."

"No, I'm fine. I need to be in a quiet, tucked-away area so I can begin the next phase of my process."

Of course that didn't stop Angela from invading it. When I first walked into her dressing room, she had all sorts of nice stuff—great chairs, a rug.

"Where'd you get all this?"

"Down in dressing room 33."

"That's my dressing room! You took my stuff?"

"Oh, that was your dressing room? Hee, hee, hee!"

"Angela, you are wrong!"

"Hee, hee, hee!"

"I don't believe you!"

Once we started rehearsing I had to trust that my old skills were all there. We had less time to rehearse than normal, a script that was twice as long, and it kept changing every day. I was scared out of my mind. My stomach stayed on edge. I lost my traditional ten pounds. Each morning I prayed and really leaned into my faith.

In the meantime, Angela could skim her script once and say, "Honey, let's run lines."

"I'm not ready yet," I'd tell her. "Please give me a little time."

"You don't have to be perfect. We can just—"

"Honey, just give me a little time, please. We'll run lines. Believe me! I just need a little more time to walk my blocking."

"Okaay…" She was very patient with me.

At the end of four weeks we began preview performances. I barely knew my lines and blocking. I was afraid that I'd completely lose my place in front of all of those people and the whole play would fall apart. I had to trust it was all in there. But I've done a lot of theater and after *Six Degrees,* when I had to go onstage after my dad's suicide and during my breakup with Ahren, my ability to focus is legendary among my peers. I wasn't comfortable with my part, but God had placed me in a situation where I couldn't do anything but depend on him. Angela and I prayed together; we knew God would take over. During the previews I worked moment by moment by moment: Say this. Now go here. Say that. Now go there. God put everything in place. When I pulled off the first show, everyone was asking, "Where did that come from?" By opening night two weeks later, I had my part down, and the whole cast was flying!

Onstage each night I got more and more confident and my performances got stronger and stronger. Working with Angela was amazing. She is a *monster* onstage—she is *so* good! And she's not just a good actor, she's a good director. Of course, even though Joe Dowling directed the play, she couldn't resist telling me what to do. But she was right—and she's my wife!—so I did what she said and it was all good. We are proud that we worked lovingly and prayerfully with each other, our cast members and the Guthrie team. The people of Minneapolis really embraced Angela and me in a wonderful way.

In the meantime, this wonderful surrogate process was unfolding. On the Monday immediately after opening weekend, we flew home to find out if Stephanie was pregnant. We had met her and Kevin only a few weeks prior, but we were choked up with gratitude when we saw them and could feel their warmth toward us in their smiles and sparkling eyes. Everyone was nervous and excited. It was such an intimate, amazing moment! We were all huddled in front of the monitor as the doctor moved the ultrasound probe over Stephanie's abdomen.

"Look, a heartbeat!" the doctor said.

"OHMYGOODNESS!" Our eyes welled with tears as we watched a small area on the screen flutter.

A moment later he said, "Oh, oh, here's another one!"

"WHAAT?" Angie screamed and looked at me wide eyed.

"Stephanie, six years ago Courtney had a dream that we'd have twins!"

"Hallelujah!"

I just shook my head. Praise God! We hugged and celebrated with the doctor and this lovely couple that was helping us establish our new family, said goodbye, rushed to the airport and flew right back to Minneapolis for the Tuesday performance. Needless to say, we were in a tremendous state of shock.

After the play closed a month later we returned to Los Angeles with a new sense of hope and expectancy.

At our monthly appointments we connected with Stephanie and Kevin. Our appointments were our rhythm, and Angela scheduled our lives and our work so we could be there with our new surrogate family. I can't begin to express how many prayers we said for our developing babies, for Stephanie's health and for this amazing couple! After all Angela had gone through to try to bear children herself, to have this process that was fraught with so many potential disasters go so smoothly for us was a complete blessing. We bonded so much at our monthly ultrasound appointments, in between appointments we started to miss being around Stephanie and Kevin! We began to think that maybe our relationship would extend beyond the terms of our contractual agreement. We came to the conclusion that they would be our family for life.

Our son and daughter were scheduled to be delivered on February 17, 2006. Since Stephanie's previous pregnancy was a Cesarean birth, this would be a C-section, too. About two weeks prior to the due date, it dawned on me that trying to get Angela to sit down with our business folks to finish adjusting our wills and trusts to accommodate the babies after they arrived would not work. So we decided to conclude all of that work before the babies arrived. After the meeting, Angela said, "Let's get something to eat."

"No, let's eat at home," I told her. "We have food in the refrigerator."

"Okay, I'll see you there."

Angela left to run a few errands and I banged out a few e-mails while sitting in the car before I heading home. Fifteen minutes later my phone rang. It was Tracy, our assistant.

"I need you to get home now. Stephanie's water broke and you have to get to the hospital."

"Oh, my goodness!"

"Is Angela with you?"

"No, she left twenty minutes ago. She should be home by now."

"Well, she's not here yet but come on home."

I boogied back to the house expecting to find Angela waiting. In true Angela fashion, she still wasn't there. Earlier she'd told me she'd forgotten her phone, so it was impossible to get in touch with her. She was probably out shopping for baby clothes that we wouldn't need because of all the gifts we would receive the next day at her baby shower. I learned that our surrogate had been at a doctor's appointment when her water broke. So she just walked right down the hall to a private room and waited for the fun to begin. Stephanie's C-section had been scheduled for four o'clock. We were an hour from the hospital and it was only one o'clock now, but we would be in Friday-afternoon traffic. There was still time but Angela would have to get home soon. My hospital bag was already packed. I grabbed this and that from around the house then called our neighbor and great friend, Mattie Lawson, to ask if she'd bring Angela to the hospital when she got home. As long as there were at least two people in the car, they could move quickly in the carpool lanes and, maybe, make it in time. Then at two, with no word from Angela, I hit the road, Jack.

Angie surfaced at about four. She was just traumatized.

"Courtney, what's going on? Where is everybody? Is everything okay?"

"Everything's fine. Her water broke. She went into labor."

"Oh, Courtney, I should have had my phone…"

"Honey, it's okay." I told her that I had made arrangements to get her there as quickly as possible. A few hours later she came running into the hospital just as the doctors told us we had to go into delivery. There must have been 15 of us in the operating room, all scrubbed up and masked. Stephanie and Kevin were huddled up talking. Tears were streaming down her face. He was telling her it would be okay. We met her mother and father for the first time, as well as her mother's mother. So there were three generations there at the same time, plus the babies. I thought, "This is just amazing!" Angela and I just looked at each other's eyes over the tops of our masks. Her eyes were big and round and moist: "Oh, my goodness!"

Standing there watching another woman give birth to our babies was absolutely surreal. After all we had been through, I thought, "Lord, this is it, isn't it? We're finally parents!" I just wanted to take it all in. Once the babies were out, everyone focused on them. The nurses cleaned and bundled them up so we could hold them. I looked at their tiny hands and fingernails, their little eyes, noses and mouths, the hair on their heads. They were perfect—positively perfect! They also showed the twins to Stephanie and Kevin so they'd know they were okay before they were whisked away. I found myself feeling torn. The babies I'd been dreaming of were here, but I wanted to be there for Stephanie as she had been for us.

"Come on, Courtney," the nurses were calling me. "Stephanie's in good hands. She's going to be okay."

Our families held hands and hugged with full hearts and mixed emotions. I was humbled by and grateful for the amazing gift she and Kevin had given us. They'd allowed us to embark upon a journey the Henry the Explorer in me could never have imagined only a short time earlier. They'll be part of our family forever.

"Go," they told me. And I did. It was time to begin my new life as a dad!

Chapter 23

Laying It in There

As new parents, Angela and I spend a lot of time thinking about how to lay the foundation for the kind of people we want our children to become. We realize we have been given a tremendous responsibility—the most important job we'll ever have. The Bible tells us to teach our children while they're waking and while they're sleeping, and that if we raise them up in the way they should go, when they get older they won't depart from it. We know that Bronwyn and Slater will need strong Biblical roots to withstand all the temptations Hollywood will present them. It's important for them to know from whence they came and to Whom they belong. To accomplish that, we will circle the wagons and surround our children with Godly people. We will teach them to "view the world through the prism of the Bible rather than to view the Bible through the prism of the world." And like other parents we'll pray our way through how to raise them.

As their father, I know that teaching them discipline is essential. Discipline needs to be taught in the home; as mother and father, it's our responsibility to lay it in there. Children don't have to learn how to lie; they lie naturally. I know; I was a "master." I would have cake crumbs and frosting all over my face, but if my father asked me if I had eaten any cake, I'd tell him, "Uh-uh." I had to be *taught* to be a good boy. If you don't put good values in there, then there's a vacuum inside. Where there's a vacuum anything can come in—and I guarantee you it's going to be something bad! But I believe that when you teach children discipline, you also teach them boundaries. When they know they have boundaries, they know they are loved. I've heard kids say, "My parents don't love me; they don't care what I do." That's so sad to me. So many adults think that by not restricting their children, they're giving them freedom; that it's a good thing to let their kids do whatever they want. But this world provides children with too many choices and many just aren't good for them. Giving kids that much freedom actually *puts them in bondage*. What they need is just the opposite—when we give them boundaries, it frees them up. When they live in the square of safety their parents carve out for them, they feel protected. Once they know they are safe and protected, they feel free to become the person God wants them to be.

It's a toughie, I know. I'm sure I will want my children to like and appreciate me just like every parent does. For now, though, I'm not going to be my children's friend. We'll all have to wait until they're grown for that. For now, I've got to do whatever I have to, to lay that discipline in there day by day. They may not always like it but we will lay it in and lay it in. I'm prayerful that suddenly it will click for them and—*bam!*—our children will self-check. They will know how to act—we're going to instill "please," "yes, ma'am" and "thank you"—and they'll know how *not* to act. I intend to prepare them to say, "No, we can't do that." They'll know when to think, "Mommy and Daddy wouldn't like it." Even though we plan to expose them to lots of wonderful things, in other ways theirs will be a very focused world. We will have to tell them that they can't do everything other people do; that they don't need to see all that there is to see or hear all there is to hear; that they can't be around everything and everybody. "Just because Johnny is doing it, doesn't mean we do it in our home," we'll tell them. "In *our* house we serve the *Lord*."

In line with that, Angela and I want to teach our children some of the "old-fashioned" ways. All these computers and technological advances are great—we think it's wonderful that you can hop on Google and find out anything in the world. But the very same computers that connect you to the Library of Congress are also wired to a world that turns into a nightmare for many people, even in the supposed safety of their own home. Obviously, we'll want to protect our children from that. When I consider the role pornography played in my life, I realize that my mind was first harmed as a young child. Technology can also take us away from things that are very important like human-to-human contact. In our family sometimes we're going to have to turn the computer and television off. Instead, we're going to look at each other and have conversations at the dinner table: "How did your day go? What did you learn? Really!" We will talk about how we are doing emotionally, which I now know was missing when I was a child. We will speed back up and use our computers and technological devices later, but the kids will still have to communicate well and do tasks like long division that require patience and their undivided attention. Although we live in a society where we can do things in a blink, somehow we also intend to teach our kids the value of time. When Angela and I grew up, we didn't have all this digital stuff. You had to dial the phone and wait for the dial to spin back around. You had to heat things on the stove and wash the dishes; there was no microwave. We will really have to consider how to teach Bronwyn and Slater the value of time when today we live in a culture where those ideas mean nothing.

The same thing is true about money. It won't matter that they have been born into privilege. That's *our* money; they're going to have to get theirs—they won't be spoiled. Our kids are going to have little jobs. They're going to be taking the garbage out and raking leaves. Even if they tell us, "Our friends don't have to take the garbage out," we plan on reminding them, "Your friends don't live here." When they're older I envision giving them a small amount of allowance money for the entire year. We'll help them figure out how to budget it, but when it's gone it will be gone. That means they will learn the value of money within the safety of our home.

"But, Dad, that's not enough."

"Well, that's all you've got."

"Oh, maaan…"

"You better start a dog-walking business!"

One of the most wonderful gifts my parents gave to Cecilie and me was the ability to dream. They constantly put us in museums and libraries and activities where our minds were tickled. Especially as artists, we'll want to expose our children to all kinds of arts and culture. If we can couple that with a love of learning, they'll be able to do anything. We'll want them to value education and understand that it's an important tool they can use to make their dreams come true. Doing well in school and developing good study habits will not be an option, since they'll form the foundation for what happens in their life. They are also particularly important for African-Americans, for whom education has played such an important role in our effort to gain access to opportunities.

Unfortunately, we still live in a world where racial prejudice exists. Therefore, we will teach our children how to interact with diverse people and navigate racism. These days racism more difficult to recognize because it's rarely black and white—it's gray. There are going to be times when our children are going to have to look someone in the eye and ask, "What did you say?" and then handle it. We're not going to teach them "an eye for an eye." It will be important for us to teach them discernment. There are some black people who will hurt you just as quickly as someone white, Latino or Asian. Above all, we are going to raise them to have a deep love of people. Angela and I know that we're supposed to love our brethren—to experience the world together as children of God. Even when people don't treat them well we will teach them to pray for them.

We are prayerful that we'll be successful in instilling these types of values. Angela and I understand that to the extent we are victorious, God will be able to take our beautiful new children and mold them so He can bring wonderful things to this world through them.

As everyone who's already a parent knows, parenting is a humbling experience. Even in the Bible there are few examples of fathers who parented well. That tells me that I have to keep growing and expanding in my relationship and parenting skills, as well as my faith. Already, these babies have turned my world upside down. Even beyond parenting they are making me change. When Angela and I first began trying to get pregnant, I also started to think about what kind of world our children would inherit. What are we going to leave for our children and our children's children, I'd wonder? I had never really thought about that. But just like when I got married and had to allow different ideas, activities and people to come into my life, I realized I'll need to do the same with the children. Today, the presence of our children gives me the opportunity to shop on different aisles in the grocery store. I had never felt the need to go down the baby aisle before; nor had I felt the need to go down certain avenues in life. Now I'm realizing that it's not just about Angela and me and our immediate family. It's about who's going to take care of them if something happens to us? And I think more about the broader spectrum now. I realize now that sometimes you have to get out there and fight for your world. I've already started to do that.

I've gotten involved with the Boys Club again. From the time I was eight to about fifteen, the Boys Club influenced my upbringing by providing a safe haven for me to hang out at on Saturdays, a place to play little-league football, go to day and overnight camps, do arts and crafts and become a camp counselor. Every child deserves to have that type of environment while they're coming up. Now I have the opportunity to reciprocate. Together, Angela and I have gotten involved with "Save Africa's Children," a humanitarian mission founded by our minister and mentor, Bishop Charles E. Blake. "Save Africa's Children" is spearheading a movement to address the impact of AIDS in sub-Saharan Africa, where the United Nations estimates that by the year 2010 about *40 million children will have been orphaned!* Now that I am a father, the thought of my children having to fend for themselves is absolutely unbearable. I can't allow that to be okay for anyone else's child. Our church is physically, spiritually and financially supporting a number of orphanages all over the continent. I have become a board member. Bishop Blake likens our outreach to the story of Joseph in the Bible, suggesting that as African-Americans we can help a generation of our brothers who are living in a "desert." If not us, who? If not now, when? Yes, we have issues here in the United States, but the problems over there are so much greater and immediate. Angela and I feel obligated from both a human and Christian standpoint. So God has laid it on our hearts, as well as on the hearts of the members of our congregation, to respond.

We are also delighted that the United Nation's Children's Fund (UNICEF) has invited us to be U.S. ambassadors. UNICEF is always on the ground when disaster strikes. They are deeply committed to taking care of people and children all over the world, as I hope people would take care of our children if a disaster were to happen here. They've asked us to choose a country we'd like to visit and begin to establish a relationship with. We are honored and look forward to using ourselves and our celebrity to benefit children in a different part of the world. When they are old enough, we envision traveling with Bronwyn and Slater, providing them with the priceless opportunity to see firsthand how children live in other parts of the world and to extend kindness and their blessings to them. I also know that at some point soon I will bring my life full circle by getting involved in foster care and suicide prevention, since both of those issues have impacted my life and family profoundly.

I think about these types of things now each time I hold my children against my chest, seeing and feeling their chests rise and fall with the life God has breathed into them. I think of the amazing journey of their existence each and every time Angela and I look into their bright little eyes, examine their tiny fingers and toes, then look at each other and marvel. We count our blessings time and time again. I know God has an amazing plan in store for all of us and it's just beginning.

Angela and I will have plenty of time to deal with all of these issues that being a mother and father bring to mind. But for now, we feel content as Mommy and Daddy. Our hands and our hearts are full....

Chapter 24

Lessons from Our Road Less Traveled

We'd never pretend to be relationship experts—as you've read, we experience relationship challenges just like everyone else. But along our journey and during this unconventional life we live, stretched between two coasts, traveling around the world, and living in—and thriving in spite of—the media fishbowl, we have figured out a thing or two about what makes a relationship endure. As a little thank-you for the love you've shown us over the years and for supporting us by buying this book, we'd like to share a few tips for having a healthy relationship and marriage. On the pages below you'll find our thoughts on a variety of relationship-related topics. Our ideas are separated into advice for single people, advice for those who are married and advice that applies no matter your marital status. You may decide to hone in on the ideas that most fit your relationship status. But we hope that at your leisure, you'll read all of the information. We all have a lot to share with and learn from each other on this amazing road we call life. We are so grateful that you've been willing to spend a portion of your journey with us.

<u>Advice for singles:</u>

If your relationships aren't going well or if you keep having the same experiences over and over, rather than trying to change

your partner, focus your attention on the plans God has for *your* life. Let Him do all the changing, beginning with you!

Angela: As human beings, we're always trying to change or control things—other people, situations, even our thoughts. It's like trying to control the wind or the weather. You can't; the weather's going to be what the weather's going to be. You'd better just dress appropriately. You might as well just put on a hat and a scarf. In other words, *you* do the changing! The only thing we are really in control of changing is ourselves. That's why it's important to sit back and figure out why things keep happening to us—what we're dissatisfied with and the reasons for it. When we work on ourselves, we gain a different perspective and see ourselves and others through changed eyes. Whereas in the past we may have been willing to accept less-than-admirable behavior—say, lying (even "white" lies) or chronic lateness—from ourselves and others, when you begin to hold yourself to a higher standard then that's not even an option. If you live up to whatever values you say are important to you, people who exhibit similar values are the only people you're going to attract. In essence, it's about how *you* behave. As you change your perspective and sense of yourself, other people—your mate, friends, coworkers—will see and deal with you differently. You don't have to stress yourself out trying to "make" them change, and your vision becomes clearer.

Courtney: If you keep experiencing the same relationship problems over and over and/or negative kinds of people keep showing up in your love life, it's not the other people that need changing. As Angela said, we attract people who match up with who we are and our values. So ask yourself, "Who am I?" and "What kind of person am I attracted to romantically?" If you just look for the physical, that's what you're going to get—a person who looks good on the outside, but may not have anything going on in the areas where it really counts. If you want to attract someone different, you have to be willing to change.

Now, I'll be the first to admit that change can be hard. We live in a society where we're led to believe that if you try something one time and don't get the results, you should give up because it doesn't work. Even though we have a tendency to become impatient, certain things take time. What do you do while your change unfolds? Engage in positive activities that help you build a strong foundation for your new life.

Between the time that Ahren and I broke up and Angela came into my life, I had to create consistent and affirming activities to help anchor my life and give it rhythm. I had to do things differently so that I wasn't having a permanent pity party, always thinking about my shortcomings and failings. When I still lived in New York, walking Bottom, going to the theater and getting therapy anchored my day. When I moved to Los Angeles, I immediately started to recreate that structure by handling fundamentals like finding the cleaners, the grocery store, a doctor, a dentist, an eye doctor. As I matured spiritually, going to church and Bible study, reading the Bible gave me spiritual roots. As you establish this type of structure and foundation—and especially a strong spiritual anchor—God will reveal to you what you are to do next, be it leave your job or go on a budget or step out on faith on something important. These activities will keep you so busy you won't have the time or energy to try to change anyone else. While God is working on these activities in your life, you can rest assured that He's working on your partner—either changing the one you have or bringing a better one to you.

Don't be afraid to spend time not being in a relationship, dating or having sex.

Angela: No matter whether you're in a relationship or not, it's very important to learn to be happy wherever you are. We all have to guard against believing that the grass is greener on the other side of the fence. Being single and being married both have their pros and challenges. Especially when you're single, you may feel lonely and wonder why you can't find someone, why nobody loves you. But married people sometimes miss being able to think only for themselves and not having to negotiate about everything. And once you have a baby, you can hardly think of yourself at all.

When you're single, I think it's important to spend some downtime between relationships and take an honest look at yourself. Do you see any patterns that you'd like to stop repeating? Do your friends tell you about behaviors you're repeating? Pay attention and consider them. One common example I've seen in people (including myself) is giving away too much of themselves early on in a relationship. I think we need to get to know each other over the course of time. Only with time do you find yourselves in a wide enough variety of circumstances and experiences to really learn about someone. It's nice to be wined and dined all the time, but when you're in a restaurant other people are waiting on you; you learn nothing about a person's serving spirit. In other words, when you're not in a restaurant, does *he* serve you or do you always have to take care of yourself? While you're alone, you can take the time to examine these kinds of issues. Do you expect someone to take care of you or is there reciprocity?

I also think it's very important to have platonic friends. We spend so much time thinking about *eros*—erotic, romantic—love because it's the easy one to spot. But there are different kinds of love and different kinds of relationships. For example *philia* love—the love of brotherly and sisterly friendship and fellowship with those you enjoy—is also very important. Friendships are very important to give you variety and insight. I know that I have some friends I keep it light and general with, and other friends I can go deeper with. As a single woman it was important to me to have guy friends who just liked me for me and where our relationship was devoid of any sexual content. Not every man in your life has to want something sexual from you. And physical attraction aside, men are very alluring. They have different interests than women, they enjoy a different kind of fun, they can clue you in about men and hip you to games other guys run. It's nice to have male friends that you just hang around with. Interacting as friends with members of the opposite sex also makes you feel more a part of the human race since they *do* make up half the population.

Courtney: Don't be ashamed to save yourself sexually for the person you're going to marry. When you're dating it can be helpful to communicate a standard message up front: "I just want to be clear that I'm saving myself for my husband (or wife), so there's not going to be any sex. I'm not even going to think about it. So let's just get to know each other." You'll know that if the person sticks around, they like you for who you are, rather than thinking they're going to get sex from you. When Angela told me that she wanted to wait on sex, I knew there was something special about her and that she had standards about herself. She didn't have to do what everyone else does. She didn't need to wear all these revealing "hoochie mama" clothes or hang out in a bar. Some men like sweet girls, women who are understated.

Until that special person comes along, it's important to have platonic friends of the opposite sex. After Dr. Kornfield encouraged me to have women friends, I've developed some great platonic relationships. When I was single I looked for women I shared interests with. I found that many of them were in the same situation I was—waiting for their train to come in. But when you become friends with someone of the opposite sex, you may have to take the lead in communicating to make sure that being buddies is all you want. So that everyone's clear and no one gets their feelings hurt, you both have to discuss where you are and what you can handle. When you both understand what the deal is, you can breathe with each other and have a wonderful, open, cool, no-tension-of-any-kind type of relationship. But in order to get to that place, you've gotta talk. You've gotta acknowledge where you both are.

Don't just live or have children together, commit to getting married.

Angela: Children are a gift from God, and any gift from God is magnificent. So that's the way we ought to treat children—magnificently. I believe they grow and thrive best when they have the benefit of a mother and father who are married to each other. Men and women are different. I don't believe that one sex is obsolete or redundant or unnecessary. I don't believe in keeping children from their parent as a punishment. That's not the way we ought to treat them. Men and women bring different things to the table and children benefit greatly from both. Now, there are many situations where that isn't able to happen. Maybe one parent disappears or is unavailable emotionally or physically, in which case you have to make the best of it. Or perhaps you decide to adopt as a single parent—there are many different ways of making a family. But I don't agree with the idea of willingly having a baby when you're unmarried. I think it's a little selfish. I think you should come to the process with a selfless spirit, thinking about what's best for the child and the ramifications of all of your actions. Once the child is here, it's important to engage in the type of growth and maturation that helps you raise a healthy citizen of the world.

Courtney: Since I wasn't raised in the church, I didn't know that God has a divine order about sex being reserved for marriage. When you follow God's plan, the only way it's possible to bring children into the world is when you're married. We're supposed to try to be holy like He is. We'll always fall short because He's perfection; yet God gives us a value system to live by. If our behavior falls outside of it, we can stop, recommit and dedicate ourselves to something higher. If you stop and take yourself to another level, God will see that and bless your relationship and family because you're trying to do things His way. You'll also get a stronger sense of who and whose you are—and that there's a plan. Once you know your behavior isn't according to God's plan, you have a choice to make. You can choose to keep doing what you're doing, knowing it's not what God wants. Or you can change. Ignore his Word, though, and the consequences are yours. You will get down the line and find that the price you have to pay not worth it. That's why the Bible tells us to always count the cost.

Before you get married, make sure to find out if you and your love share similar values, dreams and desires. The character of the person you adore is not going to change. This is why it is very important to allow God to bring us our mate, for according to Scripture: *O Lord, I know the way of man is not in himself; It is not in man who walks to direct his own steps (Jeremiah 10:23).*

Angela: Before you think about marrying someone, find out if you share a similar vision for your lives and look at the world from the same vantage point. That's the idea behind the Biblical maxim that we be "equally yoked." When you get married, two spirits are supposed to become one. The last thing you want is a two-headed monster of a marriage, where you have one body—the marriage—but two heads—two sets of thoughts—going in different directions. If this happens you'll tear the marriage and each other apart and won't move forward. When you're dating you're still an independent contractor or a solo performer. But when you're in a committed relationship or marriage, then it's all about the team; both members should be moving in the same direction. That's why as you move more deeply into a relationship, you need to learn about your mate.

There are all sorts of questions it's important to investigate. Have in-depth conversations: *Do you want children? When? Right away? Oh, I wanted to finish school first. Do you want to have them biologically or adopt them?* Or maybe you're dating someone who already has children: *Do you want to have more? You feel like you've raised your kids and are past that stage? Oh…* These are the kinds of questions you have to ask. Experts say that money is a major stressor in most relationships. Courtney came to our relationship as someone generous who would spend. I came as more frugal, more thrifty, more cautious. I paid my bills off early—I couldn't stand to have them over my head. *Ooo-wee,* that was challenging! We still deal with our money differences a bit. But we weren't going to keep our finances separate. If we truly believe we're a family, we don't want to say, "That's yours over there and this is mine over here."

Premarital counseling helps a lot because you can really shine a light on things you might not have been thinking about while you were wining and dining, kissing and hugging, and walking on the beach holding hands. I also think that before you get married it's important to see a person's credit report. Sure, you paid for dinner and that was nice, but how did you pull together the dollars that paid for the meal? You might have spent your rent money trying to impress me. Then when we marry your debt is my debt. That's why I tell people, "Get those credit reports!"

Courtney: Before you get serious with someone, take the time to see who they really are. The fact that it takes time to learn your partner is one important reason why you shouldn't hop in bed right away. If you have sex with a man, he already knows that he can get that, so he'll be quicker to move on. But if you hold out, your partner has to take the time to know who you are—that is, if he really wants to get to know you. You may feel afraid you may lose him if you don't "give it up," but that's the risk you have to take to find a decent partner. If he leaves because you didn't have sex with him, then he was going to leave anyway.

If you're already engaged and think you're going to marry someone, make sure you spend time asking all the questions you may ever want to know. Even then, everything's not going to surface until the ring's on, you're married and you're experiencing enough situations together that your really discover who the other is. But before you get married, spend time narrowing the gap between who you thought this person was and who they are in reality. You don't want to wait until after you're married to find out that someone doesn't want to have children or mow the grass. Yet it happens over and over. People think, "Oh, we're in love…" No! That doesn't cut it. Before you walk down the aisle, ask everything you need to ask.

Then, accept who the person tells you they are. The average person's basic character is not going to change. They may learn a couple of things later in life, but for most people, whoever they became in their childhood, that's just who they are. You're not going to change them. If you want a nice guy, look for a nice guy and stay away from the playboy. A nice guy may get on your nerves, but at least you can work with his flaws and foibles.

Advice for married people:

Always honor and respect your husband or wife. Remember, your mate is God's child just as you are.

Angela: Life feels wonderful during the halcyon days of a new relationship. Your face lights up when you see each other, your heart skips a beat—it's all polka dots and butterflies. The honeymoon period of any romance is exciting, passionate, hot! But over time, psychologists say—especially once people become committed or get married—the honeymoon ends and you settle into daily life. Now you have to clean the house, pay the rent and keep the water on at the same time the car's breaking down. You have to make decisions together and you may or may not see eye-to-eye. You have to deal with each other's family members. Some will be a joy; others may aggravate you to no end. You'll get on each other's nerves. The honeymoon's definitely over. And when you add kids to the equation, there are even more forces pulling you away from each other. With all of these stressful things going on, it's easy to forget just how special your spouse is, and take each other for granted. It takes effort to stay connected to each other.

I think it's important to revisit the honeymoon period during your day-to-day life. Courtney is wonderful at this. He asks me, "How did you sleep?" each and every time I wake up. And he's always saying, "Did I get my kiss today?" He's so sweet and cute! (I may only remember to ask him how he slept once in 150 times.) The way I remind myself of how special he is by sneaking glances at him. It's almost like stealing glances into his spirit, his humanity. I look at him when he's not paying attention, when he's unaware of me. Maybe that's a woman thing, observing. I watch him—his kindness, his generosity, how he interacts with others. And I appreciate him. I observe the times when he's feeling confident and times when he's not. I notice how sometimes he knows exactly what to say to me and sometimes he doesn't. You can learn a lot about someone you love by observing them, especially watching for how they treat people when they're not trying to get anything from them.

Courtney: The Bible always surprises me. I remember when I read in Proverbs: *What is required of a man is kindness.* I was stunned. The world had always told me the opposite—that I was to be strong and tough. You get no encouragement for being kind, gentle, diligent, persevering, enduring, loving, peaceful, meek or mild. People laugh at you, especially if you are a man. They'll call you weak or a punk. The world is always louder and more vocal than the Lord. Yet when I read that passage of Scripture, the idea of being a kind man resonated in my spirit; I had been raised to be kind and thoughtful—that's just who I am. The more I read, the more I learned that not only was it okay to be kind, but that Jesus was meek. Jesus wiped his disciples' feet. People mistake meekness for weakness, but they're not the same thing. Meekness is controlled strength. Now I understand that God wanted to make me into a gentleman so he could bring a very special gentlewoman to me.

In the beginning, make a decision that divorce is not an option. If you cannot take this kind of stand for your marriage with your husband/wife up front in your relationship, odds are that your union won't last.

Angela: I always tell people not to jump into marriage. I mean, you can't go into marriage thinking, "Well, I'm going to give it a try, and if it doesn't work out then so be it." Because it's easy to get married, but a marriage is too hard to make work if you're not completely committed. Plus, nobody ever talks about the fact that when you get married you tie your souls together. Pulling them apart is painful. Ask anyone who's been through it—getting divorced is hard as hell!

Before you agree to marry someone, I think it's important to check your intentions. If your marriage is to have a fighting chance, just take your time, observe and take inventory of yourself and your mate. Be honest with yourself; the only people who know the spirit of a man are God and the man himself. Think about what you each have to offer the marriage then thoughtfully evaluate whether you can work out your differences—the credit issues, the debt, the family issues, the children, whether this is a thoughtful person. Because when you're standing at the threshold of marriage, you have to have a made-up mind, not one where you're waffling or teetering. As the mother of one of my girlfriends says, "You'll come up against a lot of stuff in life that's going to work against you. You don't need to help it along."

Although I don't believe in getting divorced, I'll be the first one to admit that certain behaviors are deal breakers to me—physical, mental and emotional abuse, and drug and alcohol addiction. My mother always told me, "Grown people don't hit grown people." If you observe the spirit of anyone who's been abused, you can see that it's bad for their spirit. Their self-esteem falls, they scrunch their shoulders, duck their head, walk around on eggshells, become fearful people. That's not how God intended us to live. Witnessing that behavior is also bad for our children. They either become fearful themselves, or the individual wanting to be in control, or wrongly and tragically believe "That's just the way relationships go."

Psychologists say that people who exhibit that kind of abusive behavior are hiding behind it or using it to anesthetize themselves. Either way, it's not good for you. If they want to help themselves, you can support them to an extent. Love them from a distance—them in rehab and you at home.

Courtney: We Americans will commit to everything except getting married. We'll go through a process to get on the football team; we'll endure the discipline of becoming a ballet dancer; we'll go through the process of becoming a lawyer. But when it comes to getting married, we think, "Whatever…." We don't even find out what it means to be married. What's behind it? Why is it a commitment? Who are you committing to?

Being married is different than being boyfriend and girl-friend. You make a promise and commitment to both God and your partner that I believe you should be taken seriously. People get all hung up on having to feel "in love" all the time. But marriage is not about love *per se*, it's about commitment. That's how you can promise each other that you're closing the door behind you and that there is no way out! I couldn't bear to see the look on Angela's face if I reneged on my vows or was disloyal to her. I couldn't stand the pain of trying to explain to her how or why. So I stay focused on the job, the relationship, the promise and the commitment. They carry me through all the tough and lonely times when we're working or traveling and are away from each other. Of course, in order to make a com-mitment like marriage and the promise not to get divorced, I suggest that you take the time while you're dating to make sure the person is really right.

Having said all this I also believe that there's no excuse for abuse. If your spouse is abusive, try to get him to get some help, but if he refuses, he's got to go! There's no excuse. It has to be dealt with at the root. If he won't get any help, get away! Get away!

Stick with God's divine order for the family. Place God first; your spouse, second; your children, third; work, fourth; and yourself, fifth.

Angela: If you buy something that you have to assemble yourself, the first thing the instructions suggest is that you check that you have all the pieces. Then there's a sequence to how to assemble it. If a couple of pieces are missing, you're in trouble. And if you have all the pieces but don't follow the right sequence, you can't be sure it will work right. The same is true for our family priorities. God has an order for the family. If you want a higher position on this priority list, you're probably better off staying single. Then it will be just God and you.

Courtney: When you get married all your relationships have to shift. Mothers, fathers, sisters, brothers, friends all have to step back. The Bible tells us: *A man should leave his mother and father and cleave to his wife, and the two shall become one flesh (Genesis 2:24).* That's the primary relationship in life: the husband and wife. When Angela's sister Lynn and her husband, Al, sat us down in their living room before we got married, I'll never forget their advice reminding us of the importance of God's order. Now that I'm married and a parent, I'm clear that when it's time to make decisions you'd better know the order. Forgetting that our spouse is second after God is a major source of marital problems. If you don't know the order and put your children in front of your mate, there are going to be problems in your house. The kids need to know where they stand. I plan to tell our children, "This is Mommy's time with Daddy. Mommy is the queen, and a queen sits on her throne. So let her have her time with Daddy." By providing them with the example of how we treat each other, Angela and I will teach our children how they should be treated by their husband or wife. They will see that Daddy treats Mommy specially and that Mommy and Daddy are a "united front" when it comes to discipline. Children need boundaries in all aspects of their life, including in their time with Mommy and Daddy.

Romance and do special things for each other throughout your marriage.

Angela: It's easy to fall into a pattern of taking care of the children, the house and business ahead of taking care of your spouse. We have to make a priority of taking care of your relationship. Spend time with each other way from your family's day-to-day hustle and bustle. Do something you both enjoy, like listening to the music you fell in love to, trying out a new restaurant, going for a romantic drive. Even do something that's special to one of you but that the other person might not enjoy as much but can tolerate, then next time switch. Stepping outside of ourselves is good for us. In a marriage it can't be all about you—it needs to be all about *us!* Such tolerance teaches patience, which is required in every union.

Courtney: It's very important to carve out time for each other, to keep dating, to keep sending flowers, to do the little things. If she gets a promotion, send flowers to the office so everyone sees. If she makes a big presentation at work that goes well, take her on a celebratory date. Spend a weekend at a hotel or bed-and-breakfast. Take time to get away and nurture your relationship. Often we speak of women serving their husbands, but one important way men can do this is by serving their wives. Unfortunately in our society men who serve their wives are often called "weak" or "punks." I know I've had guys tease me and call me weak. Meanwhile, my marriage is growing by leaps and bounds and they're not married anymore. They don't realize that Jesus wiped his disciples' feet. He didn't say a mumbling word to the people who were beating and spitting on him. Yet He could flick one finger and call down legions of angels to do his bidding. The greatest in the kingdom of heaven is the child-like person with a servant's spirit!

God does not need a copilot to tell Him what to do. Figure out what He wants you to do in your marriage and "just do it." That way you have tangible and constructive activities to engage in while God is solving any challenges that face you as a couple.

Angela: Aside from doing "the right thing," I must admit that from moment to moment I'm not always sure I know exactly what God wants me to do. I *do* know that He wants me to do things decently and in order, and married relationships have an order to them that is different than when you're single.

When you're single you're supposed to put God first then yourself second. But when you're married, the order changes. Your mate becomes more important than you. Of course, this only works if you're as important to your mate as he is to you—meaning, he has to place you in second position in his life, as well. When you're both on the same page like this, you take care of each other before you take care of the outside world. When you're not on the same page, the relationship gets out of balance and the world gets in the way.

Courtney: The hardest thing is figuring out what to do while God is working out the challenges in your relationship. God does not need you to tell Him what your spouse *is* and *is not* doing. It's important to do Bible study, read Scripture, and do constructive things to anchor you. That way you're occupied, and not stressing and obsessing over what your spouse is *not* doing. In fact, don't focus on what they're *not* doing at all; instead, focus on what they *are* doing. Take the time to find that out. The things that she's *not* doing...well, those are none of your concern. That's for God to work out. It's out of your lane—you're in God's lane. Let Him do His thing with her, and you focus on the things He's lined up for you to work on. When you do that, it just about handles the whole nagging thing— there's no time or need for it. While I'm on the subject of women nagging, I look at it like this: Men aren't just *given* respect; we have to *earn* it. Women are not going to respect their husband just because they're married to them. Men must work for it by serving. Women want to feel secure, and men want to be respected. So how does it start? And who goes first? If you want to be respected as the man, be the leader in asking, "What can I do to help?" Be the leader in saying, "I'm sorry." When a woman sees that her husband puts her feelings ahead of his ego, the relationship will begin to change.

Pray together for each other and for the health of your relationship. For the family that prays together stays together.

Angela: We live in a world that tells us, "I'll get mine and you get yours," and "Take care of yourself first." Praying for another person means that you care enough about them to go before God on their behalf. When you pray together as a family, you make yourself humble before God and each other. You humble your spirit, your flesh, your carnal desires. Praying for someone else is an act of love and sacrifice. It isn't important to use the absolute perfect words. What matters is that you pray hard— almost to tears. When you get to that point, you're really praying. The Bible says, *Pray the effectual prayer. Effectual prayers of a righteous man availeth much (James 5:16).* And praying with passion takes your mind off of your own selfish needs. Praying for your mate, your children, your country, the world, is a very selfless act. Even though it's selfless, it ends up helping you in the end because it brings you closer to God and makes you feel grateful. When your mate and children are happy and fulfilled, your home is happy and healthy, and the world is a better place, it also benefits you—in part by taking pressure off of you. I'm guilty of trying to solve my own problems and issues. Truthfully, I'm just not the most capable person for the job. But I know who is....

Courtney: When you pray together as a family, you have to discuss why, what it means and whom you're praying to. There has to be a family meeting to address why you're starting prayer, who's leading the prayer, what you're saying. And most people don't start praying and not go to church. A whole host of things go on that go together and build the family, individually and collectively, like eating dinner together, and making time for family activities and trips. All of these things say "I love you" with your actions. The family that prays together stays together in part because they talk.

Advice that pertains to everyone:

Although our relationships take place on the earthly level, by nature we are spiritual beings. When we work on ourselves spiritually, God solves our human problems for us. So seek counsel, especially spiritual counsel, for the challenges you face.

Angela: When I planned to get married, I wanted to be in it for the long haul. However, since my mother's marriages didn't last, I didn't have an example of marital longevity before me. I had been a girl who liked to daydream and a young woman who loved to have flings. But marriages that work are based in reality not in fantasy. When the honeymoon ends, you have to deal with the mundane. Married couples have disagreements and you have to work them out. I wanted to move my fantasy of married life closer to reality. Marriage counseling helped prepare me by giving me some additional tools. One important thing I learned was that getting married doesn't mean you turn into clones of one another. You have different backgrounds, different thoughts, different interests, and men and women are different. I had to learn how to deal with this. I had to consider specifically, how is he different from me? How are our processes different? When Courtney wants to go to Las Vegas to see a show, he wants to drive the five hours up there; I want to fly! To him, it's all about the journey. The car, the driving—that's the fun part. I'd rather take the thirty-minute flight so we can enjoy more of the destination and be there that much longer. So I have learned to give him some of what he wants, and he gives me some of what I want. I might agree to the drive, but he understands I'm probably not going to stay awake. A long ride is like a sleeping pill to me. So it's important to have insight into what's going on. That way you don't end up in a spiritual tug-of-war. I use the term "spiritual war" because what else could it be? Courtney and I have had some seriously heated spats. And if you trace them to their origin in terms of the words spoken, they are silly! But a tone of voice that was heard or phrase that was misinterpreted led one of us to take offense. Then the ego got riled up and grew till the situation was out of control. Fortunately, we don't use language that cuts so deeply that when the storm is over we cannot recover and heal.

Courtney: There are some things I want to go through and learn from experientially, and there are some things where I don't want to have to have the experience of knocking myself upside the head. I don't want to jump from an airplane and realize, "Man, the parachute don't work!" I'm gonna do some research and make sure I have the right parachute up front. So when I decided I was ready to get married, I thought "Let me find out what marriage is—and find out what it's not!" I wanted to narrow the gap between perception and reality. Premarital counseling does that. That's where you find out stuff like your fiancé doesn't want to work—and he's the husband! "What? I thought you were going to be the breadwinner!" A lot of people find that kind of stuff out after they're married.

Unfortunately, a lot of people don't want to do any kind of introspective work. It's too much for them and it takes too long. But many of us are fractured people; we come from fractured environments. Life is all about what we do with our fracturedness. Do we fold our cards and say, "I'm done," or "I am who I am," even though it's not working? Do we curl up into a ball and call it a day? Or do we find our way out into the sun so we can find joy in life? I chose to find my way out of the pain and darkness so I could enjoy the sun!

I think it's important to seek counsel—but it's gotta be the right counsel. The Bible tells us that if you don't have good counsel, it's not wise to make a move. Dr. Kornfeld started me on the process of looking within, and Dr. Little has been finishing me off and helping me dig deeper into the Bible so I can work with myself. There's a mathematical formula. In order to build a skyscraper you have to dig a foundation of a certain depth below it. The higher the skyscraper you aspire to build, the deeper you have to go. It's like an iceberg—two-thirds of it is below the surface. God wants to take us higher in our lives, but to rise up we have to dig deeper.

Especially if in your childhood home you didn't witness an example of a relationship you'd like to imitate, find a couple that you admire and use them as a relationship mentors or advisers.

Angela: It's always good to observe things. That's what an intelligent person does. If you've never been married but want to be, it makes sense that when you see a successful marriage you ask them, "What makes it work for you?" Maybe something will resonate or there's something you can enlist. Before Courtney and I married, I thought it was important for us to be around my sisters and brothers-in-law. Individually they're magnificent people and two of them also have strong, committed, over thirty-year-long marriages! I wanted us to be in the presence of people who honor and love and care for each other. If you surround yourself with those kinds of people, I think you have a better chance to cultivate that which will nurture you as the unique individual you are and seek to become.

Courtney: If when you were growing up you didn't witness the kind of relationship you'd like to create for yourself, cultivate relationship mentors. That's a must; it has to happen. Not everyone had two parents in their life, and even those who do don't always have godly parents. If your mother or father don't exhibit the types of characteristics you aspire to have, don't turn into a victim; find people you can imitate while you still honor your father and mother. Plus, you always have Jesus to use as a model, and He'll continue to bring godly people into your life. The pastor and first lady of our church, Bishop Charles E. and his wife Mae Blake, are mentors to Angela and me. And whenever we find another godly couple we add them to our short list of godly-couple friends who urge us to continue to grow deeper into our marriage instead of turning away from it when we face challenges. And those are also the kinds of people we want to have around our children.

It's all about your attitude. Words like _please, thank you, you're welcome, I'm sorry, you're right, forgive me,_ **all go a long way. The Golden Rule still applies, so treat your partner like you want to be treated.**

Angela: It's very important to cultivate an "attitude of gratitude"—an approach to life that is thankful for all you have. When actors speak of attitude, they're speaking of the subtext, the language that's communicated but isn't spoken. No matter how much you try to pretend, when your attitude is poor it is impossible to conceal. One's attitude is a reflection of that person's spirit. Even the best actors can't hide a bad one. They may have the benefit of the most artistic makeup, amazing scenery, great lighting and a fantastic score signaling the mood—love, danger, sadness—to the audience, but even with all of these props to support them, the best thespians in the world can't "fake the funk." The audience always knows—they can always sense—when the actor isn't genuine and sincere.

In any type of relationship, the people around you—especially your mate—will either see or sense your true attitude in your tone of voice, your body language or actions. That's why it's important that when you speak your words and your tone match up. You can't call someone "sweetheart" and conceal your bad attitude. The two are antithetical. Using a loving word with a critical tone is a *sure* way to get on my nerves. To me, it's like the person doesn't want to cop to what they're really feeling so tries to fool me instead. I wonder, "What? Do you think I'm an idiot?" When you cultivate a positive attitude and find that place within yourself that is genuinely happy and grateful—for your life, for your family, for your mate, for your children—it's easy to match loving words with a loving tone. In life, since you don't have the wonderful score to lift you, the tone of your voice must be the music.

Courtney: As husbands, our job is to just to love our wives. All we need to do is ask her to tell us how to be the man she wants us to be. That takes strength; it takes a strong man to put his needs aside and just focus on his wife. Yes, we men have needs, but if we take care of our wives first, God will take care of us. And as we're gentle and patient and kind with her, she'll become secure within that love and give us the love and respect we need. My wife honors and respects me because she knows I love her. The kindness, admiration, loving looks I get from her—they all come because she knows that. And anytime she asks me anything, I'm going to say yes because she always approaches me in the right way.

God cannot operate in an atmosphere of unforgiveness. When there is an impasse, someone has to apologize so God can enter into the situation and heal it. The relationship is worth whatever "mud" we get on our faces when we humble ourselves and ask forgiveness.

Angela: Forgiveness can be especially hard because nobody wants to be thought the fool. But it is absolutely necessary if you're going to grow. Being unforgiving can stagnate your relationship and personal growth. To refuse to seek or give forgiveness is a sign that you're selfish, that it's "all about you."

I think forgiveness makes more room in your heart for love. To admit that you're wrong and ask for forgiveness is a sign of utmost strength and intelligence, especially in a woman's eye. To be able to take an honest inventory of yourself is a measure of your maturity. To know where you're shortsighted then grow from it takes character.

You can certainly melt a glacier with the words "please forgive me" spoken sincerely or a heartfelt "I'm sorry." Even saying, "I might be wrong" has calmed many a stormy sea in my life. Even in times when I knew I was not wrong, there have been times when I could give that to the person. Because forgiveness is hard. Many times we want to ask for forgiveness, but it's hard to go first. So why not be a trailblazer and apologize first? When you make that effort, the other person sees your intent. There have been many times when either Courtney or I apologized for something we didn't really do. It creates a different kind of dialogue: "You can't apologize for that; *I* was wrong, babe!" or "You weren't wrong; I was!" And that kind of conversation really melts your heart.

Courtney: Men say that they want to lead their family, to be the "head of the household." Yet many times they're not willing to take the lead in saying "I'm sorry" and asking for forgiveness. Somebody has to go first in admitting that they've made a mistake. If as the man you want to be the leader of your household, be the man in leading by saying you're sorry first. As leader, that's the man's responsibility. Once the man admits he's wrong, then God can come in and heal the situation by touching the woman's heart to be open and hear him so that things can be gentle, not bitter. I don't like it when my wife is upset with me. When she is, I know I'm going to find out what it is, so we can get back to peaceful communication. So I can apologize, and she can get that look off her face and get back to telling me what I need to do!

When you think about it, the man may be the head of the family, but the woman is the neck. The head can't go anywhere without the neck. I can't be in my position unless she's in her position and vice versa. To make that happen, the only thing I have to do is to love her. She can't find her place until I'm a loving husband rather than a judging, judgmental, bitter, angry, nagging or fault-finding husband. I have to be encouraging even when I don't know how we're going to do whatever it is she wants. Now, I'll be the first person to tell you that it takes prayer to get to that place. It's especially difficult for the man because, as the leader, he has to start the process though the woman may not be giving him any encouragement. How does he find the strength? I got it from the Good Book and a godly counselor. It was a process and a journey. I had to be taught—we all need to be taught. You literally need to be talked through it.

"A good man is hard to find," people say, and the Bible asks, "Who can find a virtuous woman?" It's easy to be the "bad boy" or "bad girl"—society gives us a lot of encouragement for that. Few people will encourage us to be our best, so acknowledge that and keep striving. Be the person that others will eventually look to as the example. Though it will be lonely and tough at times, that journey is part of the refining process. Keep the faith, and persevere.

Angela: When I was a girl playing with dolls and dressing up, I was in love with the idea of being in love. As a teenager I was attracted to people based on their physical aspects. Later, I thought men who were kind and considerate and thoughtful were boring. But after all that passion, all that drama, I realized I was burning myself out emotionally.

Love takes more than good looks and high octane to sustain it. It is more than just a feeling: love is an action. It doesn't require being whisked away to some exotic locale, but standing your ground and taking care of business with each other where you are. In time, I learned to appreciate the nerd, the Poindexter. I was able to see that the thoughtful, kindhearted, considerate person is the true prize! Some might call him the nerd but watch yourself: He may be the true prize!

Courtney: The temptations to behave badly are everywhere in this society. The government says, "don't drink and drive," but commercials seem to encourage it—"if you drink this beer, you're going to get the girl." You can smoke if you want to; advertisements make it seem like that's cool. And everyone knows that "sex sells." But there are consequences to everything. If you drink you might get into an accident. If you smoke, there's this disclaimer on the side of the cigarette package stating, "It's your own fault when you get sick." And we all see the results of our sexually permissive society with the rise in international Internet child pornography. We as society send mixed messages with all this subliminal sex. We have to acknowledge that in continuing to use sex to sell everything, we all pay a heavy price.

I saw myself as a good person, but my actions were contrary to that image I had in my mind. I had to work very hard to bridge that gap. And of course you'll get no encouragement to stay the course. Whatever is good for your spirit, the world is going to tell you is not good. *Narrow is the way to life and few find it (Matthew 7:13–14).* Yet whatever vision of yourself you see in your mind and your spirit, it's there because the Lord is trying to lead you that direction. Surround yourself with like-minded people. And take that world with you wherever you go. I do this as I travel back and forth between Los Angeles and New York. I don't allow myself to get out there by myself, away from my circle of friends who encourage me, and my motivational CDs and Christian radio station. I surround myself so I always stay focused. You know how you hear these stories: "Well, I was there—I wasn't looking for anything. She just showed up, so what was I going to do?" Well, I think what you can do is not be in those kinds of places!

It's a continuous, daily struggle for us humans to walk the path of righteousness. We are imperfect and all fall short. When that happens, get on your knees and ask for forgiveness; for *the righteous may fall seven times and rise again...* That's a marvelous thing! It means you don't have to be right all the time. You don't even have to try to be right all the time. You're going to fall. But when you do, our Father's hands are going to be right there. I've experienced it time and time again!